Adjudicating Employment Rights

Also by Susan Corby

RETHINKING REWARD (*with Steve Palmer and Esmond Lindop*)

WORKING FOR THE STATE (*with Graham Symon*)

EMPLOYEE RELATIONS IN THE PUBLIC SECTOR (*with Geoff White*)

Adjudicating Employment Rights

A Cross-National Approach

Susan Corby and Pete Burgess
University of Greenwich, UK

palgrave
macmillan

First published 2014 by
PALGRAVE MACMILLAN

Palgrave Macmillan in the UK is an imprint of Macmillan Publishers Limited, registered in England, company number 785998, of Houndmills, Basingstoke, Hampshire RG21 6XS.

Palgrave Macmillan in the US is a division of St Martin's Press LLC, 175 Fifth Avenue, New York, NY 10010.

Palgrave Macmillan is the global academic imprint of the above companies and has companies and representatives throughout the world.

Palgrave® and Macmillan® are registered trademarks in the United States, the United Kingdom, Europe and other countries.

ISBN 978–1–137–26919–5

This book is printed on paper suitable for recycling and made from fully managed and sustained forest sources. Logging, pulping and manufacturing processes are expected to conform to the environmental regulations of the country of origin.

A catalogue record for this book is available from the British Library.

A catalog record for this book is available from the Library of Congress.

Contents

Figures and Tables

Figures

Tables

Acknowledgements

The authors would like to give a big thank you to the Business School, University of Greenwich, London, for providing funding for this study and to Dr Daniela Comandè, University of Milan for contributing the chapter on Italy.

We are grateful to our numerous interviewees in several countries who were generous in their time and often candid in their assessments of their national systems.

The authors would also like to thank Andrew Levy, Andre van Niekerk, Mary Stacey, Susan Mackenzie, Alistair Dumbleton, Kevin Duffy, Michael Koch, Nadine Zeibig, Frédéric Turlan and Josee Lamers who commented on draft chapters, although interpretation and errors remain the authors' responsibility.

About the Authors

Susan Corby is Professor of Employment Relations at the University of Greenwich, UK. Formerly a trade union official, she has been a lay member of the first-instance and second-instance labour courts in Great Britain and is currently an arbitrator for a government agency (the Advisory Conciliation & Arbitration Service).

Pete Burgess is a Research Fellow at the University of Greenwich, UK. He has a background in both the academic and private sectors, in international employment research and consultancy, and in particular comparative law, industrial relations and international human resource management.

Daniela Comandè holds a PhD in European labour law from the University of Catania, Italy, and currently works as an assistant professor at the University of Milan. Before then she was a post-doctoral research fellow at the European University Institute, San Domenico, Italy.

1
Introduction: Issues and Overview

Our remit

In all developed countries, workers are protected by statutory and/or contractual employment rights, and there are institutions for adjudicating between workers and employers should disputes arise. This book focuses solely on the organisation and operation of these institutions. We do not examine workers' employment rights as such or how those rights are publicised, although such provisions contribute to the ability of the law to resolve disputes. Nor do we look at workplace institutions that provide scope for such disputes to be resolved before they enter the judicial domain, except where there is a direct and prescribed link between the workplace and external adjudication. We leave that to other books. We define 'adjudicating' broadly to include decisions by a court, by an arbitral body, by an administrative body or by an enforcement body and we restrict our attention to individual disputes of rights, not of interests, although in some countries there is an overlap in terms of the institutions used.

We begin by explaining our rationale, including our rationale for making comparisons. We then discuss our methodology before providing an overview of the many institutions covered in this book. The chapter ends by outlining the book's structure.

Our rationale

Why are adjudicatory institutions important today in the employment sphere? Traditionally, one of the key roles of trade unions has been to protect individual workers and resolve workplace disputes. During the last half century, however, there has been a decline in trade union density across all developed economies, although within this trend there are substantial national variations with Sweden experiencing only a slight decline compared with a fall of more than a half in the United States and New Zealand (see Table 1.1 on p. 2). This has been paralleled, although not directly, by a

Table 1.1 Trade union density

Country	Average density 1971–1980	Density 2011
France	21	8
Germany	34	18
Ireland	57	36
Italy	47	35
Netherlands	37	19
New Zealand	43	21
Sweden	74	68
United Kingdom	47	27
United States of America	23	11

Note: South Africa is not included as black trade unions were not lawful in the 1970s.
Source: Visser (2013) ICTWSS Database, Amsterdam, University of Amsterdam. Figures calculated by the authors and rounded.

fall in the coverage of the workforce by collective agreements, and in particular those concluded at industry level. There are a number of mechanisms, however, that mean that trade union density and collective bargaining coverage may not move identically. Although in the United Kingdom, for instance, there is broad alignment with union density at 25 per cent and collective bargaining coverage at 31 per cent (Brownlie, 2012), in France, despite low union density (8 per cent), collective bargaining coverage is over 90 per cent. This is due to the continued application of industry bargaining and the extension of industry-level agreements to non-signatory employers through administrative processes. Of course, high levels of collective bargaining coverage do not in themselves mean that the 'quality' of bargaining is high, or that there is a vigorous trade union presence at workplace level able to support individuals with grievances.

Alongside this decline in trade union density, there has been an increase in individual statutory employment rights across all the countries covered in this book. From the 1970s in particular, and in some countries earlier, there was a substantial expansion in employment protection legislation that, in many instances, generated an upsurge in individual cases brought to courts and tribunals. The United Kingdom, Ireland, Germany, Sweden, the Netherlands, France and Italy are also all members of the European Union and so are covered by the expansion of European Union employment law, which over the past 40 years has provided new individual rights, or extended existing national rights. South Africa, post-apartheid, has introduced many individual rights, akin to those in the European Union, as has New Zealand, especially as a result of its Employment Relations Act 2000. Even the United States, often seen as notorious for its lack of individual statutory employment rights, was a pioneer in introducing anti-discrimination legislation during the 1960s covering, for instance, gender and ethnicity.

As a result of these two trends in the last half century – the decline of collective regulation and the mushrooming of statutory rights in the developed world – workplace disputes are less likely now to be resolved by employers and unions acting jointly and voluntarily, but by the civil courts, by labour courts, by administrative bodies or by arbitration. The nature and operation of these institutions for resolving individual workers' disputes, however, have been largely ignored in the employment literature, although they have become increasingly salient. This book attempts to fill this gap by focusing on the institutional architecture itself.

Comparisons

We appreciate that these institutions will be shaped within an individual country by an interplay between its industrial relations context and the legal system. Accordingly, each of the ten countries covered in this study has its own chapter, in which we outline the institutions for adjudicating employment rights in their national context. Our aim, however, is also to venture a number of cross-national comparisons and contrasts in three respects. First, we consider it worthwhile to compare the basic institutional parameters of these institutions across a number of essentially descriptive dimensions: these include the overall system of labour jurisdiction, the scope and requirement for mediation and conciliation; the role of lay members in adjudication and how they are appointed and exercise their roles; and the role of the judiciary.

Secondly, in more theoretical terms, we want to explore the scope for linking the structure and operation of these institutions with theories and models that might help explain their origins, persistence or change. And thirdly, we want to offer an empirically grounded evaluation of these institutions, drawing on and measuring against certain criteria, such as accessibility, speediness and informality.

It can be argued that comparisons are well-nigh impossible, often drawing on the alleged impossibility of comparing apples and pears. We would argue that despite the difficulties inherent in such comparisons, they are useful and informative. To continue with the apples and pears analogy, both are types of fruit; and fruitarians, as well as cider and perry drinkers, could find comparisons between such allegedly incommensurable entities illuminating. The same goes for cross-national comparison, which can be instructive for academics and practitioners exposed to a variety of systems professionally and also as a means of arriving at a deeper understanding of an individual national system; it enables us to appreciate the different approaches that can be adopted and to discuss the effectiveness of different approaches, as well as to suggest theoretical explanations (Blanpain, 2007).

Moreover, despite their differences, all the countries in this book share the same broad ideological context as they operate in a neo-liberal environment (although governmental responses to neo-liberalism vary country by country). Neo-liberalism has many definitions but is used here in the sense of both a political theory and an approach to economic management based on free markets and free trade, privatisation and the breaking up of state monopolies, and deregulation (see Turner, 2008 for a full discussion). In the employment sphere neo-liberalism is linked with an emphasis on individualism and on flexibility that is reflected in the nature and extent of employment legislation.

Furthermore, all the countries in this book are confronted with virtually the same choices and challenges; for instance, how to balance access to justice with preventing unmeritorious claims; how to apportion the costs of the adjudication system between the worker, the employer and the state; whether to distinguish institutions for adjudicating employment disputes from other adjudicatory institutions; and how to square the legal presumption of equality between the claimant and the respondent with the industrial relations reality that the worker individually rarely has equality of power vis-à-vis the employer.

Other choices and challenges centre on how to resolve the conflict between a party's right to be represented by a lawyer and the aim of making first-instance adjudicatory systems non-legalistic; how to strike a balance between resolving disputes speedily and informally through alternative dispute resolution procedures and resolving disputes through litigation to ensure that the law is applied and legal norms are propagated; how to strike a balance between labour inspectors' role to provide advice with their role in prosecution and the role of non-state actors in employment adjudication systems, such as unions, employers, lawyers and civil society organisations.

Each country responds differently to these issues dependent on the way in which these problems are posed and perceived, and in relation to interests – both wider social interests and also the interests and cultural norms of the immediate actors. For instance in South Africa, when apartheid was dismantled and new employment institutions were established, access to justice was a prime consideration (see Chapter 10 in this book). In the United States (Chapter 12) arbitration has grown in the private sector, because a prime consideration for employers has been to create a dispute resolution system that is speedier and cheaper than the civil court system, but this has been at the expense of the development of the law. In Germany (Chapter 4), a prime consideration was to recognise the special characteristics of the workplace by having a wholly autonomous labour court system in which lay members sat at every level. In Great Britain, a prime consideration recently has been to place some of the cost of the adjudication system (employment tribunals) on the worker, so reducing the cost to the state (see Chapter 5). In New Zealand (Chapter 9), a prime consideration is to prevent legalism at the first-instance adjudicatory body (the Employment Relations Authority), so the adjudicator is not required to be a lawyer.

As to the role of non-state actors, in Sweden unions and employers' associations have an institutionalised role: they can bring a case to the Labour Court on behalf of a worker or an employer covered by a collective agreement; (see Chapter 11). In France too, there is some scope for unions to intervene on behalf of, or in some cases instead of, the individual at a labour court.

Methodology

This book owes its origins to an Economic and Social Research Council[1] award that included a study of lay judges in Great Britain and abroad. The study of labour courts abroad was primarily based on desk research, supplemented in some countries by interviews with organisational representatives and jurists. This research led to a broader consideration of the institutions for adjudicating employment rights and a desire to look at countries that did not have labour courts and/or used alternative adjudicatory bodies such as the civil courts and arbitration. It also led to amplifying our desk research with visits to all the countries concerned to interview key stakeholders, such as judges, advocates, trade unions and commentators in order to understand how the institutions worked in practice. Additionally, experts in the relevant countries commented on draft chapters.[2]

In making a judgement about how many countries to include, we had to make a trade-off between depth and breadth and decided to examine the institutions in ten countries: France, Germany, Great Britain (not the UK, as the institutions in Northern Ireland differ from those on the mainland), the Netherlands, New Zealand, Ireland, Italy, South Africa, Sweden and the United States. The countries chosen provide differing answers to the question of how individual employment rights are adjudicated and offer a good spread across some of the accepted – if critically – national typologies. They represent different legal origin models: common law/Anglophone countries are represented by Great Britain, New Zealand, Ireland, United States and South Africa. The other five countries (Sweden, Netherlands, Germany, France and Italy) are civil law countries, albeit exhibiting different features within this overall characterisation.

They also represent both different varieties of capitalism (Hall and Soskice, 2009) and industrial relations models (Ebbinghaus and Visser, 1997). In terms of capitalist varieties, the sample embraces liberal market economies such as Great Britain and the United States and co-ordinated market economies, but with variants: the Nordic model (Sweden), the continental model (Germany and the Netherlands) and the Latin model (France and Italy). In terms of industrial relations models, the book covers the 'Nordic corporatist' model (Sweden), 'Continental European Social Partnership' (Germany, Netherlands), 'Anglo-Saxon pluralism' (perhaps better 'Anglophone') (Great Britain, Ireland, United States, New Zealand) and

'Latin polarised' (Italy, France). As the country chapters and more detailed consideration of comparative issues show, these broad typologies embrace significant and interesting national differences; (see Chapter 2 for a full discussion).

For the convenience of the reader we mainly use generic terms, for instance civil court, labour court, professional judge, lay judge, but sometimes we use the local name, which can have symbolic implications. For instance the Swedish Labour Court is called *Arbetsdomstolen;* in France lay judges are called *prud'hommes* (literally 'good men') or *conseillers;* in Italy professional judges are called *pretori.*

Workplace dispute institutions

Adjudication

Before focusing on workplace dispute adjudication, we first consider adjudication more generally. The value of adjudication, says Lucy (2005), lies in its rationality, its impartiality and its legitimacy, but these are not simple terms. First, rationality: adjudication is not based on the tossing of a coin, or whether a witch on a bobbing stool sinks in the water, but on arguments and evidence. Nevertheless, decision-makers may differ in the weight they give to certain arguments and/or evidence and, as a consequence, rationality can be contested. As Bourdieu (1987) argued, there may also be different types of rationality drawing on different sources of reason, and the decision-makers might be systematically steered towards one approach or another depending on their intellectual formation, origins and socialisation (see Chapter 3, France).

Second, impartiality: on the one hand, a decision-maker may find it relatively easy to be impartial in the face of wealth, status or need. On the other hand, a decision-maker may find impartiality harder to achieve when faced with parties who are not equally able to put forward their case, for instance because one is legally represented and the other is not. Furthermore, decision-makers have to be partial to the rules, standards and values that constitute the legal system (see Lucy, 2005 for a full discussion of judicial impartiality). In the employment sphere, however, these values have often been anti-worker and/or anti-union (see, for instance, Wedderburn, 1986).

The third value of adjudication is said to lie in its legitimacy and this can be enhanced by having juries representative of the population so a judge alone does not decide, or by having representatives of workers and employers, that is lay judges, to adjudicate alongside the professional judge. Yet legitimacy and impartiality may not sit easily together. For instance, lay judges may provide legitimacy in that they are representative of workplace actors, but are they then *parti pris* and thus partial?

The parameters

We have already maintained that the resolution of individual employment disputes is decreasingly being carried out by employers and unions acting jointly and increasingly being conducted by adjudicatory institutions. These are largely based on what Dickens (2012) has termed a self-service model: that is, individuals make claims to an adjudicatory body to obtain compensation for a wrong. This is a reactive model, normally with damages given after the wrong has been done as redress rarely restores the status quo ante. In some countries, as we will see below, these adjudicatory bodies are labour courts, while in other countries they are civil courts or arbitral bodies.

Another model is provided by the state using public law, rather than individual private enforcement: labour inspectors, for instance, enter workplaces to ascertain whether the employer is observing certain statutory standards and, if not, they can serve administrative notices and/or take the employer to court. Labour inspectorates, or their functional equivalents, can be found in all the countries depicted in the book and their remit ranges from the particular, for instance labour inspectors for Great Britain's national minimum wage (Chapter 5), to a wide remit as in France (Chapter 3). Although possibly prompted by an employee or trade union complaint, the interaction is between the labour inspector and the employer, not the worker versus the employer, and labour inspectors can in theory be proactive, advising employers to change systemic practices to prevent a possible future failure to meet employment standards.

Labour inspectorates are supply-led; the number of workplace inspections that labour inspectors can carry out essentially depends on the number of inspectors whom the government decides to fund. In this age of austerity, many governments are increasingly limiting the resources being spent on inspectorates, with evidence for a decline in numbers. Also, particularly in South Africa, labour inspection is limited by the number of trained inspectors available.

Whereas labour inspectorates are supply-led, the courts, which governments also fund, are demand-led. Having introduced statutory employment rights and provided a means, however inadequate, for compensation for a breach of those rights, governments cannot determine the number of claims individuals may make. Governments can seek to limit demand in various ways, for instance by not publicising employment rights, by not providing legal aid, by delay (and Italy is notorious for its delays) to discourage claimants.

Importantly also, governments can limit demand for court adjudication by erecting a barrier to access by charging fees. In fact, there are fees for lodging a claim and/or for having a full hearing, whether in labour courts or civil courts in many of the countries covered in this book. The exceptions are the labour courts in Ireland, South Africa, Sweden and until recently (2013) Great Britain. France will abolish its modest filing fee in 2014.

Another way that governments can limit demand is by the institutionalisation of workplace employee representation – especially if, as in Germany (Chapter 4), there is an express injunction on workplace bodies to ensure that laws are complied with and to filter disputes before they reach the courts. At the end of the day, however, governments cannot determine demand; they can only reduce it.

Conciliation and mediation

Another way in which governments can reduce demand for litigation in the courts is by erecting conciliation and mediation gateways, through which parties have to pass, before access to a court. If a settlement is achieved through conciliation or mediation, a dispute does not have to be heard by a court. Such alternative dispute resolution is cheaper for the public purse, not least because conciliators/mediators are mostly paid less than professional judges and normally less administration is needed in terms of case management (fewer documents, for example). It can also be cheaper for the parties as the dispute is settled earlier and more informally.

Conciliation and mediation are, in practice, interchangeable terms as both are voluntary in the sense that the two sides have to agree to a settlement. Unlike a court or arbitration, a decision is not imposed on the parties by a third party. As will be seen later, in some countries engagement with the conciliation or mediation process is mandatory, that is the parties must (not may) attempt to reach a settlement through conciliation or mediation, before adjudicatory action is taken, even though any settlement remains voluntary; (see Chapter 10, South Africa; Great Britain from 2014, Chapter 5; and Germany, Chapter 4).

In both conciliation and mediation there are national variations in the mechanics. The styles of the conciliator and mediator vary between a facilitative and directive style, depending largely on the character of the conciliator/mediator and national traditions. In Great Britain conciliation is normally conducted by email or telephone and mediation by face-to-face meetings, but that distinction is not made elsewhere. For instance, normally in South Africa conciliation is conducted face-to-face, as is mediation in New Zealand.

In some countries in this book, there are separate institutions for conciliation/mediation, which are government funded. For instance in New Zealand, mediation is carried out by The Mediation Service of the Ministry of Business, Innovation and Employment. In Great Britain the Advisory, Conciliation and Arbitration Service (Acas) offers conciliation for all claims lodged at the labour court. In other countries, the court provides conciliation/mediation which is carried out by a professional judge. In Germany, there has long been a requirement to attempt to reach an amicable settlement before the judge who is likely to go on to hear the case (and therefore can indicate the possible outcome). In 2012, this was supplemented by enabling the parties voluntarily to opt for either judicial or extra-judicial mediation, with judicial mediation being conducted by a judge who would not be involved in any subsequent proceedings.

In France, it is lay judges, one from the employer side and one from the employee side, who conduct the pre-hearing conciliation. In Sweden there is both conciliation by employers and unions and, if that has failed, there is conciliation also by the professional judge within the labour court and if there is no settlement the same judge will be one of the judges hearing the case. In Great Britain too, Acas provides conciliation as noted above, but in some discrimination cases there is also judicial mediation, with a different judge adjudicating if mediation has failed.

Against this background, with the parties having passed through any relevant gateways, we now look at the courts themselves.

First-instance institutions

A key feature distinguishing one country from another is whether workplace disputes are resolved at first instance by a labour court, an 'ordinary' civil court or both. There are a number of justifications for labour courts, possibly the most significant being that because the workplace is special, in terms of its complexity and the nature and 'incompleteness' of employment contracts, it merits a special type of court that can draw on workplace understanding. Labour courts, therefore, rely on importing workplace knowledge, both specific and tacit, and often do so by incorporating lay members who, together with any professional judges, find the facts and judge the issues. Moreover, judgment by peers has been viewed, especially by trade unions, as a victory over unilateral management discretion and/or the judicial establishment.

In contrast, some countries do not have labour courts, and workers litigate in the 'ordinary' civil courts as in the United States, which also makes extensive use of arbitration; as in the Netherlands, where there is also an administrative procedure for termination of employment; and as in Italy, where employment disputes go to a specialised section in the civil courts; (see Figure 1.1 on p. 10).

A significant issue is the worker's degree of choice in respect of the forum. In the United States, workers often have the option of litigating in a federal or state court. Alternatively, on being hired American workers may be asked to sign away their right to litigate as a condition of employment, with such a right being replaced by private arbitration. Of course where such workers are asked to sign away their rights as a condition of employment, it is debatable how much 'choice' the worker in reality possesses. Italy too has a provision (law 183/2010) whereby employees can sign away their right to litigate, with such a right being replaced by private arbitration. Unlike the United States,

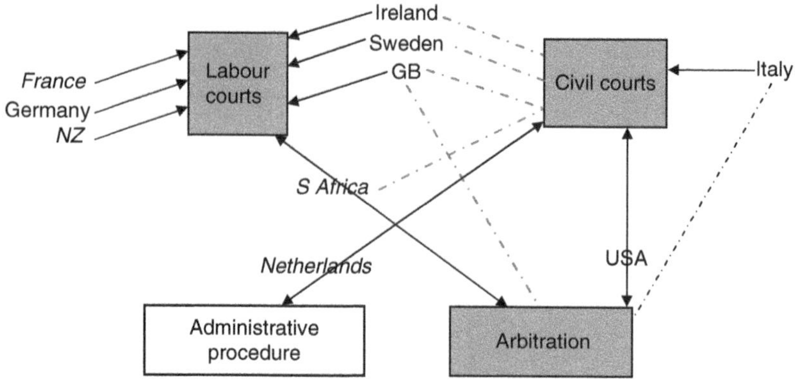

Figure 1.1 Employment rights adjudication at first instance
Notes: The dashed lines are options that are less widely used.
1. In Sweden, a union, an employer or employers' association or the Discrimination Ombudsman have access to the Labour Court on behalf of an individual, but an individual does not. Instead individuals, if unsupported, must go to the civil court (see Chapter 11).
2. In Italy there is a special section of the first-instance civil court for employment matters. Also there is some arbitration in Italy, but it is little used compared to the civil court (see Chapter 7).

however, there are safeguards: Italians cannot sign before 30 days' employment and any agreement has to be approved by a certifying commission and to be provided for by a collective agreement (see Chapter 7).

In Great Britain, an employer can now offer an employee shares in the business worth between £2,000 and £50,000 (approximately €57,938/ $76,155), exempt from capital gains tax if sold, in return for forfeiting certain employment rights, including unfair dismissal and statutory redundancy pay, and thus also the right to litigate or arbitrate over those rights. The employee, before assenting to a so-called employee–owner contract, has to have independent legal advice (Rigby, 2013). At the time of writing, this provision had found few adherents.

Elsewhere, the law generally proscribes choice. For instance, most statutory employment rights disputes in Great Britain can only go to the labour court (known as the employment tribunal). Nevertheless, British workers can choose to lodge an equal pay claim in the labour court or a civil court and they can claim 'unfair' dismissal in a labour court or in a (little used) so-called arbitration alternative. Most contractual claims in Britain go to the civil court.

In South Africa, the position is complex but legislation specifies what claims must be arbitrated (essentially dismissal for misconduct or capability) and what claims must go to the labour court. Nevertheless there is some overlap in South Africa as contractual claims may go to the civil court or to the labour court. In all the countries mentioned above, as we have said, if there is a choice of forum it is the worker's choice.

Until recently in the Netherlands (Chapter 8) the choice has been the employer's in respect of the termination of employment, not the employee's. This is because an employer may opt to use either the civil courts to dissolve the relationship or an administrative procedure under which an official, having taken advice from a bipartite panel of employer and employee nominees, can authorise a termination and a financial settlement. This choice, however, is likely to be removed from 2016, when employers will have no choice on the route to be taken, which will depend on the type of dismissal.

In Sweden, the choice of forum is not the worker's. Access to the Swedish Labour Court is confined to trade unions, the Discrimination Ombudsman, an employers' association, or an employer who has entered into a collective agreement. A worker not supported by a trade union only has recourse to the civil courts, as does an employer who does not have a relevant collective agreement or is not part of an employer's association.

In France and Germany, there are no choices: labour courts have exhaustive jurisdiction over employment disputes, with the exception of civil servants who are subject to administrative law.

Interestingly, in most of the dedicated first-instance employment rights adjudicatory bodies, the professional judge is required to be legally qualified, but in New Zealand and Ireland the first-instance adjudicators, although only dealing with employment issues, are not required to be so qualified.[3] Similarly the private arbitrators in the United States, the officials who hear dismissal cases in the Netherlands and the South African arbitrators who hear misconduct and incapacity dismissals are not required to be legally qualified.

Labour courts

In many countries, as noted above, workplace disputes go to labour courts, and much of this book is taken up with a detailed consideration of how such courts operate in France, Germany, Great Britain, Sweden, New Zealand and Ireland. Many other countries not included in this book also have labour courts, including Austria, Belgium, Denmark, Finland, Luxembourg, Slovenia and, fairly recently, Japan.

As noted above, the rationale is that the employment sphere has its own norms, rules and exigencies and that employment disputes should, therefore, be adjudicated in their own special courts. Hepple (1988), however, submits that the distinctions between labour courts and the civil courts are minimal. Evidence from our studies certainly indicates a wide range of practice in labour courts in terms of formality, the role of the presiding judge, adversarial versus investigative procedures and other dimensions. Nevertheless, overall, we have found that in general labour courts are less formal and more investigative than the civil courts as the country chapters illustrate.

Moreover, a professional judge in a civil court only occasionally deals with employment rights.[4] In labour courts the professional judge who presides becomes/is expert in labour law. Italy provides a half-way house. Employment rights claims go to a special chamber of the *Tribunale*, the first-instance civil court, but the professional judges hearing cases in the special chamber may be moved to another branch of the civil court system, so they may only have a limited opportunity to build up their knowledge of employment law before they are moved (see Chapter 7).

In some labour courts, for instance New Zealand's Employment Court and South Africa's Labour Court[5] in this book, the only adjudicator is a professional judge, but in many labour courts, the professional judge sits with lay judges (see Figure 1.2). These lay judges provide industrial expertise that can be distinguished from labour law expertise. That said, lay judges mainly provide general knowledge of the world of work, rather than particular knowledge of workplaces in specific industries. Nevertheless there is a continuum. At one end is Great Britain, where precise matching to a workplace, occupation or sector has been discouraged by the higher courts.[6] At the other end, at least in theory, is France, where there are five chambers that represent broad industrial sectors/occupations: industry, commerce and private services, agriculture, managers and specialists, and a general section.

Where labour courts include lay judges, they are normally tripartite and in the main lay judges are nominated by trade unions and employer organisations, as is the case, for example, in Germany, Ireland and Sweden in this book. France's labour courts are unusual in two respects: firstly, employer and trade union lay judges are elected, not nominated, by the social partners and also they form a bipartite court; secondly, the court only becomes tripartite with the addition of the legally qualified judge if the employer and employee lay judges cannot agree.

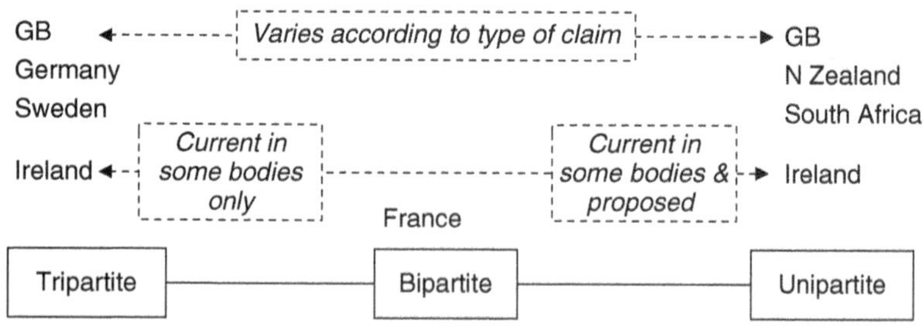

Figure 1.2 The composition of first-instance labour courts

Notes:

1. Currently in Ireland a tripartite institution hears first-instance claims only on certain matters, principally unfair dismissal. Under the proposed system in Ireland a tripartite Labour Court will be the appellate body, but there will be first-instance unipartite adjudication at the Workplace Relations Commission.

2. In France, the bipartite labour court becomes tripartite with the addition of the professional judge, if the two sides cannot agree.

Great Britain (Chapter 5) is also unusual in two ways. First, successive governments of different political hues have been whittling away the presence of lay judges. At the time of writing, the default position is that the British legally qualified first-instance judge sits with lay judges as a tripartite court in only a few types of complaints, principally discrimination cases, but he/she can depart from the default position, albeit subject to certain statutory criteria. In other countries, unlike Great Britain, where there are lay judges, they sit in all merits hearings and stakeholders who were interviewed either did not question the presence of lay judges or regarded them as desirable and a political given. In fact, the notion that a judge could determine the composition of their own tribunal was seen as a profound breach of the constitutionalist notion that the composition of a court is set by law, not the individual decision of a judge. A second unusual feature of Great Britain is that the lay judges are neither elected nor nominated by employee/employer organisations as in other countries where there are lay judges. They nominate themselves and are selected by human resources consultants and professional judges in the light of their performance in conventional human resources tests, including an interview.

The lay judges and the professional judge have equal votes in a tripartite system, but most decisions are unanimous. In some countries, where there is more than one judge and there is dissent, it is announced but in others it is not.

The appellate system

Germany has an autonomous, specialist system. Cases are first brought to the local labour court, then an appeal can be made to the regional (*Land*) labour court, with a relatively low threshold, with a final appeal to the Federal Labour Court. Thus in Germany the interpretation of employment rights, apart from the possible intervention of the Constitutional Court, is essentially immune from the interpretation of the 'ordinary' civil courts. Sweden too is immune from the intervention of the 'ordinary' courts; its Labour Court is the first and only court. In other words there is no appeal from Sweden's Labour Court. Furthermore, it hears appeals on employment matters from the first-instance civil court, so again the Swedish Labour Court is the end of the litigation road and is not subject to 'ordinary' judges in the 'ordinary' courts.

This was also the position initially in the new South Africa 1995–96 under the interim constitution, where cases went first to the Labour Court and then to the Labour Appeal Court (LAC). The final constitution, promulgated in 1996, however, said that all appeals should go to the Supreme Court of Appeal (SCA), apart from constitutional matters which should be determined by the Constitutional Court (see Chapter 10 in this book). As a result there is now a further stage of appeal from the LAC to the SCA. There are legislative proposals being considered by Parliament at the time of writing to remove the right of appeal to the SCA, making the Labour Appeal Court the final appellate body on labour matters as before.

Great Britain, like South Africa currently, has a mixed system. Appeals go from employment tribunals to the Employment Appeal Tribunal, a specialised labour court as its name suggests. Thereafter, appeals go to the 'ordinary' courts: the Court of Appeal (Court of Session in Scotland) and the Supreme Court. The New Zealand system is similarly mixed. Cases are initially determined by the Employment Relations Authority, but can be appealed to the Employment Court and then to the Court of Appeal and the Supreme Court. Ireland, which is in the throes of change, will under its new system also have a mixed appellate system (see Chapter 6 for full details).

In the Netherlands and the United States, both the first-instance courts and the appellate courts are civil only, as they are in Italy. Italy, however, like France, is somewhat of a hybrid: in both countries there are special sections in the appellate civil courts that deal with employment matters. A crude pictorial representation is given in Figure 1.3.

Where the appeal route is from a specialised labour court to a civil court, a related issue is the ease of appeal as that essentially determines the extent of intervention by the other civil courts in the labour court and the grounds on which an appeal can be brought varies country by country. In New Zealand an appeal from the Employment Relations Authority

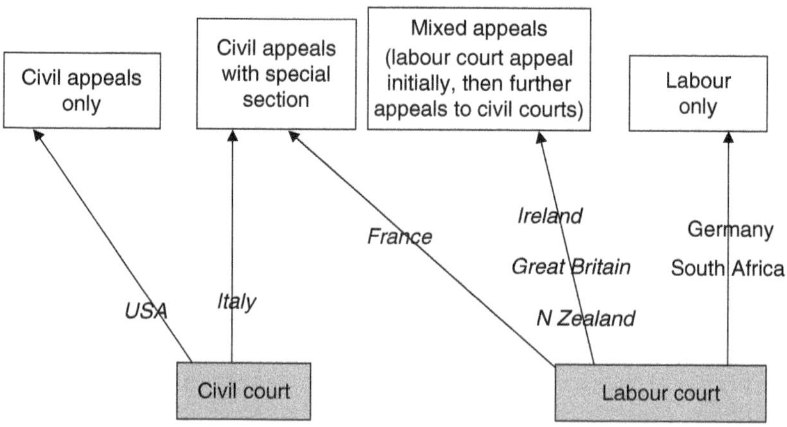

Figure 1.3 Appellate systems

Notes: 1. In Sweden there is no appeal from its first-instance Labour Court, although where a case is heard at first instance in a civil court, the Labour Court then acts as an appellate court.

2. The positions in Ireland and South Africa are depicted as if the current proposed reforms have been enacted.

3. There is no appeal in the Netherlands from employment rights cases, judicial review apart.

to the Employment Court can be brought de novo on fact and law as challenges to the first-instance decision. Thereafter in New Zealand appeals can only be brought on a point of law to the 'ordinary' Court of Appeal and from there to the Supreme Court. In Great Britain appeals at any level (Employment Appeal Tribunal, Court of Appeal and Supreme Court) can only be brought on a point of law. In France, appeals can be brought from the labour court to an appeal court (albeit to a special section as mentioned above) *de novo* if the amount at issue in each claim exceeds a certain sum (€4,000 at the time of writing) or in some other instances where the claim has a non-monetary value, such as rescinding a termination. In other instances, appeals can only be made on a point of law and go straight to the social chamber of the Court of Cassation, the highest court of appeal. In South Africa, appeals from the Labour Court to the Labour Appeal Court can be made on fact and/or law; (see relevant chapters for more details).

Another factor limiting appeals is the amount of the filing fee. In South Africa, there is no filing fee in any of its appellate courts. In Ireland there are no filing fees in its specialist labour appellate courts, unlike its appellate civil courts. Table 1.2 on pp. 16–17 sets out the institutions adjudicating unfair/unjustified dismissal disputes.

Enforcement bodies

There is some form of labour inspectorate in all the countries in this book, but the comprehensiveness of the labour inspectorate varies according to the range of topics deemed to be public law and according to the government's strategy on labour law enforcement. Historically, where workplace unionism was weak and unions looked to the state, as in France, the inspectorate had a larger role than for instance in Great Britain where unions were strong, particularly in the second half of the twentieth century. Today Great Britain has several enforcement agencies: the Health and Safety Executive, Inland Revenue (for the minimum wage); the Gangmasters' Licensing Authority for certain industries such as shell-fish gathering and horticulture, the Office of Rail Regulation, while local authorities also have health and safety responsibilities.

In some countries, for instance South Africa, the labour inspectorate's scope extends to all areas covered by labour legislation including health and safety. In other countries, for instance the United States, there is one labour inspectorate covering compliance with federal labour laws and another federal agency for occupational safety and health at work. Similarly in New Zealand there is one inspectorate for employment rights standards and another for health and safety.

In Germany, there is a division between the enforcement of health and safety standards, which is shared between the official inspectorate and sectoral accident prevention bodies, and the securing of compliance with

Table 1.2 Process for resolving non-discriminatory unfair dismissal disputes

	Pre-trial dispute resolution by another body		**Court/labour court**					
Country	**Required or considered by court**	**Govt funded C/M**	**Type of court**	**Type of judge**	**Pre-trial C/M by court**	**Court fees**	**Losing party normally pays costs**	**Type of appeal court**
France	No	No	Labour court	L & (P)	Yes	Yes	Yes	Civil, but specialised section
Germany	No	No	Labour court	P & L	Yes	Yes	No	Specialised
Great Britain	Yes	Yes	Labour court	P & (L)	No	Yes	No	Specialised initially only
Ireland	Yes	Yes	Labour court	L	Yes	No	No	Ordinary
Italy	No	No	Special branch of ordinary court	P	No	Yes	Yes	Civil, but specialised section
Netherlands	See note	No	Ordinary court	P	No	Yes	Yes	Civil

New Zealand	Yes	Yes	Labour court	L	No	Yes	No	Specialised initially only
South Africa	Yes	Yes	Labour court OR arbitration	P L	No	No	No	Specialised
Sweden	Yes	No	Labour court	P & L	Yes	Yes	Yes	None

Notes: *France*: Professional judges only adjudicate when lay judges are split evenly and thus cannot reach a decision.
Germany: The losing party pays court fees, but not the other party's legal costs. If the case is resolved in conciliation, court fees other than the initial filing fee are usually waived.
Great Britain A professional judge sits with lay judges in discrimination cases, but in other types of case the professional judge sits alone albeit the professional judge can exercise discretion and sit with lay members, after having regard to certain matters set out in statute. In some selected discrimination cases, there is pre-trial mediation. From 2014 parties are required to attempt pre-dispute resolution by another body.
Ireland: The table denotes the system to be introduced soon; the Workplace Relations Commission is set to be the adjudicatory body.
Netherlands: An employee can challenge a dismissal which has been officially authorised in the civil courts. There is no legally required mediation body, but courts may refuse to give a verdict if they think that the parties have not done enough to resolve the problem themselves.
New Zealand: If an agreement is not reached during mediation, the parties can agree to let the mediator determine the outcome, which is legally binding. Otherwise, the dispute can be referred to the Employment Relations Authority (ERA), which is a type of labour court. Decisions of the ERA can be reheard by the Employment Court.
South Africa: Conciliation is by the Commission for Conciliation, Mediation and Arbitration (CCMA). If there is no settlement the CCMA arbitrates unfair dismissal disputes on the grounds of capability, conduct and the severance of an individual only. Other unfair dismissal disputes go to the Labour Court, but only after conciliation by the CCMA has been attempted. The appellate position described is as if the proposed statutory amendment had been passed.
Sweden: If workers are not supported by their trade union and are not a union member, they go to the ordinary court with an appeal to the Labour Court.
United States: The United States is not included in this table as it has no legislation on unfair dismissal. In some organisations, arbitration is provided to resolve dismissal disputes.
Source: Adapted from Venn, 2010 but calculated by the authors.
Key:
C/M = conciliation/mediation
P = professional judge who is legally qualified
L = lay judge who is not required to be legally qualified

statutory sectoral minimum employment standards on pay, especially for posted workers, and authorisation to act as a temporary work agency, which is the responsibility of the Federal Customs Office.

Sweden, unusually, relies on unions to monitor employers' compliance with labour standards. These are mostly set out in collective agreements which cover 90 per cent of the labour force (see Chapter 11). Sweden does, however, have a separate health, safety and environmental standards body.

The powers of labour inspectors vary although they all initially seek to persuade employers to comply voluntarily. Typically there is administrative enforcement and civil penalties, with criminal prosecution only as a last resort. It is beyond the remit of this book to examine the results achieved by the various labour inspectorates. Suffice it to say, 'the results achieved reflect the means generally allocated to [them]' (International Labour Organisation, 2006: 56).

Changes

At the time of writing, important changes in respect of labour law adjudication in the countries covered here have already been introduced or are in train. One notable aspect of our research has been that virtually all the systems we considered were undergoing some form of change or had been the focus of debate. In some instances these were cost driven, often in the face of alleged high levels of claims, while others were responses to delays in the system: the details are outlined in the respective country chapters. In other cases, there have been attempts at or proposals for a more fundamental redesign of the adjudicative architecture, which has been seen as unfit for purpose. One conclusion from this might be that the impact of the juridification and individualisation of the employment relationship, which has gathered pace over the past two decades, together with the increased volume and complexity of legislation, again over the past two to three decades, has generated significant pressures for reform. We consider some examples below.

Changes introduced in Great Britain have resulted in a professional judge alone, that is, without lay judges, determining about four-fifths of all cases being heard at employment tribunals and virtually all cases at the Employment Appeal Tribunal. This contrasts with the position 20 years ago when there was tripartite composition in both these forums. Other changes introduced recently relate to filing fees and hearing fees at both employment tribunals and the Employment Appeal Tribunal and the formalisation of procedure (see Corby and Latreille, 2012 for further discussion).

In Ireland there is to be a complete overhaul: five sometimes overlapping employment rights first-instance bodies and a complex appellate structure are being replaced by a single first-instance body, the Workplace Relations Commission, with appeal to a labour court and thence to a civil court.

New Zealand's institutions for individual employment rights adjudication were changed dramatically in 2000 when employment tribunals were abolished and replaced by a three stage process: mediation, adjudication by the Employment Relations Authority and adjudication by the Employment Court. In France, changes have been proposed but not put into effect in respect of the principle of election of lay judges, given the declining rate of participation in these elections (Richard and Pascal, 2010).

In the Netherlands, proposals were made in 2012 for a radical recasting of the system for dealing with dismissals, the core business of most labour courts, in which the administrative procedure would be abolished. In 2013, after a change of government, this proposal was dropped and replaced by an alternative plan, to be implemented by 2016, in which two institutional routes will be maintained, but employers will not be able to choose which to use.

In Germany, the current position is held to be stable, with tripartite courts retained from first instance to the highest appellate level. This calm, however, has come in the wake of proposals from some jurists and *Land*-level governments that emerged in the 1990s to merge a number of civil jurisdictions into one, with the effective abolition of labour courts, certainly at appellate level. Ultimately, these proposals were not realised, mainly because of opposition from judges and trade unions.

The book's structure

This introductory chapter, after explaining the remit of this book, has sought to give a brief comparative overview of the institutions for employment rights adjudication, highlighting the different approaches that have been adopted in the ten countries covered. The next chapter provides a theoretical underpinning and seeks to ascertain whether these different approaches to employment rights adjudication can be squared with existing analytical frameworks. After that, in the following ten chapters (Chapters 3–12) we devote a chapter per country in alphabetical order. These chapters describe the institutions in the relevant country in more detail than is possible in the brief comparative overview in the first chapter. In the last Chapter (13) a comparative evaluation is offered. We explore which system is 'better' according to the criterion adopted.

2
Employment Adjudication: Comparisons and Anomalies

> Only by being contrasted with many other things, can something become wholly clear. Only by consideration of similarities and differences, and the reasons for these, is it possible to establish the essence and uniqueness of a thing.
>
> P.J.A. von Feuerbach[1]

Introduction

The country chapters in this study highlight the diversity in national arrangements for adjudicating employment disputes within a relatively small group of countries, but also point to some common features. This chapter aims to explore how this diversity and commonality might be explained. In particular, it considers whether it is possible to draw on broad social models that have a determinate effect on institutions within them and which might assist in understanding the origins, persistence or change of these institutions. We argue that such models can play a helpful role in comparing adjudicative systems and might usefully direct research into their legal and social history. Some caution, however, is in order. Abstract models still need to leave some 'allowance for the unexpected' (Hirschman, 1987: 188), and anomalies can be instructive.

As yet, institutional research has focused on welfare systems, vocational training and industrial relations more broadly (Thelen, 2010: 45). In the field of comparative law, there has been work on corporate governance (Vitols, 2001) and the employment relationship (Deakin, 2009; Rubery, 2010). In an approach closer to that envisaged here, Teague (2009) used 'path dependency' to compare conflict resolution arrangements in Ireland and Sweden.

One reason for this relative neglect might be that adjudication bodies are 'second-order' institutions that reflect broader social structures but which enjoy relatively high autonomy.[2] In the country chapters that follow, we have emphasised the role of contingency at a number of points: examples include the emergence and transformation of Dutch administrative dismissal procedures (Chapter 8) or the complex accretion of institutions in Ireland (Chapter 6). Nonetheless, how institutions have been and are being transformed exhibits numerous systematic relationships to their wider contexts, and these contexts also lend themselves to categorisation – albeit drawing on models that are not unchallenged.

We draw on three theoretical frameworks that have been subject to much discussion and debate by scholars and which, at least at first sight, have application to adjudicatory institutions for employment rights: the 'legal origins hypothesis' (LOH); national business systems, specifically 'varieties of capitalism' (VoC); and comparative industrial relations.[3] In his study of the privatisation of wrongful dismissal protection, Finkin (2008) suggested that the differences in approach to this issue evident in the United States, Britain and Germany might be explained by drawing on the legal origins theory, a political power model and public choice theory, in part adapting the three theories tested by Botero et al. (2004). We have used the LOH, but not public choice theory or the political power hypothesis, although we do refer to the latter. Instead we have chosen to look at two further institutional theories, VoC and IR typologies, as we are interested in this chapter in looking at a wide range of institutional features and exploring whether these can be linked to 'macro-social' models other than LOH. We also want to create scope for analysing deviations from these 'ideal types' using some of the concepts prevalent in institutional theory (see also Blalock, 1961: 17).

This chapter begins by outlining the three frameworks and draws them together in a summary matrix for the countries looked at in this book. Using two basic dimensions, we then explore whether the national adjudicative mechanisms delineated in this book fit with or deviate from the models. In doing this, we also consider the limitations and applicability of the models and contrast their accounts. Our discussion then looks at the anomalies and offers some thoughts on whether the models are useful for categorising and explaining national differences in employment rights adjudication.

Theoretical frameworks

Legal origins hypothesis (LOH)

There are a number of strands of LOH, and we note only some of the central aspects here. According to LOH, national regulatory approaches are significantly influenced by whether a country belongs to one of the two 'principal legal families' (Deakin et al., 2007: 133; Zweigert and Kötz, 1998): the civil law tradition (with French, German and Nordic variants) and the English common law tradition. In both cases, countries largely outside of Europe acquired their systems 'involuntarily' through transplantation and colonialism, often in hybrid forms, and also with curtailments of some of the rights granted at the centre. Based on Klerman et al. (2011), we therefore categorise

South Africa here as a 'mixed' system with elements of Dutch (civil) and English (common) law, as well as customary law.

The LOH literature focuses on a number of central differentiators, although there is debate both around these and the characterisations of the social and economic relationships that prevailed when Europe's legal systems emerged. For common law countries, principally England, Glaeser and Schleifer (2002) focus on the independence of judges and the use of juries, together with reliance on case law and precedent, and regulation through contracts and markets. Civil law countries have a tendency towards codified laws, single professional judges, inquisitorial procedures and a reliance on documentation. We explore the relevance of these features, and critiques of them, further below.

One major thrust of the LOH has been to establish links between legal systems and economic efficiency: the main hypothesis is that common law systems are more conducive to efficient corporate governance due to their adaptability and – alleged – limited scope for rent seeking.[4] In the employment field, the LOH was applied by Botero et al. (2004) to labour laws, but not their enforcement, in 85 countries using three theories of institutional choice: efficient adaptation of institutions to change, political power (in this context of labour) and the impact of legal origin. Employment laws were scored for (formal) protective impact for employees and regressed against proxy variables for the three theories: the strongest determinant was legal origin.

Deakin et al. (2007) and Deakin and Sarkar (2009) highlight a number of problems with the LOH that are of relevance in any attempt to assign countries to legal families. One concern is that it is based on a 'stylised' distinction between the two traditions that blocks a more nuanced view of differences and masks areas of overlap. First, there are significant differences *within* the two legal families: Mahoney (2001: 513) and Zweigert and Kötz (1998) note the distinctive German and Nordic civil law traditions compared with France; some aspects of Dutch law also reflect the impact of mixing French and German traditions. Deakin (2009) also emphasises these differences in terms of the contract of employment, in which systems subject to French influence were characterised by the assumption that the 'state had the power to regulate basic conditions of work' (ibid.: 48), leading to a pronounced role for public law and official enforcement, as seen in France itself and in the Netherlands.

Second, the two LOH models (that is civil law versus common law) are rarely found in a 'pure' form at least in respect of employment rights adjudication. In terms of overlap, in Germany, for example, much employment law and virtually all law on industrial action has been shaped by case-law developments of constitutional principles. Although under civil law traditions, the employment relationship is held to be constituted by statute, leading to formalised statutory types of contract, in Germany there is typically extensive scope for judicial interpretation over what is 'equitable' and 'proportionate' in the field of termination. In addition, despite a formal absence of a doctrine of binding precedent in civil law systems, higher courts in France and Germany are enjoined to ensure that case law is consistent and lower courts are limited in their scope for judicial experiment through a requirement to conform to landmark decisions issued by higher courts on certain matters in Germany and by the emergence of 'standing jurisprudence' that has high persuasive force in the interpretation of statute in both countries.

Notwithstanding these caveats, Table 2.1 denotes the national legal order of our ten countries.

Varieties of capitalism

Our second theoretical framework is based on the theory of national business systems, and in particular the varieties of capitalism (VoC) variant.[5] This holds that firm strategies are shaped by the range of institutional opportunities and constraints for resolving coordination problems, leading to distinctive paths of development and the reinforcement of these through 'complementarities' between industrial relations arrangements, training, corporate governance and collective actors. Positive feedback between firms' strategic choices and institutions creates two broad models: coordinated market economies (CME), in which coordination problems are managed by non-market methods; and liberal market economies (LME), in which these problems are resolved by competitive and contract-based inter-firm relations. External shocks arguably reinforce these clusters rather than levelling out differences.

We do not propose to engage in a critique of the VoC approach here; both the theory's authors as well as its critics have been occupied in a long period of refinement and revision. However, two aspects relevant for this study are the dichotomous nature of the theory and a time element.

On the dichotomy, VoC authors have allowed for hybrids and we make use of the 'Mediterranean' type in our typology below for France and Italy.[6] The case of South Africa illustrates some difficulties of the VoC approach with its focus on developed economies. One way of dealing with this would be to use a more complex typology, such as applying one of the models developed by Whitley (1999) initially for Asia. South Africa also could be viewed in terms of its complex heritage and the effects of adding to this a set of post-apartheid institutions that drew on international standards and perceived national 'best practices' from Great Britain and the United States in respect of conciliation and arbitration. In view of these complexities, we refrain from categorising South Africa in terms of VoC.

The issue of timing is also important. Although VoC theory is a 'longue durée' model, three of the countries in our selection that are classed as LMEs (Great Britain, Ireland and New Zealand) have experienced some 'institutional friction' between their economic model and their employment regime (Lieberman, 2002).

Table 2.1 denotes the national business system (VoC model) of our countries.

Comparative industrial relations (IR) models

For our third theoretical framework we draw on the typology of European industrial relations suggested by Ebbinghaus and Visser (1997: 336ff), which is directly applicable to some of our cases. Whereas the LOH approach is an explanation by historical genesis with path dependency and the VoC theory is rooted in assumptions about how rational firms interact with social institutions and relies on a theory of feedback mechanisms, the comparative IR model is essentially a categorisation in which types exhibit 'persistence' (ibid.: 338) from a set of distinct starting positions in the immediate post-war period. For Ebbinghaus and Visser, the core European model is seen as a social partnership model, in which labour conceded pay moderation in return for which employers reinvested profits. The precise configuration of the relationships between labour and capital, in particular whether union movements were unified and/or had access to government, determined the character of each type. Ebbinghaus and Visser (cf. Crouch, 1993) distinguish several 'basic types':

- 'Nordic corporatist', based on collective self-regulation, strong labour market actors, multi-employer bargaining, with various degrees of decentralisation, and in which the state acts as a mediator between capital and labour.
- 'Continental European Social Partnership', based (classically) on free collective bargaining, with extensive statutory employment and representative rights.
- 'Anglo-Saxon pluralism' (perhaps better 'Anglophone'), based on deregulation, weak labour market actors, workplace level industrial relations and common law contractual principles.
- 'Latin polarised', with a strong state-led sector, adversarial and politicised industrial relations and extensive statutory regulation.

Labour law adjudication: A summary comparative matrix

Table 2.1 summarises some of the main features of national systems of adjudication that are subsequently considered in terms of associations or anomalous relationships with the three frameworks briefly explained above. For simplicity, decision-making members of labour courts who are not required to be legally qualified, and who are variously described as lay judges or lay members in the ensuing chapters, are termed 'non-legal members' (NLMs) in this chapter. As we note below, although by no means the only differentiator, the role of NLMs is a significant characteristic that both distinguishes national systems and offers linkages to the wider employment relations context.

The main headings used provide an overview of the key features of labour courts (and other judicial and administrative bodies):

- the existence of a distinctive labour jurisdiction,
- whether the labour court includes NLMs (tripartite/bipartite) or not at both the first-instance level and at the first level of appeal,
- the 'national legal order' and the national business system and IR type,
- the 'direction of travel' both of labour adjudication, in terms of recent changes and proposals and employment regulation.

We have included a 'direction of travel' in order to add a time element to what otherwise can be an asynchronous (cross-sectional) account typical of 'coding' approaches to comparative law or the emphasis on institutional persistence in some variants of VoC. As Deakin et al. (2007: 142) noted in their critique of the LOH, without some element of time it is impossible to comment on the speed and nature of legal change. The introduction of a time element also allows some exploration of the associations between change and stability in labour courts and wider changes in business systems, in particular when considering some of the apparent national anomalies that arise from the use of the typologies. Table 2.1 denotes the employment adjudication system in our ten countries set against the explanatory models being used: Figures 1.1, 1.2 and 1.3 provide further detail, as do the following country chapters.

Applying the models

The dimensions

We now consider whether it is possible to associate the main features of adjudicative institutions with wider legal and economic systems, drawing on the frameworks reviewed above, and focusing on two main dimensions:

1. Existence of labour courts.
2. Presence and powers of NLMs, including in relation to professional judges.

We have chosen two dimensions in order to keep the presentation reasonably accessible and allow for a qualitative review based on the descriptions of the national systems in the country chapters. We have selected these two particular dimensions as they are significant differentiators between national systems. In labour courts, first-instance adjudication takes place in a bespoke

Table 2.1 Employment rights adjudication and explanatory models

Country	Employment adjudication regime	Labour court composition		National legal order	National business (1) and IR system (2)	Direction of travel: employment regulation	Direction of travel: adjudicative institutions
		First instance	Appellate				
Germany	Separate labour courts at all levels	Tripartite	Tripartite	Civil law	1. CME 2. Continental European Social Partnership	More individual rights via EU anti-discrimination legislation. Reaffirmed collectivism in manufacturing: increasing fragmentation in service sector	Adjudicative institutions are stable and supported by trade unions and employer associations. Radical proposals to merge jurisdictions or limit tripartism currently in abeyance
N. Zealand	Quasi-judicial investigative first-instance procedure: separate labour court for appeals	Expert investigator appointed by public authorities	Judge alone	Common law	1. LME 2. Not classified	Shift from collectivism to pluralism and individualisation, with declining trade union density	Abolition of tripartism in adjudicative bodies in 1991. Large-scale institutional restructuring with primacy of mediation before adjudication

Neths	Disputes heard in civil courts with rapid procedure. Optional admin. procedure for employer termination		N.A.	Civil law	1. CME 2. Continental European Social Partnership	General retention of collectivism with controlled deregulation of employment law and welfare reform	Recent oscillating reform proposals depend on political developments. As of 2013, two-track system to be retained but employer choice removed. Some devolution within administrative process to collective actors
Sweden	Separate labour court at first instance, with no appeal	Tripartite	No appeal	Civil law	1. CME 2. Nordic Corporatism	'Decentralization disguised as coordination' (Howell and Givan: 2011: 237) but within a strong collective framework that has retained 'institutional coherence' (Teague, 2009)	Adjudicative system is stable with no support for employment adjudication to move to civil courts
	OR						
	civil courts for some cases with appeal to labour court	N/A	Tripartite				

Table 2.1 (Continued)

Country	Employment adjudication regime	Labour court composition		National legal order	National business (1) and IR system (2)	Direction of travel: employment regulation	Direction of travel: adjudicative institutions
		First instance	Appellate				
France	Separate labour court at first instance: civil courts for appeals	Bipartite	Judge alone	Civil law	1. 'Mediterranean' 2. Latin polarised	Formal retention of industry-level collectivism, with weak TUs partly offset by state-based tri- and bipartism State intervention to shape new forms of firm-level representation	Various reform proposals recently. (1) To simplify elections to labour courts and raise participation. (2) More radically, to merge labour and other courts at first instance. Outcome of both uncertain

Great Britain	Labour courts deal with statutory and some contractual disputes. Civil courts can adjudicate on contracts	Unipartite or tripartite essentially depending on type of complaint	Judge-alone unless judge opts for tripartism	Common law	1. LME 2. 'Anglo-Saxon pluralism'	From weakly-institutionalised collectivism to pluralism, with increased 'individualised juridification' and weak institutions leading to upsurge in employment claims	NLMs no longer appointed by collective actors (since 1999) Progressive loss of influence of NLMs at first instance through enhanced powers for judges presiding alone, and at appeal level through removal of NLMs, subject to judicial discretion

Table 2.1 (Continued)

Country	Employment adjudication regime	Labour court composition		National legal order	National business (1) and IR system (2)	Direction of travel: employment regulation	Direction of travel: adjudicative institutions
		First instance	Appellate				
United States	State and Federal civil courts hear employment-related cases	N.A.		Common law 'Legal adversarial-ism' (Kagan, 2007)	1. LME 2. Not classified	Falling union density, low statutory employee protection, apart from discrimination laws	Growing practice of workplace arbitration – before employment an individual can be asked to agree to arbitrate, not litigate, employment rights disputes
Italy	Disputes heard in civil courts in specialist chambers	N.A.		Civil law	1. 'Mediterranean' 2. 'Latin polarised'	High collective bargaining coverage in an articulated system, with increasing pressure to devolve bargaining to work-place/company level	The situation is stable but in some respects this resembles a 'low level' equilibrium, with long-delays, and no consensus on finding a resolution

Ireland	Complex arrangements at both first instance (expert investigator or tripartite labour court). Appeal, mainly separate from the civil courts	Expert investigator or tripartite labour court	Tripartite for some complaints; otherwise, appeals go to the civil courts	Common law	1. LME 2. 'Anglo-Saxon pluralism'	The mixture of voluntarism and social partnership in place since the mid-1980s under pressure. Fragmentation of adjudicative institutions due to weak collective actors (Teague, 2009)	Radical measures to streamline the system in train, including abolition of first-instance labour courts and replacement by a single arbitrator/adjudicator with appeal to Labour Court
South Africa	Some types of complaints arbitrated, others go to labour court. Civil courts can adjudicate on employment contracts	Judge alone or arbitrator alone	Judges (3) without NLMs	'Mixed' Common law but with other influences	Not classified	Restructuring and pay bargaining have tested post-apartheid IR institutions, where mass direct action can still pay a significant role	The post-apartheid system is broadly stable, with conciliation-arbitration handling the bulk of initial claims, underpinned by notion of 'fairness'

forum, usually with different procedures and norms from the 'ordinary' civil courts. We have not looked at appellate systems, where the picture becomes more complex.

The presence and powers of NLMs are central indicators of the role of employers and employees in adjudication and also a proxy for other aspects of national employment systems, such as the role of collective actors. For Hepple (1988: 179), NLM expertise was one of the justifications adduced for having separate labour courts.

We also note any anomalies, or apparent anomalies, and what might be expected, and consider how these 'deviant cases' (Mahoney, 2000: 508) might be explained or whether they undermine the basis of the models. However, we draw only limited inferences about causation.

Existence of labour courts

If the LOH were to have broad explanatory force, it would be reasonable for it to suggest a relationship between legal origin and forms of labour adjudication, such as the existence (or non-existence) of a separate form of labour jurisdiction, in particular given the high proportion of individual employment rights claims as a percentage of all party v party law disputes in many countries.[7]

On a 'stylised' view, civil law systems might be expected to have more arbitral arrangements, based on investigative judges taking written evidence, and applying codified rights. In contrast, common law systems might be expected to exhibit more adversarial proceedings, a greater role for contracts and principles of tort over statute, more representation by lawyers and less by collective actors and the likelihood of a focus on using civil courts (Table 2.2).[8]

Of the five common law systems considered (United States, Ireland, Great Britain, New Zealand, South Africa), all except the United States have labour courts, as do three of the five civil law systems (Germany, Sweden and France). Italy does not have labour courts, but its civil courts have

Table 2.2 Labour courts and legal origins

	'Legal origins'									
	Civil law systems				Common law systems					
Country	**Germany**	**Sweden**	**France**	**Italy**	**Netherlands**	**GB**	**IRL**	**USA**	**NZ**	**SA**
Labour courts	Yes	Yes	Yes	No	No	Yes	Yes	No	Yes	Yes

Anomalies: Italy (civil law). All except the United States (common law).

employment chambers. This also applies to the Netherlands, which has a rapid civil procedure. In short, there does not seem to be a close association between LOH and the presence or absence of labour courts.

The VoC model would suggest that CMEs, as societies with embedded collective institutions, might have separate labour institutions with exclusive (or near exclusive) jurisdiction; that LMEs would be more likely to resolve contractual issues through civil courts; and there would be no clear outcome for the 'Mediterranean' hybrids (Table 2.3).

At first sight, the presence/absence of labour courts does not tally with the models within the VoC approach. While two of the three CMEs have labour courts, the Netherlands does not. However, it does have a special chamber in its first-instance civil courts as noted above. It also has an administrative process under which employers may apply for authorisation to dismiss, with officials taking advice from a bipartite committee of NLMs. Moreover, at the time of writing, this is likely to be reinforced in the future by a greater role for collective actors (see Chapter 8). The majority of LMEs, however, also have labour courts, with the exception of the United States. Nevertheless in Great Britain and Ireland, where there are labour courts, some contractual disputes are heard in the civil courts. Also Great Britain's labour court (employment tribunal) is becoming increasingly similar in terms of procedure to the civil courts (see Corby and Latreille, 2012 for a full discussion).

Broadly the same considerations apply in the case of categorisation by industrial relations system (Table 2.4).

Presence and powers of NLMs

We consider here whether there are associations between the presence and powers of NLMs at first instance in terms of the three approaches (LOH, VoC, and IR system). If NLMs lose powers in relation to professional judges then one of the distinctive features of labour jurisdiction could become diluted

Table 2.3 Labour courts and national business systems/varieties of capitalism

	National business systems (VoC model)								
	Coordinated market economy			**'Mediterranean'**		**Liberal market economy**			
Country	**Germany**	**Sweden**	**NL**	**France**	**Italy**	**G. Britain**	**Ireland**	**USA**	**NZ**
Labour courts	Yes	Yes	No	Yes	No	Yes	Yes	No	Yes

Anomalies: Netherlands (CME); Great Britain, Ireland, New Zealand (LME).

Table 2.4 Labour courts and industrial relations systems

	Industrial relations system								
	Continental European social partnership		Nordic corporatism	Latin polarised		'Anglo-Saxon pluralism'		Not classified	
Country	**Germany**	**NL**	**Sweden**	**France**	**Italy**	**Ireland**	**GB**	**USA**	**NZ**
Labour courts	Yes	No	Yes	Yes	No	Yes	Yes	No	No

and labour courts might become hard to distinguish from an arbitral system or a civil court with an employment chamber.

One feature alleged to characterise common law systems (in comparison with civil law systems) within the LOH approach is that they have wider scope for jury trials (Glaeser and Shleifer, 2002) and indeed jury trial is an option in the United States in federal discrimination claims. Moreover, NLMs have been termed the 'industrial jury'.[9] At first sight, however, there is no direct link between the two main legal families and the presence of NLMs (Table 2.5).

In Great Britain, however, the role of NLMs has been diminished, and in Ireland there will no longer be a role for NLMs at first instance under proposed changes, although NLMs will sit at the first level of appeal. In New Zealand the labour court included NLMs before 1991, but not since then as noted in Table 2.1.

What about civil law systems? In three of the four there are labour courts with NLMs, as already noted, while the Netherlands has an administrative procedure that includes NLMs as advisors, leaving Italy as the only real anomaly here.

One concern might therefore be to explain how and why such arrangements have arisen and persisted in civil law systems as seen by the LOH: as a theory of *origins*, this would mean tracing, through path dependency,

Table 2.5 NLMs and legal origins

	'Legal origins'								
	Civil law systems					Common law systems			
Country	**Germany**	**Sweden**	**France**	**Italy**	**Netherlands**	**GB***	**Ireland***	**USA**	**NZ**
NLMs	Yes	Yes	Yes	No	No	Yes	Yes	No	No

Note: *Some types of complaints only, as at August 2013.

links between the current situation and the key features of the civil law system. One such link might be the lesser role of lawyers in civil law systems and a consequently greater role in adjudication for representative organisations, colleagues and even relatives. In Germany, for example, lawyers were excluded from labour courts for many years.

For Germany, Sweden and France, the presence of NLMs in labour courts might also indicate that political power factors play a significant role, an explanation also noted by Botero et al. (2004). Roe (2000), for example, argued that civil law systems are essentially a proxy for 'social democracy' – that is 'nations committed to private property but whose governments play a large role in the economy ... and favour employees over capital-owners when the two conflict' (ibid.: 543) – an argument that might need to be stretched, however, to embrace Italy.

From the standpoint of a VoC approach, at its simplest and ignoring many localised features, it would be reasonable to expect CMEs (or at least the Western European version) to have strong institutions and actors to solve collective action problems, and that these actors, in turn, might have the legitimacy and/or power to acquire and retain a role in labour courts: parity of strength between employers and employees would (ultimately) be reflected in parity of decision-making (Table 2.6).

Both Germany and Sweden of the CMEs have NLMs, although they are of very different types. In Germany, NLMs are primarily drawn from the workplace and they represent a substantial group of experienced lay people: their main role is to apply the law. In Sweden, the comparatively small number of NLMs are typically employees of a social partner organisation, and about half of their caseload turns on the application of statute and about half on the interpretation of collective agreements (see Chapter 11). As to LMEs, as already noted, in Great Britain and Ireland NLMs are only found in some types of complaints at first instance.

From the standpoint of Ebbinghaus and Visser's IR typology, we would expect strong collective actors, and consequently NLMs in labour courts, in countries assigned to Continental European Social Partnership and Nordic

Table 2.6 NLMs and national business systems

	National business systems (VoC)								
	Coordinated market economy			'Mediterranean'		Liberal market economy			
Country	**Germany**	**Sweden**	**Netherlands**	**France**	**Italy**	**Ireland***	**G. B.***	**USA**	**NZ**
NLMs	Yes	Yes	No	Yes	No	Yes	Yes	No	No

Note: *Some types of complaints only.
Anomalies: Netherlands (CME); Ireland and Great Britain (LME).

Corporatism. The converse would apply in Anglo-Saxon pluralist IR systems (Table 2.7).

This is indeed the case for the partnership and corporatist models, with the exception of the Netherlands; and in the pluralist systems NLMs are limited in the types of case they sit on. However, the 'Latin' model would not necessarily entail any particular pattern of labour jurisdiction, although a high degree of social polarisation might be expected to be prejudicial to tripartism or social partnership. This might lead to France being anomalous in the IR typology, especially as its labour courts at first instance are, in fact, bi-partite.

Powers of and NLMs and judges

Finally, we look at the powers that professional judges have to make decisions when sitting alone at first instance in labour courts: in particular, we distinguish here between situations in which judges may decide on procedural matters only or whether they may also make substantive decisions in *contested* cases. As we discuss below, this is a potentially significant differentiator in terms of the power of the judiciary in relation to NLMs.

	'Judge Alone'				
	Procedure			Substantive	
Country	Sweden	Ireland	Germany*	Great Britain	South Africa
VoC	CME	LME	CME	LME	
LoH	Civil Law	Common Law	Civil Law	Common Law	Mixed Legal Origin

Note: *In Germany, judges may decide substantive cases alone in some limited circumstances, but this power is rarely used.

The results are somewhat mixed, but overall, in civil law countries and in CMEs professional judges in practice only decide procedural matters at first instance, not substantive matters. Indeed in France, professional judges have no powers at all at first instance unless the NLMs cannot agree.

Associations and anomalies

Based on this, admittedly small, selection, there would appear to be some association between the models and a good deal of the fine grain of adjudicative institutions, but by no means a complete match. These associations would be bolstered if it were possible to deal with the anomalies.

Table 2.7 NLMs and the industrial relations system

	Industrial relations system									
	Continental European social partnership		Nordic corporatism	Latin polarised		'Anglo-Saxon' pluralism		Not classified		
Country	**Germany**	**Netherlands**	**Sweden**	**France**	**Italy**	**Ireland***	**GB***	**USA**	**NZ**	**SA**
NLMs	Yes	No	Yes	Yes	No	Yes	Yes	No	No	No

Note: *Some types of complaints only as on August 2013.

As we briefly noted above, the main anomalies are as follows:

- Great Britain: a liberal market economy, with a common law system, and assigned to an Anglo-Saxon pluralist IR model – but with tripartite labour courts.
- France: a hybrid in terms of VoC, and a civil law system, assigned to a 'Latin polarised' IR model: the anomaly is the existence of bi-partite first-instance labour courts, with appeals to civil courts with no NLM involvement.
- New Zealand: a liberal market economy with a common law system, but with a labour court.
- The Netherlands: a coordinated market economy, with a civil law system and assigned to a European social partnership IR model: the anomaly is that it has no labour courts.

We review some of the findings from applying the models, including these anomalies, under three main headings: functional equivalence, the impact of the time element and path dependency.

'Functional equivalence'

The concept of 'functional equivalence' is used frequently in current comparative research, with varying degrees of rigour and in differing versions (typically dubbed 'strong' or 'weak'). Despite being pronounced 'virtually dead' (Turner, 2001), a number of variants of functionalism appear to have lived on in institutional theory, explicitly or implicitly. At base, the concept refers to processes under which different institutions in different societies take on roles and activities that act in equivalent ways to fulfil (broadly) the same function, with function defined either 'strongly' in terms of tight causal relationships or more loosely in terms of a role. It implies that a set of social requisites can be identified that must be met within different societies, and that the existence of an institution can be explained, in some way, by its wider consequences. Our observations here are confined to the analysis of employment rights adjudicatory institutions.

There is some dispute about the role of functional equivalence within the VoC model. On the one hand, Teubner (2001: 419) argues that 'functional equivalence' eventually leads back to convergence theory, in which countries move towards a common model: he rejects it on the grounds that different societies do *not* have to solve the same problems by functionally adapting existing institutions, but that, in line with the VoC approach, societies face *different* problems. On the other hand, Deakin et al. (2007: 137–8) support the use of 'functional equivalence' as a means of explaining 'how formal diversity of legal rules masks a deeper functional continuity': 'functional equivalence' is 'an indispensable tool of comparative legal analysis, and arguably of comparative analysis more generally' (Deakin et al.,

2007: 138). Occupying a mid-way position, Hancké et al. (2007: 11) argue that if the concept of complementarities, a key element in VoC, is to be retained then a course needs to be charted 'between its more functionalist interpretations and the dangers of a more open-ended unstructured voluntarism'.

The VoC position would, therefore, as a minimum predict a clustering of institutions in terms of function *within* country groupings, but not between *all* countries. That is, should institutions change within these country groupings (as a result of contingent events, such as political conflict or external influences), 'actors will seek institutional and functional equivalents' (Hancké et al., 2007: 11) in order to reaffirm or re-establish coordination, reinforcing institutional patterns that facilitate this. If functional equivalence were discarded entirely, it would be hard to retain the idea of institutional complementarity that is central to the VoC approach.

Since collective institutions tend to support the presence of employer/employee NLMs on adjudicative bodies, and often nominate and train them, NLMs also tend to 'cluster' in courts in CMEs. Some VoC theorists have accepted that political power can act to change institutions, but that 'actors still face incentives to preserve the existing system of coordination' (ibid.: 12). It is, therefore, possible to support the notion of 'functional equivalence' without advocating a set of 'universal' social needs, but only if the equivalences are confined to the main country groupings. This would still, however, leave the difficulty of dealing with hybrid systems.

Is it possible, therefore, to look at any detailed features of employment adjudication that might reflect such complementarities and/or functions? The argument that NLMs should sit on adjudicative bodies to add expertise might be a candidate, as it implies that, where there is a high demand for employee 'voice' and limitations on 'exit', characteristic of CMEs, mechanisms might need to be found to inject or accommodate such expertise. On a functionalist argument, such as Deakin's, this would be irrespective of the specific shape of the institution. This might also offer an instance of institutional reproduction via legitimation (see Mahoney, 2000: 517).

The one CME without labour courts is the Netherlands, where restrictions on employer exit from the employment contract are fairly tight (court dissolution or official authorisation). As a consequence, although the Netherlands is a country without labour courts, dismissal can draw on workplace expertise through the administrative procedure.[10] The Dutch case might be read as an example of where there is a high a degree of 'contingency' in a national system (that is, the extent to which its institutions deviate from other countries in the same grouping – in this case not having labour courts in contrast to other CMEs), other institutions take on core roles expected or required by social actors through 'conversion' (Thelen, 2003: 228ff).

The functional equivalence argument in the VoC approach could be undermined in two ways in the cases and anomalies we consider here:

- for the Netherlands, if the prospects for the future of the administrative procedure turned predominantly on short-term political vagaries. There is some evidence for this in the fluctuations in policy, depending on the make-up of governing coalitions, and the outcome is not certain.
- by attributing too much weight to functionality over contingency; for example, the establishment of labour courts in Germany and France represented a victory for labour against an authoritarian judiciary (in Germany in the 1920s) and employer-only courts in France (in the nineteenth century). While it might be argued that Germany's trajectory as a late entrant required a strong state, it would be stretching the argument to suggest that this functionally generated social partnership and the strong collective actors seen as integral to CMEs, although it might have favoured these.

Time element

Both New Zealand and Great Britain crop up as anomalies in our schemas and both also figure as exceptions in the VoC literature and that of its critics (Kesting and Nielsen, 2008: 37ff on New Zealand).

The key factor is the change in both of these systems since the 1980s. In Great Britain, trade union strength (measured in terms of union density and workplace influence) grew from 1945 to 1979 at a time when tripartism was officially promoted and the welfare state blossomed, but collective institutions remained weak compared to those in many other countries. In 1979 a new government initiated a highly deregulated model. This earlier phase, nonetheless, left a trace of tripartite institutions, but these swiftly declined in number. Although employment tribunals are one institution that has remained, a step-by-step move towards unipartism has been supplanting tripartism. This 'echo' of a tripartist past arguably accounts for the anomalous character of the presence of NLMs in Great Britain today, while the social power of the legal profession in LMEs identified by Morgan and Quack (2010) might also contribute to explaining why the role of NLMs in Great Britain has been gradually eroded over the past two decades. New Zealand has followed a comparable course, but in this case formal tripartism in the labour courts was removed completely in 1991 after a change of government, as noted above. Roe (2007: 296) argues that, irrespective of 'legal origins, institutions are trumped, and perhaps trumped easily, by modern political forces'. The changes introduced in Great Britain and New Zealand, and in train in Ireland, would appear to exemplify this.

This leaves a need to account for France, whose labour courts remain unique in terms of their bipartite make-up. It should be borne in mind that as a VoC 'hybrid', France might be expected to exhibit exceptionalism. One particular aspect in France is the extent to which conflict between employers and workers' organisations in the nineteenth century turned on who would *control* labour courts, in which over long periods employers unilaterally ruled on disputes, rather than the preferred British option of *avoiding* the civil courts. Finkin (2008: 164) argued that first-instance adjudication in France seems more akin to 'arbitration'. This would imply that French exceptionalism is not quite so exceptional, when compared with other labour courts, as the *conseils de prud'hommes* are not true comparators with German labour courts, for example.

Path dependency

All three approaches (LoH, VoC and IR systems) rely on some form of 'path dependency'. The implications of this, however, differ between the three. There are a number of variants of path dependency in institutional and historical sociology.

Mahoney (2000) stresses that unless path dependence is understood as being no more than a reminder that 'history matters', 'the specification of path dependence is always a theory-laden process' (ibid.: 2000: 508) as it requires a concept of causation. On his argument, path dependency begins within a selection process during a 'critical juncture' prompted by a contingent event (and not an 'institutional genesis' that can be explained by functional needs).

In his summary of some of the basic path dependency positions, Teague (2009) identifies 'strong' and 'weak' versions. In the strong version, institutional inertia becomes almost insuperable due to internalisation of norms by individuals and the lock-in created by sunk costs: change comes from the outside. In a weaker variant, identified with Crouch and Farrell (2004), actors can overcome their inheritance and 'recalibrate' the system, securing a new path internally and possibly through 'stealth' (Teague, 2009: 501) or hollowing-out.

Ebbinghaus (2005) also explores stronger and weaker versions of the theory, with the aim of engaging with the more common practice of historical-institutionalist research in which the long-term developmental pathway of institutions is seen as shaped by collective actors whose 'decisions are bound by past and current institutions' (ibid.: 14). Summarising a number of contributions, Ebbinghaus sees path dependency as having three elements:

Case 1. Actors establish new rules at a critical juncture, often as a result of political conflict and power relations, possibly during a crisis.

Case 2. This decision is reinforced through institutionalisation, possibly gaining support through social acceptance.

Case 3. Once institutionalised, earlier decisions structure the scope for alternatives.

For the LOH, path dependency seems to imply that a set of contingent events in the early modern period (possibly earlier) led to the establishment of legal families that conditioned subsequent institutional, and on some accounts societal, development. The weakness of path dependency explanation for an LOH account is that it needs to account for the successful self-reinforcing reproduction of this initial influence, but does not itself offer such a mechanism, nor does it enable the anomalies to be tackled, except possibly through invoking additional contingent factors. Zweigert and Kötz (1998), two of the main theorists of the LOH view, themselves adopted a functionalist position, which allowed the different legal families to be retained but within which 'different legal systems give the same or very similar solutions... to the same problems of life' (ibid.: 39).

For VoC explanations, path-dependent institutional persistence is generally attributable to increasing returns, with subsequent lock-in due to the social and economic costs, including social conflict, of discarding arrangements: all these contribute to positive feedback. This does not mean that every institution must confirm to either CME or LME exigencies, and in this sense anomalies and 'institutional friction' are possible, together with historic remnants and vestigial practices. Broadly similar considerations would apply to the industrial relations typology but in place of economistic arguments (such as increasing returns), this focuses on 'persistence' as anchored in deeply rooted 'social divisions' in which 'organisational forms... change only slowly due to their deep social and cultural roots' (Ebbinghaus and Visser, 1997: 338); see, however, the more recent and nuanced position on path dependence in Ebbinghaus (2005).

Since nearly all the adjudication systems considered here have undergone or are likely to undergo change, or have been the subject of proposals for reform, any form of path dependency would need to accommodate change but also adduce factors that promote, slow or block it. In this sense, the 'weaker' version suggested by Ebbinghaus and adopted by Teague (2009) would seem more appropriate. Some examples might include:

- The stability of Swedish arrangements based on strong institutional coherence and efficiency as an adjudicative method ('increasing returns'), as discussed by Teague in a comparison with Ireland (see Chapter 11) (Case 2, above), with the origins traceable to an institutional settlement established at a critical juncture (the 1938 Saltsjöbaden Agreement, Case 1 above).
- Adoption of a new path in Ireland by selective elimination of some institutions, but retention of those with the strongest affiliation to collective actors in a complex setting (see Chapter 6) (Case 3, above).

- In Germany, new systems installed after crises (1926 and 1953), building on pre-existing institutions, with consolidation through institutionalisation and social acceptance, with risks to collective actors from change (Case 1, above).

Final thoughts

On balance, the LOH, on its own, does not appear to offer a convincing approach to the key differentiating factors of employment adjudication. Given the overlap between civil law societies and what Roe terms 'social democratic' societies, the political power hypothesis might be a more fruitful avenue of explanation. As Roe (2007) also notes, a theory of origins is insufficient to account for present-day institutions without additional arguments from outside of the LOH, such as path dependency or an 'institutional channel' (Deakin et al., 2007) to sustain them.

The typology of industrial relations systems offers a set of stronger associations between the IR model and the main features of employment adjudication, broadly consistent with the VoC approach, although for differing reasons. Its category of 'Latin polarised', however, does not offer much of a foothold for looking specifically at labour courts, and it also shares the weakness of the VoC approach, which also has difficulty with hybrids.

We have looked at VoC as a deterministic model. However, the degree of determinism required by the theory remains open to question as some institutions might be compartmentalised from others. As such, VoC does not require all institutions to complement each other; such a claim would fly in the face of the contingency and conflict seen in national histories, also possibly eliminating the scope for new institutions to emerge (Hodgson, 2001: 53–4). This would allow legal institutions a degree of autonomy, especially in terms of their origins, while permitting linkages to wider social structures through their acquiring new functions and roles ('conversion' in VoC parlance). As such, a less deterministic VoC approach, drawing on a weaker model of path dependency and incorporating scope for the emergence of institutional friction over time, would appear to offer a more convincing account of the dimensions of adjudicative institutions that we have considered here.

This is a limited account and one open to the many criticisms levelled against the VoC approach. Whether the associations that have been found are due to the political power that CMEs open up to trade unions, or whether there are deeper links, such as the role played by employer associations in retaining – or choosing to discard – institutions as a reflection of firms' interests is one issue that remains to be further explored.

3
France

Introduction

France has a distinctive system of labour jurisdiction, anchored in a bipartite first-instance court with lay judges elected by employers and employees, and scope for appeals to forums consisting only of professional judges. Election has endowed the system with democratic roots, but has also rendered current arrangements vulnerable to erosion in the level of turnout. For a society often portrayed as characterised by an adversarial relationship between employers and – competing – trade unions, labour courts (*conseils de prud'hommes*) would appear to represent an island of constructive discourse and consensus.

The plan of this chapter is as follows. We first consider the industrial relations and legal contexts. Next we look at the labour inspectorate, a key institution in French employment relations. We then turn to the labour courts, their history, jurisdiction and structure, including the role of elected lay judges.

Industrial relations context

Industrial relations in France are notable for their focus on the state. There has been a debate extending over many years over the desirability of strengthening collective bargaining as a means of regulation.

The French trade union movement is characterised by pluralism and, frequently, inter-union rivalry based on ideological differences: although these have abated somewhat over the past two decades, there is still an organisational legacy and continuing differences in approach (see Goetschy and Jobert, 2010: 171ff.). This extends from competition over places on labour courts and works committees to a need to manage adversarial relationships in workplace representative bodies.

Union density fell from just over 20 per cent in the mid-1970s to below 10 per cent by the early-2000s. According to Visser (2011) it was as low as 8 per cent in 2010/11 (11 per cent with retired and unemployed members), with just over 5 per cent density for the private sector and 15 per cent for the public sector (see Table 1.1 on p. 2). Low union density combined with a capacity for large-scale and short-term mobilisation is a function of several factors. In the first place, French unions, with their tradition of creating an activist *cadre*, have not sought mass membership. Employee support for particular union centres is registered through voting in elections for works committees (*comités d'entreprise*) and labour courts. Secondly, unions have suffered as a result of their politicised fragmentation – one further reason why employers resist union efforts at workplace organisation. Many French firms are marked by unilateral management decision-making, but embedded in a highly regulated context offering few immediate gains from union membership.

Workplace representation has a dual aspect, with representative bodies elected by the whole workforce (usually works committees) co-existing with workplace union sections. Union sections are responsible for collective bargaining. Works committees, compulsory in all enterprises with 50 or more employees, are responsible for information and consultation, and also organise social activities.

Collective bargaining is both widespread, in terms of coverage, yet often seen as 'underdeveloped' in comparison with northern European countries. It has advanced as a means of employment regulation principally through legislative initiatives, with significant steps in 1971 and in 1983, when legislation introduced an obligation to negotiate annually with unions at workplace level provided there is at least one union delegation present. A number of issues, including sick pay, have been regulated by national agreements between the five representative union confederations and national employer associations.[1]

Collective agreements may be extended to non-signatory employers by decree. Just over half of all industry agreements are extended (Ministère du Travail, 2013), and overall bargaining coverage is estimated at nearly 98 per cent (DARES, 2006), although in many instances only minimum terms are extended (in some cases with rates below the statutory minimum wage). Workplace bargaining may derogate from industry agreements on permitted topics.

For collective agreements to be valid at both workplace and branch level, they must be signed by representative trade unions that between them account for at least 30 per cent of votes cast in workplace representative elections and have not been opposed by any trade union representing the majority of the workforce. Since 2008, the status of being a 'representative union' at a workplace has been determined, amongst things, by the share of the union's vote in elections to works committees or other workplace representative bodies: a union must obtain at least 10 per cent at a workplace (or 8 per cent for sectoral level agreements, where workplace votes are added across a branch).

Legal context

The French legal system is based on the Constitution, international treaties and European law, and domestic legislation enacted by Parliament. France has a unitary system, although many functions are organised at regional level and there is a dispersal of judicial functions across a range of tribunals. There is also a strong role for public law and regulation enacted directly by the executive, subject to consultation with the *Conseil d'Etat*, which is also the highest administrative court. As such, there is no doctrine of domestic parliamentary sovereignty (Elliot et al., 2006: 68).

The overarching framework for the operation of labour courts is set by the Civil Code, which regulates all civil procedures including contract and tort; the Code of Civil Procedure, which regulates the court system at appeal level; and the Labour Code, which contains all legislation related to employment in a unified text that was substantially reworked into a new version in force from May 2008.

There is no formal doctrine of precedent, and the power of the judiciary is theoretically more circumscribed than in common law jurisdictions. Judges are, however, required to render judgments in cases before them irrespective of any 'insufficiency' in the statute to be applied. In practice, therefore, case law, especially at higher levels of appeal, has become an important benchmark for guiding judges, and for the general evolution of law (ibid.: 79).

Public law and labour inspection

The role of public law, principally through the Labour Inspectorate (*Inspection du travail*), is a central element in employment regulation. Labour inspectors not only are the official agency for health and safety, but also enforce individual employee rights, monitor compliance with the law, and issue the required authorisations for some employer actions. Most are employed by the Labour Ministry, although the inspectorate, which is organised on a regional basis, is an inter-ministerial body shared with transport and agriculture. There are 'labour inspectors', of which there are some 775, who are responsible for oversight of firms with more than 50 employees and 'labour controllers', of which there 1,400 and who deal with small workplaces. They may enter premises without notice.

Some tasks, such as checking agreed mutual terminations, are performed by local offices of the Labour Ministry and others by the inspectorate, such as authorising some types of dismissal. Aside from this task, inspectors may not intervene in contractual disputes, for which the labour courts are competent.

Areas in which the inspectorate has an active role include:

- application of labour law at workplace level (statute and collective agreements); posting of workers; contract, temporary and agency work;

- hours of work, where they may allow hours in excess of statutory maxima and approve some flexible hours arrangements; the minimum wage (SMIC);
- checking and authorising procedural and substantive aspects of dismissals: in some cases authorising termination, such as for protected employees;
- advising employees about their rights; powers of enquiry on discrimination issues and inspection of employers' annual gender audits;
- promoting amicable settlements in the event of workplace disputes, where they have an independent right to intervene.

Breaches of the law or acting without authorisation are criminal offences.

Other dispute resolution procedures

There has not been any major growth in alternative dispute resolution (ADR) procedures for resolving individual legal disputes outside of the framework of in-company or other agreed processes, despite legislation to facilitate mediation introduced in 1995, updated in 2012 to transpose European Directive 2008/52/EC, and despite delays in the court system and the high level of appeals. The legislation enables the judge in any civil procedure, including a labour court, with the consent of the parties to appoint a mediator with a three-month window. Costs are covered by the parties, a possible deterrent given the low level of court fees (see 'Full hearing' below). In the small proportion of cases where mediation was attempted at first-stage appeal level, it was found to be successful in a high proportion of cases and to work most effectively where lawyers did not attend the hearing (Blohorn-Brenneur, 2010).

More important has been a reform in 2008 allowing termination by mutual agreement ('rupture conventionnelle') rather than through dismissal where there has been direct negotiation between employee and employer and the intervention of the labour inspectorate. Although not ADR in the strict sense, the need for such negotiations prior to authorisation has been seen as possibly fostering a climate more favourable to ADR since, as a rule, termination procedures do not allow for negotiation. In 2012, agreed terminations represented 16 per cent of all terminations of indefinite contracts, including for economic reasons, with a rise of 11 per cent over the previous year. They are particularly used in small firms, and in relation to older employees. Levels of severance pay in such cases are generally higher than in straightforward dismissals (DARES, 2013). However, some unions – notably the CGT – are sceptical about any approach that weakens the strict application of the law or that includes scope for negotiation over employment status, which they regard as rooted in employers' 'allergy' towards judicial intervention and a predilection to override the protective aspects of the law (CGT, 2010).

Labour jurisdiction

Labour courts are one form of civil tribunal alongside other first-instance specialist courts. Aside from a forum for land disputes, it is the only one with a bipartite composition in which representatives of complainants and defendants sit in judgment. There is not a separate strand of labour jurisdiction from first instance to appeal. Appeals from first instance go to the social division of the local court of appeal (*cour d'appel*), at which there is no lay involvement, which also hears appeals from social security tribunals. This conducts a retrial and can retake evidence.

Labour courts are termed *conseils de prud'hommes* – councils of 'good men', to adopt the term used when these institutions were installed in the eighteenth century (Finkin, 2008). Their origins, or at least nomenclature, can be traced back to the Middle Ages, when conflicts between artisans were resolved by the judgments of their peers. This 'feudal' model of peer justice also became an ideal during the French Enlightenment but transformed into support for a jury system modelled on England, as a 'democratic alternative' to the professional judges appointed by absolutist monarchs (Montesquieu, 1753; Moritz, 1987).

The first modern *conseil de prud'hommes* was established in 1806 in Lyon to resolve differences in the silk industry. Universal male suffrage for elections to the labour courts and a composition with equal numbers of lay judges were introduced after the 1848 revolution, with provision for alternating presidency of the forums between employers and employees.[2] The balance shifted to the employers under the Second Empire (1852–70) but employee rights were subsequently re-established. Labour courts acquired their current form in 1907 with the introduction of female suffrage and with civil courts established as courts of appeal. Although not wholly meeting union aspirations, the reform removed the provision under which appeals went to employer-only trade courts (Moritz, 1987: 144). It also introduced 'tie-breaking', under which a professional judge has a casting vote if the two sides cannot agree (Olszack, 2008: 21).

These principles have become constitutive of employment regulation in France and a key element of its legitimacy, in particular given the low level of union density, in which a bipartite system with institutional privileges might seem anomalous. David (1974, cited in Moritz, 1987: 144) notes that 'since the great conflicts at the close of the [nineteenth] century, labour courts have been seen as a historical achievement on the part of the trade unions'.

As elsewhere, one of the greatest boosts to the activity of *conseils de prud'hommes* was the development of employment protection legislation, with the most significant step in 1973.[3] In 1979, changes were made to the labour court system, with measures to support compensation and training for lay judges, and protection against dismissal. The juridification of the employment relationship gave the *conseils* an enhanced role in applying the law rather than, as before, providing a forum for reaching agreement.

Virtually all forms of dismissal are subject to statutory procedures, where failure to comply can render the dismissal void, although in 2008 new provisions were adopted for termination by mutual agreement (see 'Other dispute resolution procedures' above).

The current system

Individual disputes arising out of the employment relationship fall under the exclusive jurisdiction of the *conseils de prud'hommes* where these arise out of the contract of employment. There are only a small number of exceptions: for example, disputes over the reward for employee inventions are heard solely at a few District Courts (*Tribunal de Grande Instance*), as are challenges to attachments of earnings and claims related to profit-sharing payments. However, these account for a tiny proportion of total employment-related disputes, of which over 95 per cent are heard by the *conseils de prud'hommes*.

Conseils de prud'hommes are bipartite, with equal numbers of employer and employee lay judges. Some 80 per cent of all cases heard involve issues related to termination (including wrongful dismissal, breaches of statute law on mandatory rehiring, severance payments, unlawful dismissals, application of restrictive covenants). Labour courts also hear cases of discrimination and workplace bullying, and disputes arising during the course of hiring.

Although labour courts do not deal with collective matters, which are heard by a District Court (*Tribunal de Grande Instance*), a number of individual claims may be joined and this has been used to contest collective dismissals.

As well as dependent employees, some categories of the self-employed deemed to be in a subordinate relationship to an employer can also use the labour courts. Labour courts are also competent to resolve disputes between employees, where related to the employment relationship. Labour courts have exclusive jurisdiction over disputes concerning childcare workers in crêches or in their own homes. All such employees have written contracts of employment.

Public servants (*fonctionnaires*) not employed under private law are excluded, and are subject to the system of administrative justice.

Staff representatives (*délégues du personnel*)[4] have a right to draw management's attention to any breach of employees' individual rights (*'droit des personnes'*), a broad notion encompassing physical and psychological well-being and 'individual liberties'. If no resolution is possible at the workplace, the matter can go to a labour court. In such cases, the judges may issue an order to ensure that 'all appropriate measures' be taken to rectify the breach: this can include requiring management to conduct an investigation with staff representatives.

Individual employers may also bring a claim against an employee – albeit an extreme rarity. Typically, such claims arise where an employee has not complied with a restrictive covenant or not kept to an agreed notice period.

Trade unions may not generally bring a claim independently, except in two circumstances. Firstly, they may act as a party (*action en intervention*) where an employee who is a union member has made a claim and this has an impact, direct or indirect, on the collective interest of the occupation in question (Code du travail, L. 2132–3). Whether the union's action is admissible is decided by the court. In addition, on some issues a union may act in place of an employee, or employees (*action en substitution*), without the employee being directly involved in the case. The employees must be clearly named in the action and receive any compensation awarded. These instances include discrimination and harassment, equal pay, redundancies, rules on fixed-term and temporary employment, and collectively agreed provisions (Boulmier, 2011: 39–41).

Organisation of labour courts

Labour courts are organised territorially, and parties attend depending on their place or work and/or residence: in all, there are 210 courts. To take account of 'social and economic realities', each court is divided into five sections in line with the sector of the employer, with sections for industry, commerce and private services, agriculture, managers and specialists (*cadres*), and a general section.[5]

Employees and employers stand for election for a specific chamber. In practice, sectoral knowledge plays only a marginal role, in part because the sectors are very broad and in part because the system does not operate strictly on sectoral lines when allocating judges to cases, with the residual 'general section' playing a major role. Industry specifics have also become less significant with the spread of general employment protection legislation. In practice, to reduce delay if a case is due to be heard, a hearing will be convened with any available members, irrespective of chamber.

In 2011, of the cases that were listed, aside from interim hearings, 37 per cent were heard before a commercial chamber, 25 per cent at an industrial chamber, 21 per cent by the general section, 16 per cent by the white-collar section, and 1.6 per cent by the agriculture section.

Each section has a conciliation panel and a 'judgment panel' for full hearings. Each also has a president and a vice-president, who normally chair hearings. The president and vice-president are lay judges (see 'Composition' below) and are elected for a period of one year from among all the elected lay judges in a particular court, each by the respective college of employer and employee members. The posts are held alternately by employer and employee members.

There is a national body (*Conseil supérieur de la prud'homie*), made up of nine representatives of trade unions and nine employer representatives, with five officials from the relevant ministries (labour, agriculture, justice). It can carry out studies and make proposals for the operation of the system. It is also consulted on proposed measures that impinge on the labour court system.

Lay composition

Each first-instance court consists of at least four lay judges, with equal representation from the employee and employer sides. Lay judges ('conseillers' or, on occasions, 'juges') are elected, and represent employees and employers.[6] Elections are held every five years by direct suffrage. The period of office is renewable, but members may not serve beyond ten years after they have ceased employment: retirement for many employees is between 60 and 63.

Given the significance of elections as an indicator of institutional strength for union and employer organisations, these commit substantial resources to the process. Organisations must seek to achieve an improved gender balance by reducing the gap between the proportion of women elected, and the female proportion of the relevant electorate.

All employees, job seekers, or employers, have the right to vote, provided they are older than 16, registered both as voters in France and as electors in accordance with their section and locality. Elections are held on the same day in each district during working hours. Employees have paid time-off to vote; around a third of electors vote by post. Voting is by a complex system of proportional representation. According to Richard and Pascal (2010), current arrangements have encouraged a large number of employee organisations to put forward candidates, although – as noted below – the main trade union centres account for some 70 per cent of all employee member positions.

Those eligible to stand for the employee side must be aged at least 21, be of French nationality and not be deprived of core civil rights, such as the right to vote. They must be employed under private law and may be trainees or retired (but may not hold office more than ten years after ceasing employment). Candidates for the employer side must either employ one or more employees, be partners, act in managerial capacity, or be a director.

The election held in 2008 was for 14,500 lay positions. Turnout was 25.6 per cent, a decline from the approximate 60 per cent turnout in the 1970s. On the employee side, the electorate was 18.7 million, of whom 4.7 million voted. By section, the highest turnouts were in industry and amongst managers and professionals (*cadres*), with turnout of around 30 per cent (34 per cent in industry).

The rate of declining turnout appears to have accelerated in recent years for employees, with a 38 per cent drop between 1992 and 2008 (Richard and Pascal, 2010: 24). This development has been seen as a challenge to the legitimacy of the system, and prompted an official review (see 'Reform proposals – Rapport Richard' below).

For employers, the electorate was 518,700, of whom 161,000 voted – a turnout of 31 per cent. Interestingly, employer turnout appears to have increased, although this is might be attributable to a contraction of the employer electorate (from 720,000 to 518,000) due to the exclusion of small firms.

In the past, these elections constituted the main indicator of union representativeness. However, this changed in 2008 when legislation was introduced establishing more formalised criteria for representativeness.[7] Table 3.1 gives the percentage of votes cast for worker lay judges by the trade unions.

Lay judges are not paid directly by the state unless sittings are outside normal working hours, when they receive a fee of €7.10 an hour: this rate is also paid directly to members who no longer work or who are unemployed when they attend a sitting at any time. Employee lay judges have paid time-off, and this is reimbursed by the state subject to statutory limits for each type of activity (30 minutes for conciliation, an hour for a full hearing, five hours for writing up a judgment). Employees elected for the employer college (such as senior managers or HR directors) receive double the fee quoted when they sit during the working day, again paid by the employer who is reimbursed by the state, and the ordinary rate for time spent outside usual working hours; alternatively, they may claim 1/1607 of their annual income. Travel expenses are directly reimbursed by the state. Employee members are entitled to 36 paid working days for training (and a maximum of two weeks in any one year). Training is financed by the state and delivered by an authorised organisation.

Any termination of a member during their period of office and for six months after requires authorisation by the Labour Inspectorate.

Table 3.1 Votes cast for worker lay judges by each trade union

Trade union	**1987**	**1992**	**1997**	**2002**	**2008**
	In per cent of total votes cast (numbers rounded)				
CGT	36.4	33.4	33.1	32.1	34.0
CFDT	23.1	23.8	25.4	25.2	21.8
CGT-FO	20.5	20.5	20.6	18.3	15.8
CFTC	8.3	8.6	7.5	9.7	8.7
CFE-CGC	7.4	7.0	5.9	7.0	8.2
UNSA	–	0.1	0.7	5.0	6.3
Others	4.4	6.7	6.8	2.7	5.2

Source: Ministry of Labour.

Procedures

Time limits

Although this book focuses on the institutional architecture of adjudication, not the legislation itself, time limits nevertheless bear on access to adjudicatory institutions and a dramatic change has taken place in France in recent years. Between 2008 and 2013, the previous period of 30 years in which an employee could challenge a non-economic dismissal or seek damages was reduced to two years for new claims.[8] The 2008 reform also allowed contractual parties to conclude contractual time limits that differ from those specified in law, in some cases with a permitted range from a minimum of one year to a maximum of ten years. Before 2008, an employee had a period of 30 years within which to bring an action to establish that she or he was the victim of discrimination, harassment or bullying and claim damages. This was also reduced to five years, to run from the date at which the discrimination became evident to the employee where the employment contract is still in force. The time limit for claims for bodily injury remains at ten years.

Conciliation

Before a labour court hearing, there is a mandatory requirement for conciliation, which is held in private and requires the personal attendance of the parties: parties may also be represented. It is held before two lay judges, one representing the employee side and the other the employer side, together with a clerk. The conciliation hearing is chaired by the president or vice-president of the local labour court. If neither the president nor vice-president is available, the hearing is chaired by one of the members, as designated by the president or vice-president. If no such decision has been made, the chair is taken either by the member with the longest experience or, if this is equal, by the oldest.

The conciliation panel can declare the claim to be void if the complainant or their representative does not attend without good reason. Similar considerations apply to the defendant, in which case the matter may be referred direct to judgment proceedings. There are a limited number of circumstances in which the conciliation stage may be omitted if the complainant wishes, principally where there is a concern to achieve a rapid outcome, such as an employee's request to convert a fixed-term contract into a contract of indefinite duration.

The conciliation panel also exercises a special role in the event of a collective dismissal. If a number of applications are made by individual employees with the same respondent, these may be joindered. The presiding judge can also join claims submitted by individual employees with the same respondent employer if there is a link between the claims and it is 'in the interests of justice' for them to be heard together. This is quite a common event, and reduced the total claim volume by some 14,000 cases in 2011 – probably as a result of jointly heard economic dismissal cases.

There is only one formal conciliation hearing, although the parties may come to an agreed settlement at any time. If a conciliated outcome is achieved, this is recorded in a statement signed by the parties, but not the panel members, based on minutes of the discussion taken by the clerk of the court (*le greffier*). Any agreed outcome can be implemented immediately. A conciliated outcome may only subsequently be challenged if the conciliation panel has failed to meet its statutory obligations, such as informing the parties about their legal rights. Aside from that, or fraud, a conciliated outcome is binding.

Following conclusion of a national collective agreement in January 2013, in June 2013 the government legislated to introduce scope for a prescribed lump sum payment linked to seniority to settle all outstanding claims and which can be offered during conciliation over a contested dismissal. The proposed rate would be equivalent to two months' salary for less than two years in post, rising in stages to a maximum of 14 months' for more than 25 years' service: this is substantially more than current penalties for unlawful dismissal and would not be expected to be binding, but rather represent the upper limit for freedom from tax and social security contributions. This is intended to raise the conciliation rate and avoid the need for a full hearing. At the time of writing, this was being considered by the Constitutional Council.

In addition to facilitating a conciliated outcome, the conciliation panel can also: require submission of documents; order payment of wages due or any other financial consideration (such as for paid leave or severance); call experts; and ensure evidence is preserved. When acting in this capacity, the conciliation panel becomes a public forum, although in practice this requirement is met 'symbolically' by opening the door of the room in which the hearing is held (Boulmier, 2011: 173).

In order to prepare a case for a full hearing, the panel may additionally appoint one or two members of the chamber as *rapporteurs* to prepare a verbal or written report on the case to highlight the key issues for the full hearing. *Rapporteurs* may, but are not required to, attend the subsequent hearing as judges. This practice has been criticised on the grounds that the *rapporteurs* may have already come to a conclusion about the case before a properly constituted hearing has been held. If there are two *rapporteurs*, one must be from the employer side and one from the employee side.

If conciliation fails, or only succeeds in part, the case, or any outstanding issues, will go before the 'judgment hearing' (*bureau de jugement*), as outlined below.

In contrast to some other national systems, fewer than 10 per cent of disputes are resolved at the conciliation stage, albeit with substantial variations between labour courts. This low rate of successful conciliation has been attributed to both the lack of training and of time on the part of lay judges as well to the fact that in eight of ten cases, the employer does not attend and is represented by their counsel. In addition, the same lay judge will also probably sit at the full hearing, possibly inhibiting the parties from exposing their positions (Blohorn-Brenneur, 2010).

Full hearing ('bureau de jugement')

Although a full hearing may follow directly from a failed conciliation, this is rarely practicable and the court clerk will then usually notify the parties and convene a hearing at an available date. The full court must have at least four lay judges – two from the employee side and two from the employer side. (Providing parity is maintained, a hearing may have more than four members, but this is rare.)

As with conciliation, chairing alternates between an employer and an employee president or vice-president of the local chamber on a rota system, with a fallback procedure by experience and age.

Hearings are normally held in public,[9] and matters are dealt with orally – although written positions and supporting documents may be exchanged between the parties and referred to in proceedings. Some labour courts may impose limits on the period within which written material can be communicated.

In the past there were no costs or fees. This changed for proceedings initiated after 1 October 2011, when a charge of €35 became payable by the party initiating proceedings. This is in the form of an excise stamp (*timbre fiscal*), which can be bought at tobacconists, at a public service office, or online. Anyone in receipt of legal aid is not required to pay. The sums collected are intended to contribute towards the costs of providing legal aid, and are not seen as a fee for defraying the costs of proceedings. Overall, the fee offsets some €60 million of the overall €379 million legal aid bill. In July 2013, the Minister of Justice announced that the fee would be abolished from 2014, and that the missing revenue would be found temporarily from within the budget, and in the longer term from another source, such as a levy on lawyers or on certain types of legal contract. It was emphasised by the Minister that abolishing the fee was a 'question of social justice' (Ministère de la Justice, 2013).

Claimants must cover the costs of legal representation. These typically have a fixed and a contingency fee element (approximate €1,200 and 10 per cent of any award at a first-instance hearing). It is possible to claim legal aid subject to income limits.[10] Claimants can also be represented by a union. Where a complainant loses, the labour court can require payment of the cost of proceedings and a portion of the other party's representation costs. However, there is some judicial discretion in this area.

Following the hearing, lay judges deliberate and announce their judgment either on the same day or shortly after, unless they consider there is a need for additional measures (such as supplementary reports or referring the case to the criminal courts). Deliberations and voting are secret, and court clerks are not permitted to attend. A judgment must be reached by at least three judges (in a panel of four), and is written up by the chair, with dissent not being announced. Interviewees for this study noted that writing the judgment is often seen as a challenging task by lay members, but also as representing an important achievement for the lay side. Lay members assist each other and writing up a judgment is seen as a rite of passage to becoming a 'real judge'.

Court clerks (*les greffiers*), who are legally qualified, play an important role in advising judges and helping transcribe judgments as well as in managing relationships with the parties to the case.

If the lay judges cannot agree (that is, no majority is achieved) the case proceeds to another hearing to 'break the tie' (*audience de départage – 'settlement hearing'*). This is held with the same lay judges but with the additional attendance of a professional judge who acts as 'the fifth member'. It is intended to allow a stalemate to be broken without the need for formal appeal. This practice is fairly infrequent, with a rate of 18–20 per cent of cases heard, with annual and regional fluctuations (Ministère de la Justice, 2012).

According to Boulmier (2011: 205), this low proportion demonstrates a high level of internal cohesion on the part of lay judges as well as some resistance to the intervention of a professional judge. Swierczek recorded one lay member as saying: 'It's like being an old couple who are forced to live together and listen to each other' (Swierczek, 2010: 124). An employer member commented: 'If I behave just as an employer judge, with all my a priori views about union members... that will just reinforce their convictions and certitudes' (ibid.).

In short, despite representing different interests, and against the background of a fairly high level of political militancy on the part of union representatives, lay judges are able to reach unanimous decisions without a professional judge. The low rate of tie-break points to a relatively high level of internal legitimacy. However, this also needs to be set against the relatively high rate of appeals (see 'Outcomes'). This, in turn, suggests firstly, a low level of external (performance) legitimacy and, given the low level of electoral turnout, possibly diminishing regime legitimacy.

The rate of referral to a 'tie-break' hearing appears to have increased in recent years. While this might appear to suggest a diminishing lack of consensus in the bipartite hearing, it has also been related to the changing composition of cases, with more economic dismissals based on employer arguments over competitiveness that are less amenable to bipartisan consensus.

A tie-break hearing rehears any outstanding issues. There are some conflicting views about the conduct of these proceedings. On one account, professional judges do not simply add their vote to one side or the other but participate fully in a rehearing at which the lay judges also engage in debate. Other accounts note an 'acceptable' level of discussion, but also that professional judges do not find it easy to adapt to the 'collegial style' held to characterise bipartite proceedings. One lay member noted that judges 'look down on us' and imply that the decision should 'be left to a pro' (Swierczek, 2010: 69–70). For their part, lay judges 'almost unanimously lament the lack of competence of professional judges in deciding employment cases' (ibid.).

This raises the wider issue of how lay and professional judges view each other. Whereas lay members have the legitimacy of being elected, and of their workplace knowledge, professional judges have formal legal knowledge and arguably see their professional identity, and the 'judicial space' (Bourdieu, 1987), as disrupted by the exclusive role of lay members at first instance, where the line of demarcation between the 'vulgar vision' (ibid.) of individuals about to come under the jurisdiction of the court and 'juridical actors' is blurred. Some judges expressed a preference to sit alone and had criticisms of lay members.[11]

'Rapid procedure'

Where swift action is seen as necessary, there is a rapid procedure, known as 'référé prud'homal'. This is applicable for issues such as non-payment of wages, failure of an employer to provide a leaving certificate or a statement of grounds for termination, and actions that block access to social security. It can also be used to prevent an immediate and evident contractual breach, such as dismissal of an employee for being on strike. In such cases, each court has a special panel, consisting of one employee and one employer judge. They decide whether the issue is urgent, not the merits of the case.

There is an option of, but no requirement for, conciliation and the application is made direct to the panel hearing the application, either by a bailiff or by a party on application to a court official. Lay judges can order steps be taken to remedy the problem or to avoid an imminent detriment, provided the defendant does not enter a serious objection. There is also scope for an application for an injunction from a civil court judge.

Appeals

Either party to the case has a right to appeal the first-instance decision if the amount at issue exceeds €4,000 (taking each claim of the same type separately, not the aggregate of all claims) or for certain other instances where the claim has a non-monetary value, such as revoking a disciplinary sanction or rescinding a termination irrespective of the monetary value involved. This sum will usually be indicated in the first-instance judgment. The appeal must be lodged within a month of the first hearing decision. If the sum is below the required amount, the appeal must go the social chamber of the Court of Cassation but only on the grounds that the first-instance court did not correctly apply the law.

According to the European Commission for the Efficiency of Justice (2012: 218) 42.5 per cent of employment dismissal cases were appealed and the rate of appeals has been rising steadily. Appeals in the employment area are also higher than in other fields of civil law and account for around a quarter, of the workload of the appeal courts (Ministère de la Justice, 2012a).

As noted above, there can be mediation by a third party (not a judge) at the appeal stage, but it is not compulsory. If a party refuses, or if mediation fails, the case is heard by the social chamber of the court of appeal (*la chambre sociale de la Cour d'appel*), with a typical delay of one to two years. There is no lay involvement at the appeal stages.

Further appeal can be made on a point of law to the court of cassation (*Cour de cassation*) in Paris, which is a general court, and at which legal representation is mandatory.

Discrimination cases

Provisions forbidding discrimination in recruitment, and on pay, training, promotion and any change or renewal of the contract of employment on a range of protected characteristics, including trade union membership, are contained in the Labour Code (Art. 122–45), together with specific provisions on disability. Cases are heard at first instance by labour courts, and any dismissal found to be discriminatory may be declared void, with the option of using the 'rapid procedure' to obtain an injunction. Discrimination is also one of the grounds that permits a union to act directly on behalf of an individual at a labour court.

Up until 2011, there was an independent body to combat discrimination (with the acronym HALDE). This was dissolved in 2011 and subsumed within the office of the 'Defender of Rights' (*Défenseur des Droits*), an independent body under the constitution. The *Défenseur* may intervene to 'reinforce' the application of the law, but may not bring a claim directly (Défenseur des Droits, 2012: 107ff.). Its powers are primarily investigative, based on cases referred, but it may make recommendations to enable a dispute to be amicably resolved. Based on its findings in a case, the *Défenseur* may also present observations on particular areas of law or in support of a claimant to the relevant jurisdictions, including an individual labour court considering a case, as well as more generally to develop and consolidate case law. The *Défenseur* may also be invited by the *Conseil d'Etat* to offer observations on a set of related cases.

Reform proposals – 'Rapport Richard'

In view of the decline in turn-out since the 1970s, M. Jacky Richard, a member of the *Conseil d'Etat*, was asked by the Ministry of Labour to report on the method of electing lay judges in order 'to preserve the unique model of justice based on [lay] judges from the world of work' and to make recommendations to 'strengthen the legitimacy of the institution and its members'.

Richard and Pascal (2010) identified several factors contributing to falling turnout. These included practical voting arrangements, declining overall participation in public life, the remoteness of elections from the everyday world of work, and a perception by employees that elections were part of a wider political and inter-union contest in which they were increasingly uninterested.

Richard outlined three reform options:

- Maintain the current system but simplify voting (internet voting, removing voting by section, and simultaneous elections for workplace representatives).
- Union appointment of employee judges based on representativeness.
- Indirect election depending on type of organisation: for example, in small firms, election could be by a college of electors composed of existing staff representatives. There would be tiered structure for the employer side.

The trade unions are generally seen as opposed to changing the current system, with the exception of the CFDT.

In the summer of 2013, some deliberations of two working parties on judicial reform entered the public domain. One of these groups was tasked by the Ministry of Justice with exploring options for merging local district and specialist courts (the TGI and TI) and to include in this what it termed 'social judicial bodies', which would encompass *conseils de prud'hommes* as well as social security tribunals. One observation was that the government needed to respond to the lengthy delays in the *conseils* that hampered access to justice. The proposal, albeit still embryonic, was immediately condemned by trade unions and judges (Liaisons Sociales, 2013). Any such radical step would be resisted not only by trade unions but also probably by employers. However, it suggests that the present structuring, as well as the details of the electoral system, of the *conseils de prud'hommes* may not be entirely sacrosanct.

Outcomes

In 2011, 205,000 new cases were dealt with, including 'rapid procedure' referrals, of which there were just under 41,000. This overall total was 6 per cent down on the preceding year. Of the 165,000 cases lodged, excluding 'rapid procedure' cases, only about half went to a hearing, with the remainder being joindered, struck out or withdrawn. Only some 7 per cent of the total lodged were resolved at conciliation, with 10 per cent withdrawn, and as many as 15 per cent struck out. Some commentators have argued that a proportion of those withdrawn are also settled amicably using other civil code options after an initial conciliation that might have failed (see Contrepois, 2009: 10 Ftn 17). It takes an average of 14 months to resolve a case (Ministère de la Justice, 2012). In the event of an appeal, this can extend to over four years.

About half of all first-instance decisions are appealed, as noted above. In just over 73 per cent of cases, the *conseil* found for the plaintiff, who is almost always the employee, not the employer, suggesting a fairly high level of employer appeals.

Conclusion

The French labour court system remains unique in that first-instance judges are directly elected, representing employers and the employee side, and that first-instance hearings and pre-hearing conciliation are conducted exclusively by these representatives. A professional judge will only be called in if no decision can be reached. Elected lay judges also have procedural responsibilities, such as preparing cases for a full hearing. In contrast to other countries, the rate of resolution by conciliation, at some 10 per cent, is low (see Table 13.4). Despite the potential for the first-instance courts to suffer from constant stalemates, this is not generally the case, and offers an interesting instance of the capacity for the two sides to agree without the presence of a professional judge. However, the rate of appeals is comparatively high.

Although reforms have been mooted to streamline elections for lay judges, there has been no proposal to abolish them or lay participation – a step that would be seen as overturning an institution, fought for by trade unions, that is deeply embedded in the system of employment regulation and an element of French political and republican culture.

4
Germany

Introduction

One of the distinctive features of the adjudication of employment disputes in Germany is the existence of a separate structure of labour jurisdiction that deals with the vast bulk of employment disputes, individual and collective, aside from those related to civil servants. The system provides for first-instance local labour courts, a regional (appellate) (*Land*) level, and a final Federal appellate court. There is lay representation at all levels.

The system co-exists with, and for some types of case is also integrated with, workplace institutions for employee representation. Some collective agreements also contain staged procedures for resolving individual grievances.

The system of labour jurisdiction has been broadly stable for many years, with operational reforms instituted from time-to-time, but with no fundamental change in the scope or composition of labour courts, although there have been radical proposals to restructure the courts in recent years. As such, although stable, labour jurisdiction has been seen as contested (Rehder, 2007a).

Although there is no official mediation or arbitration service, the court system encourages agreed resolutions at all levels and, since 2012, allows for private and intra-judicial mediation. First-instance court proceedings also begin with a conciliation hearing before moving to a full hearing if no agreement is reached.

We first look at the context, before focusing on the first-instance labour court and appeals, concluding with some comments on recent developments.

Background

Industrial relations context

German industrial relations are characterised by a complex mix of legal regulation and case law, but with a commitment to free collective bargaining. Trade union density was 18.3 per cent in 2010, compared with a peak of 36 per cent in 1991 (Visser, 2011).

In the 'classic' form of German industrial relations, employee interests are represented through a dual system of works councils in workplaces and collective bargaining between trade unions and employer associations at industry level. As outlined below, this constellation has been steadily eroded in recent years.

Directly elected works councils represent the whole workforce in an establishment, except senior managers. They are not mandatory, but once established are entitled to information, consultation and, on some matters, joint decision-making ('codetermination'). They may conclude workplace agreements on specified issues, such as 'social plans' to mitigate the impact of organisational and business changes, collective redundancies and other issues subject to codetermination (such as social facilities, arranging working hours, health and safety). However, they may not strike. If no agreement is reached, a binding ruling can be issued through arbitration procedures. Unless permitted by collective agreement, or where a collective agreement has not definitively regulated an issue, works councils may not bargain on pay or other basic terms.

Some 43 per cent of the workforce in West Germany (36 per cent in the East)[1] work in establishments with a works council (Ellgut and Kohaut, 2013: 286). Works councils are more prevalent in large workplaces: while 81 per cent of workplaces with over 500 employees have a works council, this applies to only 6 per cent with fewer than 50 staff. Overall, only one in ten eligible establishments has a works council. Nonetheless, compared with other countries, workplace representation remains widespread. Even in relatively small workplaces (100–199 employees), workplace and workforce coverage is over 60 per cent.

Board-level codetermination, confined to large undertakings, shapes strategy and policy, but has only a limited impact on day-to-day industrial relations.

Collective bargaining is well entrenched in many sectors when compared with the United Kingdom or United States, but has lost ground over recent decades. There are mechanisms to extend industry agreements to non-signatory employers, but these are also less effective than in the past. There is no national statutory minimum wage. Setting minimum pay in workplaces not subject to collective agreement occurs through a procedure originally intended to set pay levels for posted workers.

Multi-employer bargaining has been in decline for some time. In 2012 it covered 53 per cent of the workforce in West Germany (36 per cent in the East): this compares with 70 per cent in the West (56 per cent in the East) in 1996 (Ellguth and Kohaut, 2013: 284). Company bargaining accounted for 7 per cent of the workforce in 2012 in the West (East, 12 per cent). Some 40 per cent of employers not subject to a collective agreement stated that they were guided by industry agreements when setting terms and conditions.

One consequence of these developments is that the 'classic' German model of works council plus industry-level agreement is now a minority phenomenon, covering 29 per cent of employees. Just over a third of employees in West Germany and just under a half in the East have neither a collective agreement nor a works council (ibid.: 287).

Works councils play a role in filtering individual disputes and procedures in the event of a contested dismissal are influenced by the works council's stance.

Legal context

The 1949 constitution, the 'Basic Law', provides for five jurisdictions, each with a supreme court: criminal and ordinary civil law, administrative justice, tax, social security, and employment. Appeals on consistency with the Basic Law are heard by the Federal Constitutional Court. There is lay involvement at many levels in these jurisdictions.[2] The current system of labour courts was established under the 1953 Labour Courts Act, last amended in May 2013. However, its origins in its current form date back to the Weimar Republic. Lay members are referred to as 'judges' (*Richter*).[3] Some commentaries dispute the term 'lay', which is sometimes used in German ('*Laienrichter*'): rather, employee and employer members are seen, as one commentary notes, as non-stipendiary judges appointed on the basis of their 'specialist knowledge and workplace experience' (Bader et al., 2012: 41).

Public law and labour inspection

Public law to enforce employment standards can be found in a number of areas.

In the field of health and safety, there is a dual arrangement in which statutory labour inspection, mainly responsible for enforcement, co-exists with the so-called autonomous system for setting standards, undertaken by industry health and safety associations (*Berufsgenossenschaften*). The two pillars cooperate within a national health and safety strategy. Associations are financed by levies on employers: they deal with standards, prevention, rehabilitation and compensation and make some 700,000 workplace visits each year.

The labour inspectorate enforces statutory standards, which tend to be directed at the wider public rather than directly with employees and frequently derive from EU standards. It is organised at regional level, may be sub-divided into industry specialisms, and has a variety of designations. Its main role is to ensure that the actors in the system comply with their legal requirements, using a range of powers as well as offering advice, conducting workplace inspections, and direct enforcement and sanctions in the event of breaches.

Works councils have a statutory right to codetermination on workplace health and safety, as well as a general duty to ensure that laws are complied with.

Enforcement of entitlement to a minimum wage rate, as well as other statutory rights, under the Posted Workers' Law is the responsibility of the Federal Customs Office, whose officials can exercise police powers, such as entry to premises. Under this law, an agreed branch-level minimum wage determined by trade unions and employer associations can be extended by decree to all employers in that branch, and will apply to all employees, including those posted to Germany from abroad. This is different to the usual extension procedure in that the branch needs to have been expressly incorporated into the statute: at present, such branches cover some three million employees, including care and cleaning, as well as providing minimum rates for the temporary work sector. The Customs Office is also responsible for combating illegal employment and enforcing the registration and authorisation of temporary work agencies.

Other dispute resolution mechanisms

Germany has no official agency for mediation, conciliation or arbitration for individual or collective disputes, reflecting the negative experiences with compulsory arbitration that began in the Weimar Republic (1919–33).[4]

However, there are mechanisms in the industrial relations system that help resolve disputes before they reach the courts, of which the most important is the works council system, which provides for a number of rights for individual employees. Employees have a right to take grievances to the employer and works council, and many issues are dealt with at this stage. In undertakings with at least 20 eligible employees, the employer must inform the works council before any appointment, grading or re-grading or transfer. If the works council refuses consent, the employer can appeal to a labour court for a ruling. Works councils must also be consulted before every dismissal. We outline the procedures that apply in this instance further below.

Individual grievance procedures in collective agreements

Collectively agreed conciliation procedures generally cover collective issues, such as a failure to agree. Nevertheless, some agreements provide mechanisms for individual disputes but these may not limit or supersede any statutory rights enjoyed by works councils (in particular on grading).

Some regional agreements in the metalworking industry contain procedures for individual disputes arising out of the application of the collective agreement. In one example, workplaces with more than 200 employees are to establish conciliation panels with equal management and employee representation. If no agreement is reached, the issue will be referred to the works council. If these options fail, the issue may be referred to the labour courts or a higher-level conciliation panel composed of representatives of the signatory organisations.

Agreed conciliation clauses may also specify that disputes, individual and collective, will be dealt with through conciliation, unless the matter falls within the competence of the labour courts. Nonetheless, the parties (that is, the employee and employer) may still take a potential labour court matter to a conciliation panel and ask for a ruling.

Alternative dispute resolution

The main focus of ADR is the scope for mediation, which has seen several recent initiatives. The Mediation Act, 2012, which transposes the EU Mediation Directive (2008/52/EC), is intended to promote extra-judicial settlement in a range of civil law disputes, including employment. Although such options have always been available, the law established a framework for procedures and certifying mediators. The law introduced scope for 'intra-judicial mediation' by a professional judge but outside of judicial proceedings.[5] The considerable scope for settlement in labour court proceedings means that these changes are likely to have a smaller impact in employment than in other fields (see 'Mediation' below).

Labour jurisdiction – basic principles

Those entitled to bring a case under the Labour Courts Act are dependent employees, trainees, homeworkers or others deemed dependent on an employer. Trade unions and employer associations may also be parties in some cases, as can works councils. Established civil servants (*Beamte*), of which there are some 1.9 million, may not use the labour courts.

There are two types of labour court procedure: *Urteilsverfahren* ('judgment proceedings') and *Beschlussverfahren* ('decision proceedings'). The former is by far the most common, accounting for over 90 per cent of referrals and includes individual disputes. Decision proceedings deal with collective matters in public law, such as works councils, board-level representation, and organisations' right to conduct collective bargaining. We deal here only with 'judgment proceedings'.

The system operates at three levels:

- Local labour courts (*Arbeitsgericht*), which operates through chambers, consisting of a presiding professional judge and two lay judges.
- *Land* labour courts,[6] with the same composition as local courts but requiring lay judges to be more experienced. In practice, this level represents the

final appeal forum, with only a few legally significant matters appealed to the Federal Labour Court.

- Federal Labour Court, which operates on the basis of 'senates' (sometimes translated as 'bench'). The requirements for lay members are more demanding than for lower instances. The court composition is also different, with a presiding chair, two professional judges, and two lay members, one from the employee side and one from the employer side.

We deal with the conduct of the proceedings in each instance below (Figure 4.1).

Labour Court membership

Courts at all levels have a tripartite composition: professional judges and employee/employer lay judges.

Professional judges (*Berufsrichter*)

Professional judges are career judges. The route to becoming a judge begins with legal study at a university, which concludes with the first official examination, part of which is academic and part of which constitutes a 'state examination', which is the first stage in acquiring a licence to practice law. Students may opt to take specialist modules in labour law. During vacations, students must participate in three months of practical activity. Potential professional judges must then spend two years in preparatory work, known as *Referendariat*, during which they can specialise in a particular area of law. After this, there is a second state examination, set and marked by the *Land* legal authority. Success entitles the graduate to apply for posts as a professional judge: after appointment there is a three- or four-year probationary period, depending on the *Land*, during which they can be dismissed without cause. This is followed by two years in which they can be required to leave office if deemed unsuitable. Finally, they are appointed for life. Competition for posts is intense and primarily based on academic performance. Just under 40 per cent of presiding judges are women, with a higher proportion in younger age groups. German professors of law may also serve as judges.

Rehder (2007b) noted that the distinct perspectives of labour court judges, who had worked solely in that jurisdiction, have been diluted in recent years by the incursion of non-labour jurists, with a background in contract law, into first-instance courts.[7] As yet, however, this has not applied to the Federal Labour Court, where the share of 'full-blooded' labour lawyers has increased since the 1960s. Labour court judges are also appointed earlier in their careers than in the past, leading to a more thorough socialisation in the culture of labour adjudication. Some 65 per cent of Federal Labour Court judges have also completed a doctorate. Succession planning for future Federal Labour Court positions is fostered by the fact that recently appointed judges in lower labour courts may be seconded for up to two years to the federal

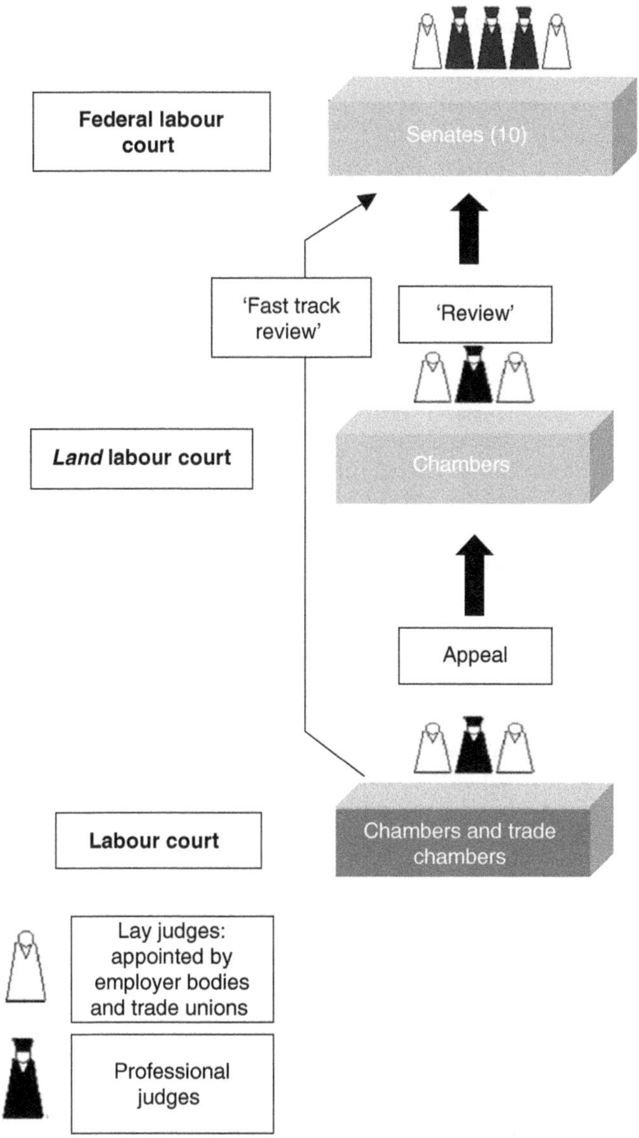

Figure 4.1 Structure of German labour courts

level as research staff, enabling their qualities to be gauged. Some individuals have been known to move directly from a local to the federal court.

Presiding judges wear robes but lay judges in most *Länder* do not. However, this is an external distinction and does not affect their judicial decision-making role.

Lay judges (*ehrenamtliche Richter*)

Selection and nomination

Lay judges are appointed from lists submitted by trade unions, other employee associations, and employer associations. The principle of appointment rather than election was established during the Weimar Republic, when elections might have politicised the judiciary. In addition, given the scale of labour courts, any ballot for lay judges would mean considerable administrative expense. Unions and employer associations, it is argued (Bader et al., 2012: 38), are sufficiently significant and legitimate to warrant their role as nominating bodies.

For a first-instance court, a person must be at least 25 years old and live or work in the area where the court is located; be 'fit to hold public office' and not have been sentenced to more than six months' imprisonment; and be eligible to vote in Federal elections. There are additional criteria for being an 'employee' or 'employer'. The statutory definition of suitability for office is a very broad one derived from the Basic Law. Organisations must document that the criteria are met, and the authorities will check and ask for further evidence if they consider it necessary.

The nominating organisations determine which individuals will be included in their list, and are responsible for assessing their competence to exercise the role There is no formal means for appraising the experience of parties in the system, either before nomination or when sitting.

At lower levels, lists are submitted to the *Land* authorities by regional branches of employer and employee organisations. The authorities must ensure that there is 'an appropriate balance of minorities', viewed by Bader et al. (2012: 47) as referring to smaller trade unions rather than demographic groups. Organisations may only nominate as many candidates as there are places, but *Land* authorities are not bound by the list and can request more nominations (for instance, to ensure that the economic structure of the district is reflected) (Bader et al., 2012: 41–2). Appointing authorities usually select in the order of the lists provided by nominating organisations, often compiled with the most experienced individuals at the top. Officials interviewed for this study noted it was difficult to fill all available places, so rejection was rare.[8]

The authorities must ensure that women and men are '*appropriately* considered' when composing courts, which, in the view of some commentators, takes precedence over any *Land*-level requirement for *equal* provision. Bader et al. (2012: 45) cite a proportion of 45 per cent as 'guideline', reflecting the proportion of women in the workforce. In North-Rhine Westphalia, the proportion was 21 per cent (NRW, 2009). There are no other diversity requirements, although some unions make particular efforts to be more inclusive.

The number of lay judges to be appointed is a matter for the *Land* authorities. Bader et al. (2012: 47) estimate that each chamber tends to have

26–28 lay judges and that each sits four to six times a year, in each case for a day. Lay judges are allocated to chambers by the court president in consultation with a committee of lay judges, and these try to match their experience and knowledge with industry-specific chambers, where these have been established (see 'Full hearing (streitige Verhandlung)' below).

National organisations (BDA and the Ministry of the Interior for private and public sector employers and DGB for its affiliated trade unions) are responsible for nominations for the Federal Labour Court.

Status and rights

Lay judges are appointed for five years, but once appointed they may be, and typically are, reappointed when their period of office expires. There is no limit on how often a lay judge can be appointed. Once retired, a lay judge can only continue until their period of office expires. They must be granted time off, both for attendance at a hearing and reading case documents. They are paid a fee per hour (from leaving home or workplace until they return), plus travel costs and are protected against dismissal with notice during their period of office and also against any detriment as a result of their activity.

There is no statutory obligation on the authorities to provide preparatory or ongoing training[9] for lay judges. As a rule, training is provided by unions and employer associations, with some financial support from *Land* governments, usually covering some 75 per cent of costs (Bader et al., 2012: 125–6). Employee lay judges are entitled to reasonable time-off for training conducted by unions.

Legal commentators are generally supportive of lay involvement. Bader et al. (2012: 2) note that the presence of lay members creates confidence in the 'correctness and persuasiveness' of judgments in which lay judges from the parties' milieu were involved and rejected the argument that removing lay involvement would save money, given the 'comparatively small sums involved' (ibid.). Lay involvement 'raises the transparency of the structures and procedures and improves the acceptability of decisions' (ibid.).

Trade unions are entirely supportive of lay participation. And there appears to be no movement on the official employer side to change existing arrangements in terms of retaining lay participation at all levels.

Resolving and adjudicating individual rights disputes

In the absence of an official mediation or arbitration service, works councils play an important role as a first stage in resolving differences, as noted above. In the case of dismissals, this is formally integrated into the legal channel for claims. The works council must be consulted on all proposed dismissals, with the reasons, the proposed date of termination and details of the employee's social situation. Any dismissal effected without notification is void. The works council can express reservations about the dismissal and in some cases may formally oppose it. If the works council formally opposes it, which happened in 28 per cent of cases in the research by Höland et al. (2007: 103), it must notify the employer in writing within a week of being consulted about an ordinary dismissal (three days for summary dismissal). If the employer proceeds despite works council opposition, the council's opinion must be appended to the notice of dismissal to the employee. If the works council has formally opposed the dismissal and the employee has initiated court proceedings within three weeks of written notice being given, the employer must continue to employ the person, if they request it, until final settlement of the case, with some limitations. Parallel to this, under employment protection legislation (*Kündigungsschutzgesetz*), an employee who wishes to contest a dismissal can, if they wish, notify their objection to the works council. If the works council accepts this, it must seek a resolution between the parties. A text of the work council's opinion must be provided to the employee and employer if requested, and should also be forwarded to the labour court. Höland et al. (2007) found that works council objections were found invalid in around 40 per cent of cases, of which just under two-thirds were due to an inappropriate legal basis for the objection.

Initiating labour court proceedings

If a claimant initiates proceedings, the procedure begins with a local labour court.[10] The claimant can submit a claim via a lawyer or directly to the court. There is no prescribed form for this, except that it must be in writing and indicate the plaintiff, and the aim of and reasons for the claim. A claim can also be submitted verbally to a court official, who will submit it but may not give legal advice. Labour courts often have a model claim form for downloading.

Time limits

For dismissal, the employee must submit a claim within three weeks of receiving written notice but may apply for an exemption if they can establish justifiable reasons. A late application must be made within two weeks of resolving the problem but with a maximum of six months from the end of the three-week limit.

Time limits for other claims are specified in the Civil Code. The usual limit is three years, from the end of the year in which the claim arose. This applies, for example, to all wage payment claims. Much longer periods apply for tortious liability (from 10 to 30 years, depending on whether an actual injury occurred).

There is a two-month time limit for claims under equal treatment legislation, unless a different period has been set by collective agreement.

Statutory time limits may be superseded by contractual time limits in individual contracts of employment or collective agreements. One important difference is that statutory time limits only apply if one of the parties invokes them; otherwise the court may disregard them and the claim does not lapse. Contractual time limits must be taken into account by the courts. A court may, however, deem a claim to have been forfeited if it considers a claimant has delayed for too long.

Fees and costs

No deposit or advanced court fees are required before bringing a case. Fees are only paid by the losing party after a judgment has been given and are, therefore, waived if an agreed settlement is reached. Fees are split if the judgment assigns some culpability to each side. Fees were negligible up until 2004, but were then substantially increased.

There is a statutory sliding scale for fees related to the 'judicial amount' (*Streitwert*): this is determined either by the sum claimed in the application or, where there is no direct sum of money involved, such as correcting an inaccurate reference, by the court. In the event of a dismissal, where the maximum compensation that can be awarded by the court is one year's pay, the judicial amount is three months' pay. For example, for a contested dismissal where the employee earned €40,000 a year the fee would be €392 (based on a judicial amount of €10,000).[11]

There are no restrictions on representation at the first-instance level and the parties bear their own costs of legal representation and any other expenses.

At the appellate levels, the losing side must pay both the fee and the counter-party's legal costs.

Lawyers' fees are also regulated by statute. There is a base rate, depending on the sum at issue, that is 'the judicial amount', and a multiple, depending on the action taken during proceedings. For example, in the termination case noted above, the lawyer's fee would add up to €1,215 for bringing the claim and attendance at the hearing, plus administrative costs of €20 plus any travel costs. A lawyer can additionally charge for any initial consultation, with fees negotiable, but these will be offset against the total fees charged. Contingency fees are not allowed.

If a party cannot afford legal representation 'without detriment to maintaining themselves and their families' and are not represented by a union or employer body and do not have access to such representation, on application the presiding judge can assign a legal representative if the counterparty is represented. In 2011, there were 67,000 applications and 93 per cent were granted. In such instances, court costs are also usually waived. However, the court will only authorise this if the prospects for the applicant are good. Depending on income, costs can either be wholly waived or repaid in instalments.

Mandatory pre-hearing conciliation

Once a case is lodged by the claimant and before the respondent is required to respond in writing, the parties must attempt to reach an amicable resolution in a preliminary conciliation hearing (*Güteverfahren*), held in the presence of a presiding judge but without lay members. In contrast to mediation (see 'Mediation' below), the presiding judge will offer their assessment of the prospects for the case and, if no settlement is reached, will chair the subsequent full hearing. Conciliation proceedings, which are usually very brief and not subject to rules of evidence, also provide an opportunity for each side to prepare for the hearing, but also allow a claim to be withdrawn without further formality (Dendorfer, 2011: 857). Such a hearing can be held in public, but may be in private if appropriate.

Further conciliation hearings can be scheduled at the judge's discretion. If one of the parties fails to attend, or if conciliation fails, the proceedings move 'immediately' to a full hearing, attended by the lay judges: if this is not possible because they are not present, the presiding judge must arrange a hearing at the earliest opportunity. In practice, it is very rare for a full hearing to follow immediately, given the need to compile documents and ensure that the lay judges assigned to the case are available: the interlude is three to four weeks at a minimum, and usually six to eight weeks. The same judge will be assigned to the full hearing as undertook the conciliation hearing. The attending party can also apply for a default judgment that a presiding judge can issue alone. If the complainant does not attend, the respondent can ask for the case to be set aside (see 'Presiding judge sits alone'). If neither party attends, the case is suspended, but a party can apply for a full hearing to start within six months of conciliation: otherwise, the complaint is deemed to be withdrawn.

Dismissal cases can be heard under an accelerated procedure. The conciliation hearing should be held within two weeks of the claim being submitted. If this is unsuccessful, the presiding judge will ask the respondent to reply with evidence within two weeks if they consider that the respondent has not yet adequately done so. The judge can also give the complainant two weeks to produce a written opinion on the respondent's statement. Evidence submitted after this period is only admissible at the presiding judge's discretion. A very high proportion of such procedures ends with an agreed settlement – around 88 per cent of all those that are proceeded with and higher than other types of case. Once minuted, this concludes the case. An out-of-court settlement can also be brought to a presiding judge to be formalised.

Mediation

Scope for mediation was introduced in 2012. This has two forms. In the first, known as 'intra-judicial mediation', the presiding judge can suggest that the parties conduct conciliation before a different judge, who is appointed by the court but has no power to make a judicial decision. This individual, termed a 'conciliation judge' (*Güterichter*) to distinguish them from professional mediators, is entitled to deploy 'all methods of conflict resolution, including mediation' (Labour Courts Act, 1954: 6). Two judges may be appointed from a pool to assist both parties ('co-mediation'). Proceedings are suspended while this takes place. If the parties come to an agreement, this can take the form of a judicial settlement (or withdrawal of the claim). There are no additional costs to the parties for using 'intra-judicial mediation' and any court costs due for a full hearing are dropped if a settlement is reached at this stage. Proceedings are confidential.

Alternatively, at the conciliation stage the judge may suggest external mediation or any other procedure for extra-judicial conflict resolution using paid external specialists. If this is accepted, the court procedure is suspended. A date for a full hearing may be set on application by one of the parties, otherwise court proceedings begin again after three months, unless mediation is still underway.

As yet, experience with these new arrangements is limited, and the options do not represent a fundamental breach with the existing practice in labour jurisdiction of pursuing agreed settlements. In the decade or so preceding the 2012 legislation, the *Land* of Thuringia successfully operated a system of 'intra-judicial' mediation as a pilot project, in which professional judges were given training in mediation.[12]

Presiding judge alone

The presiding judge may decide on their own in some circumstances outside of a full hearing. There are no instances where a presiding judge can decide a disputed case alone on its merits *unless* the hearing follows immediately after conciliation; it is possible to conclude the case; and both parties agree to apply in writing to the presiding judge to do so (LCA, Para. 55: 3). According to interviewees for this study, this is very rare and would normally only occur if the case involved major issues of law that might be expected to move rapidly through the court system, and where the two parties, usually trade unions and employer associations, want to test the law.

The presiding judge can also issue a judgment on their own in the following, procedural, circumstances (including if they are sitting with lay judges):

- if the complaint is withdrawn or waived,
- if one or both parties fails to appear and a default judgment can be made,
- to determine the labour court at which a case should be heard or assign costs,
- to correct any of the facts as stated in a judgment, if these are inaccurate or contradictory, provided neither party has requested a full hearing.

The judge may also instruct the parties before the full hearing to provide written evidence, request an expert opinion, or for a party to attend for questioning.

Full hearing ('streitige Verhandlung')

Courts sit as chambers (*Kammer*). The full hearing has a tripartite composition: a presiding judge chairing and two lay judges, one nominated by the employer side, the other by trade unions. All have equal status as judges in full hearings.

A court may establish chambers to deal with particular sectors (*Fachkammer*): this can embrace a whole sector (such as the public sector or construction) or specific groups (such as technical staff). Lay judges in such chambers should be drawn from individuals with a relevant background. Chambers can also be established for localities. Allocation to the numerous general chambers of large courts may be made purely on the basis of complainants' place-of-residence. Before establishing chambers, there must be consultation with local employer associations and trade unions. In practice, *Fachkammer* are only established in large first-instance courts (such as Berlin) where there is a sizeable body of appropriately experienced lay judges. In many courts, it is not feasible.

The procedure in first-instance hearings is oral. Evidence must be presented directly to the chamber. In 'judgment proceedings', that deal with individual disputes, the procedure is adversarial, but in 'decision proceedings', for resolving public law matters related to employee representation, it is inquisitorial. Evidence is only given on oath if the chamber considers it to be especially important. Witnesses who gave evidence at conciliation must do so again; however, parties and their representatives may refer to written submissions for brevity and there is an expectation that the presiding judge will brief lay judges in a short pre-hearing. These will not be witness statements but other supporting material (Bader et al., 2012: 94).

Local labour courts often issue guidance for lay judges. For example, the labour court in Cologne asks lay judges to 'signal discretely to the chair if they wish to interrupt proceedings to withdraw for consultations. Differences of opinion should not be aired in public' (*Merkblatt,* Arbeitsgericht Köln).

Judgments and other outcomes

Because of the many agreed settlements and withdrawals, 'contentious' judgments account for only a tiny minority – just 8 per cent – of claims lodged. Some 60–65 per cent of cases in 'judgment' proceedings end in an agreed settlement (Statistisches Bundesamt, 2012), rising to some 85 per cent of new applications if withdrawn claims or other unspecified resolutions are taken into account (these amount to some 15 per cent of applications). Practitioners note that 80–90 per cent of cases that are proceeded with are settled in conciliation before the hearing. The law also encourages the parties to reach an amicable resolution during the hearing, also culminating in an agreed settlement.

All three judges have an equal vote. They may not abstain. There is no requirement for unanimity but dissent is not announced. Formal voting is extremely rare and some 90 per cent of judgments are thought to be unanimous (Bader et al., 2012: 4), although there are no definitive statistics. Lay judges should be present when a *summary* judgment is read; if they are not, a summary judgment must be *signed* by the presiding judge *and* the lay judges. The *full* judgment, with the statement of facts and grounds, is signed by the presiding judge alone.

Appeals

Land (regional) labour courts

Any party that loses a case in a local labour court can appeal to the relevant *Land* labour court (*Landesarbeitsgericht*) both on matters of fact and law:

- if the judicial amount exceeds €600;
- if the case deals with the existence, non-existence or termination of an employment contract (but not for a claim by a job applicant to be engaged).

An appeal can also be lodged with the leave of the first-instance court: this must be granted if the case is of 'fundamental significance'; is between collective bargaining parties over the status of a collective agreement; where the issue turns on industrial action or freedom of association; if the court intends to depart from a judgment of the superior *Land* court or any other judgment affecting the parties to the case made by any other court. Parties must be represented, either by a qualified lawyer or a representative of an employee or employer organisation.

According to our calculations based on 2011 labour court statistics (Statistisches Bundesamt, 2012), some 40 per cent of dismissal case judgments are appealed. According to the European Commission for the Efficiency of Justice (2012: 218) there was a 3.77 per cent rate of appeal to *Land* labour courts from first-instance decisions for employment dismissal cases in 2010, but our analysis suggests this percentage is based on the percentage of all claims submitted at first instance.[13] As noted previously, the majority of cases are settled or withdrawn.

Land Labour Courts also operate through chambers with a presiding judge and two lay judges, representing employers and employees. Appointment is as with first-instance courts, except that the individual should be at least 30 years old and have five years' experience in a first-instance court. There is also only limited specialisation of chambers at *Land* level: if pursued, the main distinction is between the public and private sector, or specific chambers for areas of law.[14]

Judges are equal in status. While at first instance the full judgment is signed only by the presiding judge, in *Land* Labour Courts it is signed by all three.

The proportion of agreed settlements tends to be lower at the appellate level. For example, some 30 per cent of contested dismissals were resolved by formal judgment at *Land* level, compared with just 11 per cent at first instance (Höland and Zeibig, 2007: 250).

The Federal Labour Court (Bundesarbeitsgericht)

Appeals to the Federal Labour Court can be brought by individuals, trade union organisations, and employer associations and leave to appeal is granted if certain criteria are met. For example, the case must be of fundamental significance for the development of law or of public interest. Appeal is also possible if a *Land* court's decision deviates from that of a higher or parallel court. A case can be referred from the first instance to the Federal level if it is of fundamental importance and deals with certain issues in collective labour law (identical to those for appeal to a *Land* Labour Court). Application to the Federal Constitutional Court is permitted to test the compatibility of a statute with the Basic Law, or whether a rule of international law is applicable in Germany. Parties must be represented either by a lawyer or a representative of an employee or employer organisation who is qualified to serve as a presiding judge through having completed the second state examination.

The Federal Labour Court operates through 'senates' (*Senate,* or 'bench'). There are currently ten senates, each of which deals with a specific area of law. A 'Grand Senate' can be convened if a senate intends to make a judgment that departs from that of another senate or the Grand Senate, or there is a matter of fundamental legal significance that requires either the development of the law or consistency between rulings. A Joint Panel of all the supreme courts of each jurisdiction can sit to establish consistency between jurisdictions.

The Federal Labour Court is also tripartite and lay judges are appointed through nominations from trade unions, other social or occupational employee associations, and employer bodies: a Federal lay judge must be at least 35 years old 'with particular knowledge and experience in the field of labour law and the world of work', should have served for at least five years as a lay judge in a first or second-instance court, and should have been active 'for a considerable period of time' as an employee or employer in Germany. They are appointed by the Federal Minister of Labour for five years. Both professional and lay Federal Labour Court judges are equal in status and all must sign the judgment.

The court composition also differs from lower instances, with a presiding chair, who is a professional judge, two other professional judges and two lay judges, one from the employee side and one from the employer side. Each lay judge will be present for two or three sittings each year. Sittings normally last one day, and documents are made available beforehand. Some 14 days before the hearing, the three professional judges may indicate their likely judgment and their reasoning to the lay members assigned to the case, based on the case papers – effectively signalling the final outcome. Professional judges might also consult lay members with particular expertise, for example in collective agreements, to help interpret an issue.

Discrimination cases

Claims made under anti-discrimination legislation, the General Law on Equal Treatment, 2006, arising out of the employment relationship, including discrimination in the recruitment process, fall under the competence of the labour courts, with no special procedures (Federal Anti-Discrimination Agency, 2009). Associations representing the interests of people with protected characteristics may also *support* plaintiffs in court proceedings, provided they have at least 75 members. Cases brought under the Disabled Persons Equality Law are heard by social courts, and associations representing people with disabilities may bring a claim direct to the court on issues such as access. However, a discriminatory dismissal on grounds of disability will be heard by a labour court.

Employers have a number of statutory duties to prevent discrimination and resolve instances, including transferring employees or termination. This includes provision of a person or department to which employees may refer on grounds of discrimination under a protected characteristic. The Federal Anti-Discrimination Agency was established under the 2006 Law on Equal Treatment. Its main role is to offer advice but also to seek to resolve conflicts arising out of alleged discrimination. It does not bring cases, and nor does it have the right to conduct any form of judicial or quasi-judicial hearing.

Recent developments

The period from the mid-1990s saw a number of proposals both by the then Federal government and some *Land* governments to undertake a fundamental reshaping of the judiciary ('Grosse Justizreform') to reduce the five jurisdictions to a smaller number, with various scenarios: in some of these labour courts were to be merged into the 'normal' civil jurisdiction; in others social and labour courts would be merged, and in yet others there would be a consolidation of administrative justice, leaving labour jurisdiction as a separate pillar. Any such change would need a constitutional amendment. A detailed discussion and exchange amongst labour law academics and practitioners can be found in Rieble (2005) (also see DGB (2005)). Rehder (2007a) sets the proposed reforms in the longer-term context of the establishment of a separate, yet 'fragile', system of labour jurisdiction.

The principal arguments for the integration of labour jurisdiction into the civil courts have been (i) costs (ii) flexible deployment of judges (iii) uniform procedures (iv) simplification to raise public acceptance. All of these have been challenged by opponents. Amongst labour law jurists, one argument that gained a few adherents, although it remained a minority position, was that tripartism should be retained at first instance, but with only legally-qualified members at the appellate stage or with a merging of appellate courts from civil and labour jurisdiction. Supporters of the status quo have argued that, in practice, at the Federal appellate level many 'lay members' are, in fact, legally qualified and may be practising lawyers or in-house legal counsel for nominating organisations.

Whereas the trade unions and, by and large, the judiciary were opposed to any change that would weaken lay involvement and dilute the specific role of labour courts and labour court judges, employer associations have been more ambivalent and, in the view of some commentators, contradictory (Sawall, 2007: 324ff.). The current position of the main employer association, the BDA, is that it favours some rationalisation of some of the separate civil law jurisdictions, but wishes to retain a distinct labour strand together with lay representation at all levels. As such, there is still a social partner consensus over the participation and role of non-legal members in separate labour courts.

The number of cases referred to labour courts has been falling since the mid-1990s (from 659,000 in 1997 to 404,000 by 2011). Reforms to accelerate procedures took effect in 2008, mostly technical in nature. Nevertheless, labour courts deal with cases more swiftly than any other jurisdiction in Germany. Significantly, these reforms did not impinge on the fundamentals of lay participation and mostly turned on procedural matters. Stakeholder observations at hearings on the amendments broadly supported the proposals. The German Trade Union Confederation (DGB) used the opportunity to reiterate its longstanding call for an easing of the scope for organisations to bring claims in pursuit of members' individual rights, as is the case in France in some instances (see Chapter 3), albeit unsuccessfully.

Conclusions

Labour courts constitute a distinct and separate system of law that co-exists with a fairly strongly institutionalised system of employment regulation and industrial relations. Lay participation exists at all levels, despite some proposals for change that did not win the support of the main stakeholders within the system, which is broadly seen to be working well. There has been some extension of the scope for presiding judges to decide on certain matters alone, but these are confined to procedural issues. Compulsory preliminary conciliation hearings, heard and assisted by a presiding judge alone, appear to act as an important filter for the courts, and most cases initially referred are settled at this stage. This has recently been complemented by scope for external and judicial mediation.

5
Great Britain

Introduction

Until the 1970s the law was used only in exceptional circumstances in the employment sphere and the rights and interests of British workers were protected by trade unions and the collective agreements which they had concluded with employers. In the last four decades, however, there has been a significant decrease in trade union density and coverage of the workforce by collective agreements has waned (Brownlie, 2012). Concomitant with this decline there has been a growth in individual statutory rights mainly, but by no means wholly, emanating from the European Union. As a result, British employment relations, which half a century ago were voluntarist and collective, are now subject to legal adjudication mainly, but not exclusively, by labour courts known as employment tribunals (ETs).

There are several features of British labour courts which distinguish them from their counterparts abroad. First, although originally tripartite (a professional judge and lay judges), now a professional judge sits alone without the lay judges in many types of case; moreover, where there are lay judges they have been recruited as individuals, not nominated or elected by the social partners (see France (Chapter 3), Germany (Chapter 4) and Sweden (Chapter 11)).

Second, Great Britain has a complex system of employment rights adjudication. For instance, although ETs provide the main forum for claims at first instance, the civil courts also have a first-instance role in some employment-related adjudication and there are also quasi-judicial bodies and inspectorates in the employment field. The third feature is that Britain does not have an autonomous labour law adjudicative system: appeals at the two highest levels go to the 'ordinary' civil courts, unlike Sweden and Germany (see Figure 5.1). Fourth, recent changes to the employment rights adjudication system have reduced ETs' accessibility.

The plan of this chapter is as follows. We first look at ETs and the Employment Appeal Tribunal and the latest changes to these labour courts,

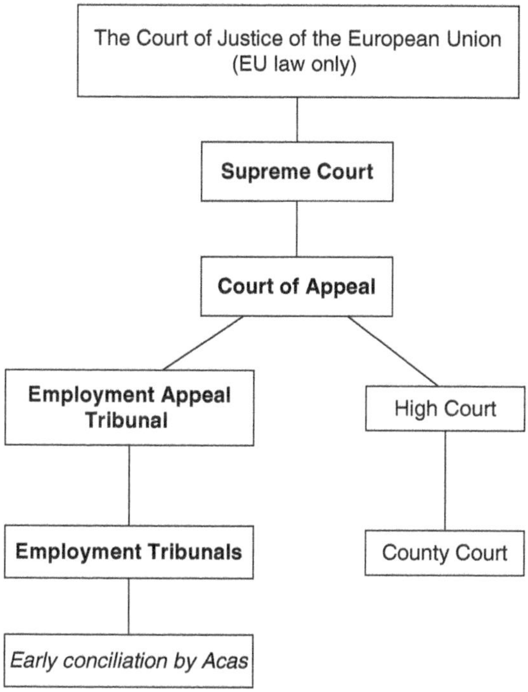

Figure 5.1 Great Britain's court structure

Notes:

1. In Scotland, the Court of Session replaces the Court of Appeal. The Sheriff Court replaces the High Court/County Court, but England, Wales and Scotland all have employment tribunals and are covered by the Employment Appeal Tribunal, while the Supreme Court covers England, Wales, Scotland and Northern Ireland in respect of civil cases.
2. The bulk of employment rights cases go to the courts shown in bold type.
3. The Supreme Court was previously known as the House of Lords.

together with some empirical evidence. We then consider the civil courts and quasi-judicial bodies, before making some concluding observations. We confine this chapter to Great Britain, which consists of England, Wales and Scotland but excludes Northern Ireland (all four together make up the United Kingdom). Northern Ireland's system of employment rights adjudication differs in a few respects from that in mainland Britain, that is, England/Wales/Scotland.[1]

Background

Otto Kahn Freund, considering employment relations in Britain in the 1960s, noted that the impact of the law in the workplace was 'only a fragment' and '[a]s a power countervailing management the trade unions are much more effective than the law has ever been or can ever be' (Kahn-Freund, 1977: 9, 10). In the last 30 years, however, British employment relations have changed dramatically and Kahn-Freund's view no longer holds good. UK union density declined from a peak of 50 per cent in 1979 to 26 per cent in 2012, but for UK private sector employees in 2012 union density was 14 per cent, as opposed to 56 per cent in the public sector, while collective agreement coverage in respect of an employee's pay was 29 per cent (BIS, 2013a). At the same time statutory individual rights at work have grown apace covering *inter alia* redundancy pay, unfair dismissal, discrimination on grounds of gender, race, disability, age, religion or belief and sexual orientation, whistle blowing, equal pay, maternity pay and leave, time off rights for trade union activities and for public duties. As a result, the locus for the resolution of employment disputes has mainly shifted from the collective bargaining arena to the ET, that is, a body that in the first instance adjudicates on statutory rights.

In fact ETs[2] were established well before this expansion of statutory rights. They were set up under the Industrial Training Act 1964 and their origin 'is shrouded in silence, if not in mystery' (Clark and Wedderburn, 1983: 174). They were 'children of civil servants' and not created at the request of employers, unions or political parties (Wedderburn, 1986: 264), but as they were established in the heyday of corporatism, they were constituted on a tripartite basis – a lawyer and lay people representing employers and employees.

The role of these tribunals at the outset was essentially as administrative tribunals, for instance to adjudicate on appeals by employers in respect of the imposition of training levies, on certain aspects of dock work and on disputes in respect of the Redundancy Payments Act 1965. Although the latter was an employee/employer dispute, the State had an interest because at that time any redundancy payment made by the employer that complied with the Act was refunded to the employer by the State (Dickens et al., 1985; Meeran, 2006). From the 1970s, however, the nature of the ETs' jurisdiction changed from the individual versus the organs of the State to party versus party when they were given a new jurisdiction, unfair dismissal, a change recommended by the Royal Commission (1968).

When ETs were first established, appeals went to the 'ordinary' courts, but first the tripartite National Industrial Relations Court (NIRC), and then from 1975 its successor, the tripartite Employment Appeal Tribunal were established to hear appeals from ETs on points of law. Further appeals on points of law can be made to the 'ordinary' common law courts: the Court of Appeal (Court of Session in Scotland) and the Supreme Court (Figure 5.1). In the last 25 years there have been various changes affecting employment rights adjudication, but the main focus of this chapter is the current position.

Employment Tribunals

Composition

Employment Tribunals (ETs) are chaired by a professional judge, who has to be legally qualified (for instance as a qualified barrister or solicitor) and to have experience in a law related activity (Judicial Appointments Commission, n.d.). So a person cannot become a judge immediately after qualification as there are no initial rungs on the judicial career ladder, for instance as a trainee judge, unlike in many other countries; (see, for instance, Chapter 11).

When ETs were first established they were always tripartite as noted above. At every hearing the chair was the legally qualified person who sat with lay members[3] (equivalent to lay judges in other countries), one drawn from a panel nominated by the Confederation of British Industry (CBI), the main employers' organisation, the other drawn from a panel nominated by the Trades Union Congress (TUC) to which most unions were affiliated.[4] Their very presence was intended to help to overcome the mistrust by labour and the unions of traditional courts[5] and engender public confidence, as they would act as a counter-balance to a purely legal perspective, important at a time when trade unions were more powerful than they are today. Second, lay members would be sensitive to the wider, industrial relations context and this would be reflected in their decision-making.

These lay members are effectively lay judges, and are now required to take the judicial oath. Furthermore, the three members of the tribunal, that is the professional judge and the two lay judges, have equal voting rights.

In 1999, however, the role of employer and employee organisations was all but ended and today lay members (i.e. lay judges), instead of being nominated by employer and employee organisations, apply individually and nominate themselves to the employer or employee panel and are recruited and selected through an open recruitment and appointment process. This nomination system distinguishes lay judges in Great Britain from their counterparts in other countries (see, for instance, France (Chapter 3), Germany (Chapter 4), Ireland (Chapter 6) and Sweden (Chapter 11)).

The British system of lay member appointment involves advertisements, job descriptions and person specifications, with applicants filling out an application form and then being assessed by formal processes which draw on a conventional human resources repertoire (competency frameworks and formalised tests/interviews) overseen by the Judicial Appointments Commission and conducted by human resources consultants with the help of professional judges. This process has occasionally caused problems, for instance when managers have nominated themselves to the employee panel because they are union members, although their role at work is as a manager (Department of Trade and Industry, 2003).

Somewhat paradoxically, however, although in Great Britain labour market actors do not play a part in the nomination and selection of lay judges, tripartism has not been totally obliterated: as noted, there are still two panels – employer and employee – and at the final stage the Minister appoints, but only does so after consulting with organisations representative of employers and employees.[6] Such consultation, however, is not undertaken when lay members are re-appointed after their three year term; such reappointments are virtually automatic until the lay member reaches the age of 70.

Tripartism, however, has not only been vitiated by the erosion of the institutional role of the key labour market actors. It has also been vitiated by governments of varying political hues empowering the professional judge to sit alone in an increasing number of types of complaint. At the time of writing, the professional judge is now required to sit alone, that is without lay judges, both in all preliminary hearings (PHs – see below), and very many types of full hearing, subject to the exercise of judicial discretion in the light of certain matters laid down in statute.[7]

The types of cases where the professional judge is required to sit alone include redundancy payments, holiday pay and most recently (April 2012) unfair dismissal, which comprised over a quarter of all claims accepted by ETs in 2011–12 (Ministry of Justice, 2012a).[8] As a result, the default position is that the professional judge now often only sits with lay members in discrimination cases. This move to empower the professional judge to sit alone in ETs reflects the long-standing practice in the civil courts (the County Court and the High Court) where a professional judge sits alone.

The lay members do not receive the papers in advance and, only in some long cases, is reading time allowed. They receive £174 per day at the time of writing[9] with a half fee for half a day's sitting or for a full day's training. Training is provided by the Employment Tribunals Service and the amount of training is normally one or two days per year.

Before the full hearing

A worker/employee, and in a few cases an employer, may make a claim[10] to an employment tribunal. From spring 2014 the government is introducing a provision whereby claimants, before lodging a claim with the ET, will be required to submit key details of their dispute to the Advisory, Conciliation and Arbitration Service (Acas) which will seek to conciliate and normally will have one month to do so. This is known as 'early conciliation'.

Acas is a government-funded, but independent, agency, controlled by a tripartite governing council of employer representatives, union representatives and independents. If the parties decline to take part in this early conciliation, or if the dispute remains unresolved, a worker can then submit a claim using a pro-forma either online or in hard copy to one of the 26 hearing centres.

The time limit for making a claim is set out in the relevant statute but is normally three months from the incident giving rise to the claim (and up to one extra month is now being added to allow time for early conciliation).

Acas, as well as being empowered from 2014 to seek to resolve the matter by early conciliation, has since 1975, and continues to have a statutory duty to provide conciliation after a claim has been lodged and can do so up to the time of the full hearing. In 2011–12 Acas successfully conciliated in 33 per cent of claims, but with variations between types of complaints. For instance 42 per cent of unfair dismissal claims were settled by conciliation, while a further 24 per cent were withdrawn, sometimes after Acas intervention (Ministry of Justice, 2012a).

Apart from conciliation by Acas, which is more often than not conducted by telephone or email, there may be judicial mediation which involves a face-to-face meeting lasting up to a day, with the parties having separate rooms and the judicial mediator shuttling between the parties. Judicial mediation, however, is only used for selected cases: the criteria for selection include that the full hearing would have been scheduled to last three days or more and that the parties are willing to engage in mediation. If judicial mediation is unsuccessful, the case proceeds to a full hearing with a different judge from the judicial mediator who takes no further part in the case after the mediation. There are some 200 judicial mediations a year in England and Wales with a success rate of 70 per cent (Sullivan, 2012); however, this high success rate is based on a pre-selected pool, whereas Acas's lower success rate is a percentage of all claims. Whether this rate of success will continue after fees for judicial mediation have been introduced (see below) remains unclear at this juncture.

Before a full-hearing there is generally a case management discussion, now called a preliminary hearing (PH) in the more complex and lengthy cases, generally a face-to-face discussion between a professional judge and the claimant and respondent or their representatives. PHs are designed to ensure that the subsequent full hearing runs smoothly, so as a result of a PH a professional judge will fix timetables, give orders to the parties, for instance witness orders or orders for the discovery of documents, and identify the issues to be resolved.

In addition, a PH may be held to resolve a number of preliminary issues, for instance, whether a person is an employee and/or has the necessary service and is thus entitled to make a claim of unfair dismissal, and whether a person has a disability. If a claim has no reasonable prospect of success it may be dismissed in full or in part. Furthermore, if it appears that a claim has 'little reasonable prospect of success', a party at a PH may be required to pay a deposit of up to £1,000[11] as a condition of proceeding to a full hearing and given a warning that they may be liable for the other party's costs (if legally represented) or preparation time (if not legally represented). Such a deposit is forfeited if the party then loses at the full hearing.

The full hearing

A full hearing on the merits of the case takes place some six months to a year after a claim has been made. The parties do not have to be legally represented at a hearing (unlike the 'ordinary courts' where only lawyers can represent), although many are. According to a survey in 2008, 34 per cent of claimants had a legal or professional representative at a full hearing compared to 73 per cent of employers and 9 per cent of claimants were advised by a trade union at some stage (Peters et al., 2010). The length of hearing varies by type of complaint and the same survey found that 28 per cent of hearings that resulted in a decision lasted two days or more. That figure, however, includes pre-hearings, which overall are normally shorter than most full hearings.

The procedure is mainly adversarial although the employment tribunal also has a duty to ask questions of the witnesses if it appears relevant to do so. As in the civil courts, witnesses in employment tribunal cases attend on oath and in England and Wales (but not Scotland) submit written statements in advance (a practice introduced a decade ago) and these written statements are now normally taken as read and provide the basis for cross-examination. The judge takes an official note which he/she may be required to make available in full or in part at an appeal. The hearing, however, is not recorded as in some other countries (see South Africa (Chapter 10) and Sweden (Chapter 11) in this book). Whether the judge sits alone or there is a tripartite tribunal is determined by the type of complaint, subject to judicial discretion (see above).

The judgment, that is the decision together with reasons, can be delivered orally on the day by the judge after an adjournment. If so, the judgment (not the proceedings) is recorded and can be transcribed later if requested by the parties. Alternatively the judgment is reserved and sent in writing to the parties a few weeks later. Where the ET is composed of three members, one person can dissent and the dissent and the reasons for it are set out in the judgment. Dissent, however, is rare: according to Selwyn (2008), 96 per cent of decisions are unanimous. Whatever the ET composition, however, and whether or not there is dissent, only the judge signs the judgment, unlike in Sweden's labour court (see Chapter 11).

Costs do not follow the event. In only a few cases (3 per cent) does the ET require the losing party to pay the winning party's costs, for instance because a party has acted abusively or if the bringing or conduct of the proceedings were 'misconceived' and the tribunal considers it reasonable for the losing party to pay costs (Ministry of Justice, 2012a).[12] The ceiling on costs a tribunal may award has been raised from time to time and at the time of writing is £20,000.[13] If the ET wishes to award more than £20,000, at present it transfers the case for an assessment of costs to the County Court but this is scheduled to change to enable ET judges to deal with the assessment. Full costs, however, may not necessarily be awarded as the ET may (but not must) take account of a party's ability to pay.

In most cases the successful party will receive compensation for loss, that is a sum of money, but ETs are not themselves responsible for the enforcement of their awards. Accordingly a person who wishes to force a reluctant employer to pay the amount due must do so via the ordinary courts. From April 2010, a successful claimant can ask a High Court enforcement officer to commence proceedings in the county court on the claimant's behalf and to seize and sell the employer's goods if payment is not made. A publicly available register provides details of any enforcement action and may affect an employer's ability to obtain credit and/or may be widely publicised in the media (Morris, 2012).

A decision can be reviewed by a tribunal only in strictly limited circumstances, for instance if new evidence has come to light since the conclusion of the hearing but only if its existence could not have been reasonably known or foreseen, or if a party had not received notice of the hearing or it is in the interests of justice (IDS, 2006).

Employment Appeal Tribunal

There is an underlying public policy principle in Great Britain in all judicial proceedings that there should be finality in litigation. Accordingly, an ET decision can only be appealed on a point of law, unlike in many other countries (see Germany (Chapter 4), for instance).[14] Only one in 20 of all fully heard ET claims is appealed (Renton, 2012: x), although our analysis based on data from Ministry of Justice (2012a) gives a slightly lower figure of 3–4 per cent, that is 1 in 25 or less.

An appellant has 42 days from the date of the ET judgment and reasons to lodge an appeal with the Employment Appeal Tribunal (EAT) and the EAT sits normally in Edinburgh and London. After an appeal has been received, a judge (or the registrar with an appeal to the judge) conducts a 'sift', that is, a filter, looking at various papers including the notice of appeal and the ET's judgment, and there are several possible outcomes. First, an appeal can be rejected (for instance because it is out of time or does not reveal a point of law); second, it can be set down for a preliminary hearing where the appellant has to show an arguable case and, where that is done, the case then goes to a full hearing; and third, a case can be set down straight away for a full hearing. If an appeal is rejected at a sift an appellant can have a one-hour oral hearing before a judge to persuade him/her that the appeal should proceed to either a preliminary or full hearing. In the year to 31 March 2011, over half of all appeals were rejected after a sift and/or short oral hearing (Ministry of Justice/HM Courts and Tribunal Service, 2011).

At an EAT hearing, a legally qualified person is in the chair, normally a High Court or circuit judge. As noted above when the EAT was established in 1975, every case was heard by a judge and two lay members (one from the workers' side and one from the employers'). Then the default position became that where a case was heard at an ET by a judge alone, it was judge alone at the EAT. In 2013, however, the government removed lay members (i.e. lay judges) from **all** cases at the EAT, subject to judicial discretion. Such discretion is exceptional: in every other country in this book, the law, not a judge, decides a court's composition.

When sitting, which is becoming a rare event, lay members receive £303 per day,[15] but that does not include preparation time as they receive the papers some five days in advance, nor perusing a draft judgment after the hearing. Once a year the EAT provides training for lay members for which they receive a half fee.

Similarly as with ETs, lay members were originally nominated by the main labour market actors. Now individuals apply and are interviewed and selected and nominate themselves either to an employer or employee panel in a manner similar to their counterparts below.

Before reviewing a case, the EAT may invite the ET which decided the case at first instance to clarify its reasoning and/or findings and to this end it may ask the parties to put forward, and if possible agree, questions for the ET (the so-called Burns-Barke procedure). The EAT only hears the parties' submissions and any replies to the Burns-Barke questions, not any evidence, and so it very rarely grants permission to obtain the ET judge's notes of the original hearing in full or in part, even though it has the power to do so. Where allegations of bias are made the ET's comments are sought on the specific allegations.

Three quarters of all accepted appeals are heard within 26 weeks (Ministry of Justice/HM Courts and Tribunals Service, 2011) and procedure at a hearing is adversarial. As a result of a full hearing the EAT can disallow the appeal, make a ruling on a point of law and remit the case in full or in part to the original tribunal or a differently constituted one so that the case can be reheard, or overturn the employment tribunal decision and decide the case itself. It rarely does this, however, as it has not heard all the facts.

Also as in ETs, the hearing itself is not recorded. The EAT's judgment, that is, the decision with reasons, can be delivered orally on the day by the judge after an adjournment. If so, it is recorded and can be transcribed later if requested by the parties. Alternatively it is reserved and handed down to the parties a few weeks later. Where the tribunal is composed of three members, one person can dissent and the dissent and the reasons for it are noted in the judgment. As at first instance, however, dissent is extremely rare and whatever the EAT's composition, only the judge signs the judgment.

Costs do not follow the event and the costs regime is similar to that in ETs (see above).

Recent changes

Successive governments have been concerned to reduce the number of ET claims, for two main reasons: to reduce the costs of the system and to reduce the so-called burdens on business. In 2011–12 there were 186,300 claims to ETs, a litigation rate of 0.8 per cent according to our calculations (number of claims divided by working population), although Gibbons (2007: 15) gives a rate of 0.4 per cent. Whatever the precise figure, the litigation rate in Great Britain is not higher than that in many other countries in this book (see Table 13.3).

In 2010 a new government was elected with the aim of reviewing employment law to 'provide maximum flexibility and promote competition without compromising fairness' (BIS/HMCTS, 2011: 2). This has resulted in several employment law changes which diminish worker protection and are beyond the scope of this book.[16] Some changes, however, have a direct impact on ETs and the EAT.

We have already referred to one recent change: the removal of lay members from unfair dismissal cases in ETs from April 2012 and the removal of lay members from all cases at the EAT, albeit a professional judge has discretion to opt to sit with lay members, thus departing from the default position. This does not fit easily with the findings of a survey carried out in 2011. It found that over half of all ET and EAT professional judges were of the view that a three-person labour court generally has a greater legitimacy than a judge sitting alone, while 60 per cent of ET professional judges said that lay judges provided a balance between legal and worker/employer perspectives (Corby and Latreille, 2011) (Table 5.1).[17]

We have also already referred to another recent change – the introduction of early conciliation by Acas, which establishes a hoop for potential

Table 5.1 GB tribunals' legitimacy

	ET		EAT	
	Judges	**Lay members**	**Judges**	**Lay members**
Strongly agree	13.3	66.5	12.5	71.8
Agree	42.0	31.3	37.5	28.2
Neither agree nor disagree	22.9	1.6	25.0	–
Disagree	19.1	0.3	18.8	–
Strongly disagree	2.7	0.4	6.2	–
Base	188	1136	16	39

Note: 'A three-person tribunal generally has greater legitimacy than a judge sitting alone'.
Source: Corby, S. and Latreille, P. (2011) *Survey Evidence: ET and EAT Judges and Lay Members*, http://www2.gre.ac.uk/about/schools/business/research/centres/weru/publications [accessed 23 November 2012].

claimants to go through before they can submit their claim to an ET. The most far-reaching change of all, however, is the introduction of fees for taking a case, which reduces accessibility. Until recently there was no fee required, but the Government imposed a fee structure at first instance (ET) and appellate level (EAT) from 29 July 2013 as follows (Ministry of Justice, 2012b):

Employment Tribunals (ET)

- Level 1 claims (e.g. unpaid wages, payment in lieu of notice, redundancy payments etc.)
  - the issue fee: £160 (approximately €187, $255),
  - the hearing fee: £230 (approximately €269, $366),
- Level 2 claims (e.g. unfair dismissal, discrimination)
  - the issue fee: £250 (approximately €292, $398),
  - the hearing fee: £950 (approximately €1,111, $1,512),
- judicial mediation: £600 (approximately €702, $945).

Employment Appeal Tribunal (EAT)

- £400 (approximately €467, $636) to lodge an appeal,
- £1,200 (approximately €1,401, $1,908) for a hearing at the EAT.

A claimant is remitted from paying these fees in full or part provided he/she satisfies a disposable capital test *and* then a gross monthly income test, but a partner's or spouse's capital and income counts and it is thought that very few will be able to satisfy the tests to obtain full remission.[18] A judge, after a hearing, will have the power to order a losing respondent to reimburse the claimant for those fees in full or in part.

In addition, from April 2013, the government reduced legal help and legal aid. Legal help is a scheme, funded by government, under which a lawyer can advise on a case, write letters and prepare documents, provided that a person meets certain financial and eligibility criteria. From April 2013 such legal help in the employment sphere, was only available for discrimination cases. Legal aid is a government funded scheme providing for legal representation at a hearing. Legal aid has never been available at an ET, but it has been available, subject to financial and eligibility criteria, for all cases at the EAT. From April 2013 it has only been available for discrimination cases at the EAT and the higher courts.

Other recent changes (April 2012) such as doubling the caps both on deposits ordered as a result of a PH and on costs[19] and withdrawing payment of state-funded witness expenses also can provide a financial disincentive to those seeking to access ETs, while taking witness statements as read adds to the formality of proceedings.

This, however, is not the end of the government's quest to save costs to the public purse and/or to deter claimants. They include new ET rules (in draft form at the time of writing) aimed at shortening hearings; for instance, a judge being given the power to timetable oral evidence and impose guillotines and to strike out proceedings at any stage (BIS, 2013b).

The government has justified many of these changes on the grounds that such arrangements already apply in the civil courts, so eroding the distinction between ETs, that is, what are known as labour courts in other countries, and the 'ordinary' courts (see Corby and Latreille (2012) for further discussion). Accordingly, we now turn to the role of the civil courts.

The civil courts

Employment rights adjudication is not confined to ETs and the Employment Appeal Tribunal (EAT). The civil courts, the County Court or the High Court (Sheriff Court in Scotland) hear cases at first instance and the higher civil courts hear appeals on points of law from the EAT, or the first-instance civil courts.

In their first-instance role, the civil courts dispose of personal injury claims, and claims in tort including whether trade unions and their officials have immunity in planning and organising industrial action, while claims relating to contractual issues are heard initially either by the County Court or the High Court (Sheriff Courts in Scotland). There are 220 County Courts and the bulk of their work (and that of the High Court and the Sheriff's Courts) is not related to employment.

The main criterion determining whether a case is heard in the county court or the High Court is the size of damages being sought and fees relate to the amount claimed. In April 2011 for instance, if the amount claimed was over £5,000 to £15,000, the fee was £245. If the amount claimed was over £100,000 to £150,000, the fee was £885, with additional fees for a witness summons (£35) and for a hearing (£1,090).[20] No court fees are, however, payable if the claimant's annual income is below a certain level or if certain state benefits are received.

Adjudication on contract claims, however, is not limited to the civil courts. ETs can hear some breach of contract claims outstanding on the termination of the employee's employment, albeit subject to a limit.[21] Some contractual matters such as the enforcement of restrictive covenants are excluded from the ETs. Cases concerning the application of the equality clause implied into every contract of employment to achieve equal pay between men and women may be brought in the ET, or if the claim is out of time for the ET, the High Court or County Court. There is thus a degree of dual jurisdiction and overlap between the civil courts and the ET and there can be some forum shopping. As can be seen just from this brief description, the system of employment rights adjudication is complex.

As to appeals, whether cases at first instance follow the employment tribunal/Employment Appeal Tribunal route or whether they follow the County Court/High Court route the next stage is an appeal to the Court of Appeal (Court of Session in Scotland) on a point of law only and then to the Supreme Court, where the test for an appeal is a point of law of general public importance.

The Court of Appeal is based in London and the Court of Session is based in Edinburgh and both Courts normally comprise three professional judges. Leave to appeal is only granted if permission is given either by the Court itself or by a more junior court and only a minority of appeals concern employment. The last appellate court for England, Wales and Scotland is the Supreme Court, based in London. It hears about 100 appeals a year of which about six are employment related (Taylor and Amir, 2009).[22] It takes at least 18 months from receipt of an ET judgment to the handing down of a Court of Appeal judgment and a further 18 months or more for a Supreme Court judgment to be handed down. Of course these timescales are lengthened if a preliminary reference is made to the Court of Justice of the European Union.

Professional judges in the civil courts normally have previously been barristers (advocates in Scotland) when they perhaps never or rarely represented in employment law cases or had experience as employees (since barristers are self-employed) and their main role as judges is not adjudicating in employment law cases. So they tend to have little or no knowledge of employment relations norms and instead to apply common law concepts and norms.

Quasi-judicial bodies

To further complicate British employment rights adjudication, the Advisory, Conciliation and Arbitration Service (Acas), as well as providing conciliation before an ET hearing, also operates as a quasi-judicial body in order to provide a more informal and less adversarial adjudication process than the process in employment tribunals. In short, from 2001 Acas has had a scheme to provide arbitration in respect of unfair dismissal and in 2003 it launched a further scheme to provide arbitration in respect of flexible working, with both schemes providing an alternative to adjudication by an ET. Yet the parties seem to prefer the more court-like ETs to the more informal Acas arbitration. Since these schemes' inception, that is, in over ten years, there have been less than 80 unfair dismissal arbitrations, compared to 47,900 unfair dismissal claims to ETs in one year alone (2010–11) and only three flexible working arbitrations.[23]

Another important quasi-judicial body is the Central Arbitration Committee, but as that body only deals with collective/trade union issues, it is outside the scope of this chapter and this book.

Enforcement authorities

To add to the labyrinthine systems of employment rights adjudication in Great Britain, there is a patchwork of employment rights inspectors who can issue enforcement notices in respect of specific employment rights and/or in specific industries and in the last resort criminally prosecute, but there is no single inspectorate or enforcement agency covering all or most employment rights. For instance inspectors from the Health and Safety Executive (HSE) can issue enforcement notices and bring criminal prosecutions for a breach of the health and safety legislation in respect of manufacturing plants, construction sites, farms and laboratories. Its diminishing resources, however, impair its effectiveness (see Tombs and Whyte (2012) for a full discussion).

Likewise local authority environmental health officers and the Office of Rail Regulation (ORR) can issue enforcement notices and bring criminal prosecutions for a breach of the health and safety legislation, with the former responsible for offices, hotels and restaurants and warehouses; and the latter for rail transport. In 2009–10 these three enforcing authorities issued 15,881 enforcement notices, while the HSE and ORR completed 922 prosecutions resulting in an 80 per cent conviction rate (Health and Safety Executive, 2010).

Similarly, so-called compliance officers from HM Revenue and Customs (HMRC) can issue enforcement notices requiring employers to increase pay rates and to pay back-pay to workers whom these officers have found to have been paid below the national minimum wage. In 2008–9 it issued 96 enforcement notices. Although employers can appeal against these notices to an employment tribunal, their rate of success has been low (Low Pay Commission, 2011). In addition, since 2006 HMRC has prosecuted a handful of employers in the criminal courts (Morris, 2012).

To add to the patchwork, there is also a Gangmasters' Licensing Authority (GLA) to protect workers from exploitation in selected industries: agriculture, horticulture, forestry, shell-fish-gathering, food and drink processing and packaging. A licence is given if the gangmaster meets certain standards, for instance on health and safety, accommodation and the payment of National Insurance. GLA inspectors can issue enforcement notices if they find that workers are being exploited. During the year to 31 March 2011, GLA inspectors identified 845 workers who had been exploited. In financial terms the exploitation amounted to almost £2.5 million (Gangmasters' Licensing Authority, 2011). At the time of writing the government is planning to remove from the scope of the GLA what it calls low risk activities or sectors, such as cleaning contractors and forestry, which could save around £60,000 a year.[24]

Last but not least is the Equality and Human Rights Commission. Although its main legal work is supporting claimants, it has the power to conduct formal assessments and to issue compliance notices in connection with a breach by a public authority of its general duty to eliminate discrimination and advance equality of opportunity in respect of age, gender, disability, pregnancy and maternity, gender reassignment, race, religion or belief and sexual orientation. For further details, see IDS (2010). Its enforcement activities are being curtailed, however, because of drastic reductions in budget. By 2015 it will have lost nearly two-thirds of its initial resources when it was established in 2007 (Hepple, 2012: 56).

Conclusions and prospects

One noticeable feature of the British system of employment rights adjudication is that it is not autonomous. As we have shown judgments of the specialist ET can be appealed to the specialist EAT. Further appeals, however, go to the 'ordinary' courts: the Court of Appeal and the Supreme Court. Because of the doctrine of precedent, the common law concepts of the higher courts (the Supreme Court and the Court of Appeal) are injected into the way the judges in the ETs and the EAT adjudicate employment relations disputes. Yet judges in the higher courts may have had little experience of employment law and are often ignorant of employment relations norms.

Another noticeable feature relates to the fact that the British employment rights adjudication system is not straightforward and has developed in an *ad hoc* way, unlike, for instance, post-apartheid South Africa (Chapter 10). As we have seen there are a number of sometimes overlapping bodies, resulting in a claimant having options. For instance claimants can decide whether in a dismissal dispute to opt for unfair dismissal (a statutory right) with adjudication by Acas arbitration or adjudication by an employment tribunal, or to opt for wrongful dismissal (a contractual right), rather than unfair dismissal, with adjudication by the High Court. In addition there are a number of quasi-judicial bodies and piecemeal and partial inspection/enforcement authorities.

A further feature has been the government's focus on reducing the burdens on business and the cost to the public purse by reducing the budget and thus the activities of enforcement authorities and similarly by reforming ETs. As we have shown above, lay members have been incrementally excluded by governments of differing political hues from adjudicating in ETs and the Employment Appeal Tribunal (EAT). The present government's justification for excluding lay members from ETs relates to cost savings (BIS/HM Courts & Tribunals Service, 2011: 31). According to that argument, if lay members were excluded from *all* employment tribunal cases, this would lead to further cost savings, so the prognosis for tripartite ETs is poor.

As to reducing the burdens on business by reducing the number of ET claims being lodged and heard, again this has a long history: pre-hearing assessments to screen out cases were introduced in 1980 and were the forerunner of pre-hearing reviews first introduced in 1993 (see above), while the grounds for awards of costs were expanded in 1980, 1993 and 2001 and the ceiling on costs was raised in 2001 and 2012 (Corby and Latreille, 2012). Most controversial of all, however, is the recent change to introduce fees in respect of ETs and the EAT and again further changes cannot be ruled out. The government has pointed out that the civil courts in England and Wales aim to attain 100 per cent of costs from users net of the remission system in 2014/15 (Ministry of Justice, 2011). The fees introduced by the government in 2013 for ETs and the EAT do not equate to full cost recovery, but there is nothing to prevent the government from raising the fees substantially in future. Moreover, against an economic background of austerity projected to last for at least several years more, the government's main emphasis is likely to continue to be on cutting the cost to the public purse, rather than improving the accessibility of adjudicatory institutions.

6
Ireland

Introduction

At the time this book was concluded, Ireland stood on the cusp of radical change. Over the past few decades, the Republic became characterised by a complex institutional landscape for resolving employment disputes, both individual and collective. Many structures and procedures evolved in an ad hoc way, with institutions often adapted or created to deal with specific concerns – in some cases leading to the same body having differing roles and powers depending on the issue. The desirability of rationalising this matrix was acknowledged several years ago, but during 2013 proposals to simplify the system were poised to go through the *Oireachtas* (parliament) providing for first-instance adjudication by a new Workplace Relations Commission and appeals de novo to a reformed Labour Court.

Having outlined the context, we describe the current system and then we examine the proposed new system, including the new bodies, their role and powers and some criticisms. We conclude that the simplification of bodies that the proposed new system will introduce is long overdue and is set to benefit workers, employers and the state.

The context

The Irish state was first established as the Irish Free State in 1922, but became the Republic of Ireland in 1949, based on a written constitution. Today, Ireland is a small country (under two million employees), with its economy heavily dependent on the presence of US multinationals (Eurofound, 2013).

At its inception, industrial relations in Ireland were characterised by a broadly voluntarist approach and most collective agreements are not legally binding. Nevertheless, until recently Joint Labour Committees, which are independent tripartite bodies, issued Employment Regulation Orders (EROs) which determined legally binding minimum rates of pay and conditions of work in low wage sectors such as catering, hotels and cleaning where union density is low, but EROs were declared unconstitutional in 2011 (Eurofound, 2013).

Similarly Registered Employment Agreements (REAs) ceased to have legally binding effect after a decision of the Supreme Court in May 2013. REAs were registered with the Labour Court (see below) and covered an entire industry, irrespective of whether or not employers were members of the relevant employers' association. They were most prevalent in electrical contracting, construction, retail and printing (Eurofound, 2013; NERA, 2013).

EROs and REAs apart, industrial relations voluntarism has been tempered by social partnership in the last 25 years. In 1987, with unemployment and the national debt soaring, the government brokered a national social partnership agreement between trade unions and employers called the Programme for National Recovery. Since then there have been successive national social partnership agreements, each of approximately three years duration, the last one being the Transitional Agreement concluded in late 2008. These agreements set wages policy, after negotiations between the Irish Business and Employers' Confederation (IBEC) and the Irish Congress of Trade Unions (ICTU). Although these wages policies were not legally binding on all employers, compliance was high. Importantly also these national agreements determined macro-economic and social policy and, as well as the social partners, the participants included voluntary and community groups, agricultural representatives and small business associations (Donaghey and Teague, 2007; Eurofound, 2013).

From the mid-1990s, the Irish economy grew rapidly, but this halted in 2008 when the Irish banking system failed and Ireland's property 'bubble' burst, against a background of international economic and financial turbulence. One result of the economic and financial crisis was the breakdown of the social partnership model in 2009 and a movement from multi-employer national level bargaining in the private sector to company level bargaining. (Previously where there was company level bargaining, this essentially shadowed the wages policy set in national social partnership agreements.)

Nevertheless, in 2010 an agreement was reached for the state sector, The Public Service Agreement 2010–14, which aimed to provide major productivity improvements and efficiencies, as well as industrial peace. The agreement includes commitments to redeployment, acceptance of significant workplace changes and changed working hours (Labour Relations Commission, 2012).

Other important developments in the last 25–30 years have been the decline in trade union density and the growth of legislation. In Ireland, as in the vast majority of developed countries, trade union density has declined sharply from nearly half of all employees in the 1970s to 32 per cent in 2011, with collective bargaining coverage currently estimated at 44 per cent (Eurofound, 2013). Using Visser (2013), we calculate union density at 36 per cent for 2010–11 (see Table 1.1 on p. 2). At the same time over the last 30–40 years there has been a growth of individual legal employment rights based on a diverse range of sources; the common law, the written constitution, domestic legislation and legislation emanating from the European Union, which Ireland joined in 1973. Such laws include legislation on unfair dismissal, redundancy compensation, protection against discrimination on the grounds of sex, race, sexual orientation, disability, age and religion, maternity protection, parental leave and limitations on working time and atypical work.

Against this background sketch, we now turn to the way such legal rights are adjudicated at the time of writing (August 2013).

The current position

As noted above, the present system has evolved over time in a piecemeal fashion in response to European Union developments, the evolution of national level social dialogue, domestic legislation and the changing nature of employment (Bruton, 2011). Currently, there are five redress/enforcement bodies for the resolution of individual employment rights disputes:

- Rights Commissioner Service
- Employment Appeals Tribunal (EAT)
- Labour Court
- Equality Tribunal
- The National Employment Rights Authority.

In addition there are other bodies that deal with employment rights in the 'ordinary' civil court system: the Circuit Court, which has first-instance and appellate jurisdictions, and the High Court and the Supreme Court, where appeals can be made on a point of law. Moreover, there is a Labour Relations Commission (LRC), which provides an industrial relations conciliation and advice service and workplace mediation for the resolution of workplace disputes that have not been referred to other bodies for adjudication. In addition, the LRC issues codes of practice, carries out research, publishes advisory guides and contains the Rights Commissioner Service noted above.

Figure 6.1 sets out the position in diagrammatic form and we now consider the adjudicatory/enforcement bodies mentioned above.

Rights Commissioner Service

Rights Commissioners were established in 1970 to resolve disputes involving individuals and small groups of workers on small-scale industrial relations problems, but over the last 40 years their role has changed (Labour Relations Commission, 2012). Now their main focus is the resolution of complaints brought by individuals alleging a breach of certain statutory employment rights, particularly unfair dismissal cases if the parties agree, but additionally

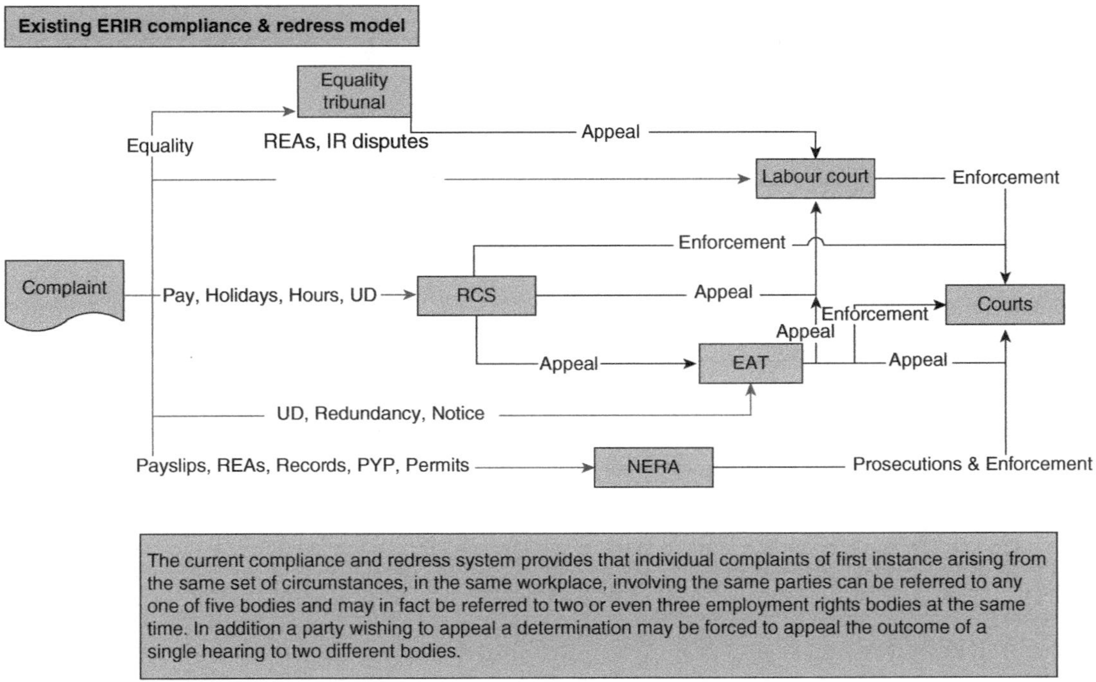

Figure 6.1 Ireland's current adjudication and compliance structure

Source: Reproduced with the kind permission of the Ministry of Jobs, Innovation and Enterprise from the *Blueprint to Deliver a World Class Workplace Relations Service* (Bruton, 2012a: 40).

Key: EAT = Employment Appeals Tribunal; ERIR = Employment Rights and Industrial Relations; NERA = National Employment Rights Authority; PYP = Protection of Young Persons; RCS = Rights Commissioner Service; REAs = Registered Employment Agreements; UD = Unfair Dismissal they cover a number of other employment rights under some 40 pieces of legislation including cases concerning maternity protection, parental leave, the minimum wage, working time, payment of wages, fixed-term and part-time contracts, disputes of alleged dismissal in circumstances where an employee has less than 12 months' service and appeals against a disciplinary sanction imposed by an employer (Bruton, 2012b).[1]

A Rights Commissioner hears a dispute alone and hearings are held in private, unless the dispute has been referred under the Payment of Wages Act, 1991. Hearings are not adversarial and written submissions are not required, although they are often provided. A Rights Commissioner cannot require the submission of documents,[2] or the attendance of witnesses and where witnesses do attend, their evidence is not given on oath. There are no restrictions on representation so the parties can be represented by a lawyer, trade union, employers' organisation, friend or family member. Rights Commissioners issue their findings either as decisions or as non-binding recommendations. Before adjudicating, Rights Commissioners often try to help mediate on the day of the hearing and have off-the record conversations with the sides separately (Mallon, 2012), returning to their adjudication role if there is no settlement.

Rights Commissioners are fee-paid on a *per diem* basis and, as noted above, they are based within the Labour Relations Commission. They are nominated by the social partners and subsequently appointed by the Minister. At the time of writing there were 14 Commissioners, seven from the trade unions and seven from the employers. The number of referrals to the Rights Commissioner Service grew steadily in the five years from 2006, peaking at 15,671 referrals in 2010, but fell in 2011 to 9,206 referrals, with a reduction in the delays in obtaining a hearing. 'At the end of 2011 an offer of a first hearing for referrals was in the region of about six to eight weeks' (Labour Relations Commission, 2012: 27).

Either party may appeal against a decision, with the options and time limits dependent on the type of case: no grounds are required to make an appeal but appellants will be required to indicate grounds when submitting documentation to an appellate body. Appeal is to the Labour Court or the Employment Appeals Tribunal, depending on the case.

Employment Appeals Tribunal

The Employment Appeals Tribunal (EAT) is a statutory body established to adjudicate individual rights disputes, not collective disputes. Originally established in 1967 as the 'Redundancy Appeals Tribunal' to resolve disputes over redundancy, it was given its current name in 1977. Paradoxically, however, despite its name as an appellate body, the EAT also has first-instance jurisdiction.

The EAT's main first-instance jurisdiction (over a fifth of its claims) is unfair dismissal. This is because a party to a dispute may object to a Rights Commissioner's investigation of a case brought under the Unfair Dismissals

Acts and go straight to the EAT. In 2011 roughly half the unfair dismissal claims went to the Rights Commissioner and half at first instance to the EAT (Employment Appeals Tribunal, 2012). Redundancy disputes and disputes over minimum notice periods, however, are also adjudicated by the EAT at first instance (see Employment Appeals Tribunal, 2012; Labour Relations Commission, 2012, for further details).

As to its appellate jurisdiction, the EAT hears appeals from certain decisions of Rights Commissioners essentially on unfair dismissal and such appeals form 12 per cent of its work. It also hears appeals from decisions of the Deciding Officer under the Redundancy Payments Act (for instance, by an employer in respect of a rebate and from an employee in respect of the identity of the employer) and appeals from a Minister in respect of insolvencies (Employment Appeals Tribunal, 2012).

The EAT is tripartite, with a legally qualified chair (or vice-chair) and two members, one drawn from the employers' panel and one drawn from the trade union panel. In 2011, apart from the chair, there were 43 vice-chairs, 41 members nominated by the Irish Congress of Trade Unions and 41 by organisations representative of employers. All its members, vice-chairs and even its chair are part-time and appointed by the Minister for a fixed term. According to several interviewees, they are all political appointees irrespective of any track record in employment law. As one interviewee said: 'not only every time the government changes, but every time a minister changes, a whole new lot of people are appointed'.

The EAT conducts hearings in some 36 locations around the country, sitting half the time in Dublin and half the time outside the capital. In 2011, it received 8,458 referrals and disposed of 6,723 cases of which a third were redundancy cases and a quarter were unfair dismissal and minimum notice cases. The waiting time between the claim and a hearing was on average at least a year. As to representation, a party may appear in person, be represented by counsel or a solicitor, by a representative of a trade union or employers' association or, with leave of the EAT by any other person. Some two-thirds of employees and almost the same proportion of employers have legal representation in unfair dismissal cases, although legal representation is less common in other types of cases (Employment Appeals Tribunal, 2012).

Hearings are normally open to the public. Evidence is given on oath and judgments are entered on a publicly accessible register. The EAT may not award costs against any party to an application except where, in its opinion, a party has acted frivolously or vexatiously (Employment Appeals Tribunal, n.d.).

The Equality Tribunal

The Equality Tribunal was established in 1998 as an independent quasi-judicial body to mediate and rule on claims of unlawful discrimination in employment, pensions and in the provision of goods and services.[3]

The bulk of the claims (77 per cent in 2011) relate to alleged discrimination in employment or the seeking of employment and pensions, not goods and services, with discrimination on race the most frequently cited ground out of nine protected characteristics.[4] In 2011 38 per cent of the cases were settled in mediation and a further 29 per cent were withdrawn or closed during mediation (Equality Tribunal, 2012). Decisions are publicly accessible, but the names of witnesses are redacted, although not the names of the parties except in certain types of cases such as sexual harassment or unless the parties request anonymity.

Before making a claim, a person who feels they have been discriminated against is entitled to ask the respondent (the employer) for information to help them decide whether to refer the matter to the Equality Tribunal. There is a form for this, and a reply form. The respondent is not obliged to respond, but a Tribunal hearing the case may draw inferences if there is no response.

Although called a Tribunal, in fact adjudication is by one person called an Equality Officer, who is a civil servant and both mediates and adjudicates. There are currently about a dozen Equality Officers, according to an interviewee but the same Equality Officer never mediates and adjudicates in the same case and mediation proceedings remain confidential.

For adjudication purposes, the Equality Officer may require the production of relevant documents, enter premises and require any individual to attend a hearing. There are no restrictions on representation, but the majority of both complainants and respondents are not legally represented (Equality Tribunal, n.d.). Hearings are investigative, not adversarial and are held in private. They are not necessarily held in Dublin as the Equality Officer will normally arrange a mediation/hearing at a location accessible to both parties. Costs are not awarded and the average award was €2,522 in 2011 (Equality Tribunal, 2012). Appeals from an employment decision of the Equality Tribunal go to the Labour Court and a party can apply to the Circuit Court for an enforcement order if a decision is not complied with within 42 days. Appeals from the Equality Tribunal about goods and services go to the Circuit Court. Accordingly, we now briefly consider the Circuit Court.

Circuit Court

The Circuit Court is a branch of civil jurisdiction and can hear at first-instance common law claims for breach of contract, such as wrongful dismissal. As with Great Britain, but unlike New Zealand (Chapter 9), the employment institutions do not have exclusive jurisdiction of employment issues. The Circuit Court, however, may not impose damages above €38,092 unless agreed by the parties, or where the case is a direct referral in a claim of discrimination on the grounds of gender, when the amount of damages is unlimited.

The Circuit Court also hears appeals de novo from the EAT, where the latter has had first-instance jurisdiction in cases of unfair dismissal, and has certain enforcement powers.[5] In the case of gender discrimination, a plaintiff can choose either the Circuit Court or the Equality Tribunal. In contrast to claims taken to the Equality Tribunal, Circuit Court hearings are held in public and there is a fee.

The country is divided into eight circuits with one judge assigned to each circuit, except in Dublin, where ten judges may be assigned, and Cork, where there may be three judges.

National Employment Rights Authority

The National Employment Rights Authority (NERA), an enforcement and inspection body, was established in 2008 following the 2006 social partnership agreement 'Towards 2016'. It is an Office of the Department of Jobs, Enterprise and Innovation, with 105 staff in 2012, headquarters in Carlow, and regional offices in Cork, Dublin, Shannon and Sligo (NERA, n.d.; NERA, 2013).

NERA aims to secure compliance with a raft of employment rights legislation, including the minimum wage, working hours, payment of wages, and fixed term work through five main functions: information, inspection, enforcement, prosecution and the protection of young persons (NERA, n.d.).

NERA inspections are carried out in response to complaints or after sectors have been identified by risk analysis. In addition, it carries out a small number of inspections on a random basis. In 2012 it carried out 4,689 inspections involving 91,778 employees (some 5 per cent of employees). It is NERA policy to seek voluntary compliance and the number of prosecutions is low; only 1.5 per cent of employer inspections resulted in a prosecution (NERA, 2013).[6]

Where an employee has received an award after a hearing before a Rights Commissioner, the EAT or the Labour Court, and the employer has failed to pay the amount due, NERA on behalf of the Minister can bring proceedings in the civil courts for enforcement. Other functions of NERA relate to the issuing of licences in respect of employment agencies and the protection of young persons (see NERA, 2013 for further details).

The Labour Court

Established in 1946, the Labour Court has two distinct roles, one dealing with industrial relations issues[7] where it makes recommendations, the other with employment rights where it makes decisions. Calculated on the number of references there are twice as many industrial relations issues as employment rights issues, that is, a 2:1 split. Calculated on hearing days, employment rights cases form about half its workload because of the complexities often involved (Bruton, 2012a: 29). In employment rights issues, the Labour Court hears appeals de novo from the Equality Tribunal in employment cases and appeals against decisions of the Rights Commissioners, and complaints that decisions of Rights Commissioners were not implemented, in respect of the organisation of working time, the national minimum wage, part-time work, fixed-term work and health and safety.[8]

Where there is a de novo appeal a party can submit fresh evidence, but not change the nature of the claim and although the Labour Court is supplied with the first-instance judgment, this only provides background as the case is heard afresh. In both 2010 and 2011, appeals from Rights Commissioners on the organisation of working time was the largest category of employment rights cases heard by the Labour Court (Labour Court, 2012). Appeals from the Labour Court go to the High Court and Supreme Court on a point of law only.

The Labour Court is not a court of the law in the conventional sense, despite its name. There is no requirement for the chair or deputy chairs to be legally qualified and appellants and respondents sit around tables in a U-shape, rather than tables facing the judges, as is usual in a court room. Another symbolic difference is that the adjudicatory dais is only slightly raised.[9] A court secretary takes notes in longhand but these notes are not verbatim and if the parties wish, they can bring in their own stenographers, although this happens only rarely according to the chair of the Labour Court.

The Labour Court is a tripartite body. In 2011 there were nine full-time members: a chair and two deputies appointed by the Minister,[10] three employer side members nominated by IBEC and three employee side members nominated by the Irish Congress of Trade Unions (ICTU) and all were full-time (Labour Court, 2012). In addition, there is a registrar (legal adviser). The Labour Court normally sits with three members, that is, in three divisions: a chair (or deputy) and an employer side member and an employee side member, but very occasionally it sits as a full court with all nine members (Labour Court, n.d.).

Labour Court cases are usually heard in private (Labour Court, n.d.) and one division sits outside Dublin in most weeks of the year, while other divisions sit outside Dublin on a regular basis, typically in one out of every three weeks. In 2011 the Labour Court sat in 17 locations, often using hotels or government buildings. The parties are asked to make written submissions at least seven days before the hearing which is normally held within 12 weeks of referral (Labour Court, 2012). The Labour Court has no jurisdiction to award costs in the conventional sense such as the costs of professional representation, but it can award expenses incurred in attending a hearing if it finds that the case was frivolous or vexatious. Its decisions, with reasons, are published, with 85 per cent being issued within six weeks of the hearing.

At present Labour Court appeal hearings last a day, while EAT appeal hearings last four or five days. This shorter time period, according to the chair of the Labour Court, is because the Labour Court requires written submissions seven days in advance and its procedure is less formal. Decisions are always unanimous at the Labour Court, whereas at the EAT a decision can be by a majority (although this occurs infrequently), with dissent announced as is the tradition in the 'ordinary' courts.

The appellate system

We have shown that the first-instance adjudicatory system is complex, but the appellate system is almost as complex. In summary, appeals from certain decisions of the Rights Commissioners go to the EAT, as described above, with further appeals going to the High Court on a point of law. Appeals from the Equality Tribunal and certain decisions of the Rights Commissioners go the Labour Court, as we have briefly described above. Thereafter appeals from the Labour Court go to the High Court on a point of law only. Except in employment equality cases there is no further appeal from the High Court to the Supreme Court. Accordingly, in order to be able to appeal beyond to the Supreme Court, some parties tactically apply for a judicial review of a Labour Court decision.

Appeals from first-instance unfair dismissal decisions of the EAT go to the Circuit Court de novo (see above) and then to the High Court de novo. In fact there are very few. The EAT was notified of four appeals to the High Court in 2011 and 128 appeals to the Circuit Court (Employment Appeals Tribunal, 2012).

The proposed system

The need for reform

Readers so far will have realised that the adjudication of employment rights in Ireland is complex and will not be surprised to learn that it has been 'the subject of much analysis involving eight reports in as many years' (Bruton, 2012b: 4). One criticism is that workers often do not know which body has the power to adjudicate their claim and, if they have referred the claim to the wrong body, it may become time barred before the error is discovered. Another criticism is that currently a number of claims have to be heard in different bodies, depending on the statute involved, and cannot be conjoined, even though they stem from the same set of facts. This is a growing problem because increasingly a complaint has a number of jurisdictional bases.

Confusion to users is exacerbated, be they claimants or respondents, because there is a lack of consistency between these adjudicatory bodies regarding the degree of formality of hearings, rules of evidence, the use of adversarial or inquisitorial procedures, whether hearings are held in public or not, and whether and in what format the decisions are published. For instance, the Equality Tribunal is mandated to adopt inquisitorial procedures, while the EAT adopts essentially adversarial procedures and has been criticised for being over-legalistic, according to two interviewees. Rights Commissioner decisions are not published, but Equality Tribunal decisions are published with the names redacted and EAT decisions and Labour Court decisions are published. A further criticism is that the state does not enjoy economies of scale because of the multiplicity of forums.

In the face of this complexity, the Minister for the Department of Jobs, Enterprise and Innovation (DJEI), Richard Bruton, issued a consultation document in 2011, receiving 67 submissions (DJEI, 2011), after which the Minister issued a 'Blueprint to Deliver a World-Class Workplace Relations Service' (Bruton, 2012a). He then made a submission to the *Oireachtas* Select Sub-committee, setting out how he intended to proceed (Bruton, 2012b) and at the time of writing (August 2013), legislation is being drafted. In short, there will be major overhaul which will result in a two-tier structure: one body at first instance, the Workplace Relations Commission, and an appellate body, the Labour Court. We turn to each of these in turn (Figure 6.2).

The Workplace Relations Commission

The Workplace Relations Commission (WRC) will be established as an office of the DJEI. All employment-related complaints, which can be lodged without charge,[11] will first be received and screened[12] by the Registrar of the WRC

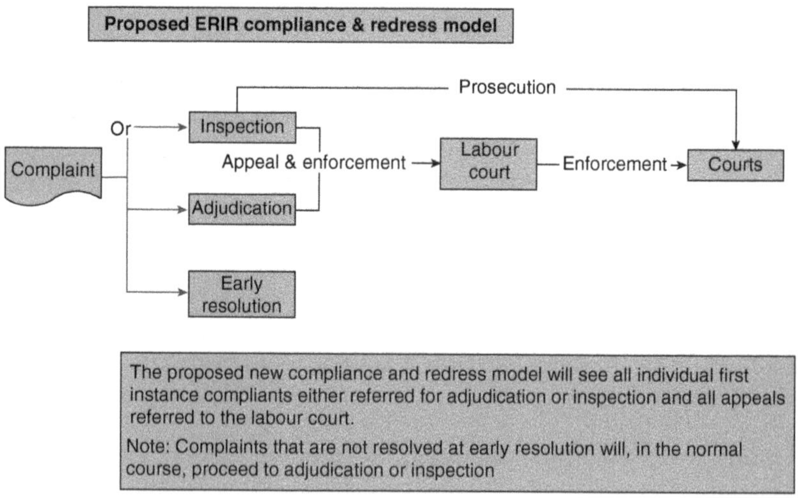

Figure 6.2 Ireland's proposed adjudication and compliance structure
Source: Reproduced with the kind permission of the Ministry of Jobs, Innovation and Enterprise from *Blueprint to Deliver a World Class Workplace Relations Service* (Bruton, 2012a: 41).
Key:
ERIR = Employment Rights and Industrial Relations

who will be a qualified and experienced lawyer. There will be a consistent time limit of six months for the initiation of all complaints requiring adjudication (unless there are exceptional circumstances) replacing a range of time limits currently prescribed in various employment statutes. Normally the Registrar will pass on the complaint to the Early Resolution Service, whose staff will engage with the parties (or their representatives) to the dispute to seek to conciliate.[13] In the main, conciliation will be conducted by telephone or email; resolution will be attempted through a 'meeting directly with the parties...only in exceptional cases' (Bruton, 2012a: 16). It seems that the Early Resolution Service will probably have a set time limit (currently not determined)[14] for the attempt at conciliation, after which a case will be referred back to the Registrar for adjudication/enforcement as appropriate.

All complaints requiring adjudication will be heard by a single person, a WRC adjudicator, who will replace the Rights Commissioners, the Equality Tribunal and the first-instance jurisdiction of the EAT. Existing Rights Commissioners, who work on a *per diem* basis (see above), and officers of the Equality Tribunal (permanent civil servants) will initially be the adjudicators. Any new recruits (and there is a recruitment embargo at the time of writing) will be selected and appointed following a transparent process that applies to all public appointments. They will not be nominated by the social partners as has been the practice for Rights Commissioners. Both current adjudicators and future recruits will not be *required* to be legally qualified, although at least some may in practice be so qualified.

The terms and conditions of new recruits have yet to be determined (for instance, whether they will be fee paid or employees and, if the latter whether on indefinite or fixed term contracts). It is envisaged that there will be a rigorous accredited training programme for existing adjudicators[15] and any new recruits and all adjudicators will be required to be qualified to deal with the full range of complaints that can be referred to the WRC.

It has not yet been determined whether, in the course of an adjudication hearing, adjudicators will have the flexibility to engage in conciliation and assist the parties to settle the matter, as is the current practice in the Rights Commissioner Service and the Equality Tribunal. Normally hearings will be held in private, unless the WRC adjudicator decides otherwise following a request from a party, in line with the practice at the Equality Tribunal and the Rights Commissioner Service, but not the EAT. Adjudicators will be empowered, but not obliged, to take evidence on oath and summon witnesses and documents.

As before in the Rights Commissioner Service and the Equality Tribunal, there will be no restrictions on representation and the adjudicator will not be empowered to order costs.

A detailed operations manual to which adjudicators must adhere will be publicly available and the Minister will be empowered to make regulations relating to the conduct of hearing (Duffy, 2012). The emphasis will be on an inquisitorial approach. Nevertheless, although 'hearings . . . will not follow strict rules similar to courts of law, fair procedures should be followed' (Bruton, 2012a: 18).

The adjudicator will take notes but only for his/her own purposes.[16] To standardise decisions there will be a template, requiring a reasoned explanation for the decision, and the Minister is setting an ambitious target for the communication of decisions to the parties: 90 per cent within 28 days from the date of the hearing. Decisions will then be published on the publicly accessible WRC website, but with some names and any identifying features redacted (currently the convention for decisions by the Equality Tribunal, although the EAT normally does not redact). Decisions will be appealable in the Labour Court (see below).

The WRC will also be an inspection and enforcement body. To this end its so-called Compliance Officers will incorporate the functions currently carried out by NERA, but there will be some modifications. Essentially, compliance with the Compliance Notices will be a matter for the Labour Court. In short, Compliance Officers, after having asked employers voluntarily to comply, will be empowered to issue a Compliance Notice setting out the steps that the employer must take to effect compliance within 21 days. An employer may appeal to the Labour Court within the 21-day period against all or part, of the Notice. If the employer fails to take the actions set out in the Compliance Notice, the Compliance Officer can go to the Labour Court, which can order the employer to carry out certain steps. Failure to implement an order will be enforceable in the District Court.

In addition fixed charge notices are to be introduced. If an employer fails to rectify certain matters within 14 days, such as failing or refusing to provide a payslip to an employee,[17] a Compliance Officer will be empowered to serve a fixed notice charge, currently planned to be in the region of €150 (Bruton, 2012a: 21). A Compliance Officer can refer failure to pay the fixed charge to the District Court.

The WRC will have other functions ancillary to its adjudication and compliance remit: it will provide advice and information, including being responsible for drafting codes of practice; it will operate an online and telephone advice service; conduct research; and conciliate collective disputes.

The WRC already has a Director Designate, Kieran Mulvey, currently the chief executive of the Labour Relations Commission. The WRC will be organised in four divisions: corporate, adjudication, compliance and collective mediation. According to the Director Designate, there will be a 'Chinese wall' between adjudication and compliance, assisted by the fact that the Compliance Division will have its headquarters outside Dublin, in Carlow – the current location of NERA – whereas the other three divisions will have their headquarters in Dublin. For adjudication and collective mediation the WRC will travel outside Dublin and preferably use hotels or occasionally court rooms, although according to the Director Designate of the WRC: 'we've got a little bit of feedback from our people... they don't want to be going into courts of law'. Compliance Officers will inspect premises throughout Ireland.

The Director of the WRC, who will be appointed for not more than ten years, will have executive and statutory responsibility for the WRC, but there will also be a statutory tripartite advisory board, comprising four representatives of employers, four representatives of trade unions and ministerial nominees, including a chairperson. The latter will be appointed for a non-renewable term of five years and the eight members will be appointed for a fixed term of two years, renewable. The board will be required to prepare an annual work programme in consultation with the Director for submission to the Minister and to present an annual report to the Minister who will lay a copy before each house of the *Oireachtas* (Bruton, 2012b).

The Labour Court

The Labour Court will be the appellate body in respect of all decisions of WRC adjudicators except in regard to discrimination over goods and services. Accordingly the EAT will be abolished; its appellate functions will transfer to the Labour Court, except that the EAT's redundancy appeals will transfer to the Social Welfare Appeals Officers, and the EAT's first-instance functions will transfer to the WRC. In addition, the Labour Court will obtain a new role in respect of Compliance Notices (see above) and retain its existing role of providing statutory mediation and conciliation under the Industrial Relations Acts. Some interviewees for this study said that the Labour Court, rather than the EAT, was chosen as the appellate body under the proposed system, because it has proved more time efficient than the EAT (see above) and less legalistic.

Appeals to the Labour Court from WRC decisions will be de novo with a 42-day time limit from notification of the WRC decision to the submission of an appeal (replacing a range of time limits). Appeals will remain free of charge, albeit an appellant who failed to attend a WRC hearing personally or through a representative will have to pay a €300 fee.

There will be a pre-hearing review carried out by a chair or deputy on paper for case management purposes, such as identifying the issues and estimating the hearing time. Occasionally the chair or deputy chair sitting alone may convene a case management conference with the parties, or the parties' representatives, or consider an adjournment application. All hearings will be tripartite as at present (chair or deputy plus one trade union side member and one employer side member). Furthermore, all employment rights hearings will normally be held in public;[18] evidence can, but not must, be taken on oath and decisions will be published, normally with the parties' names, but not the names of any witnesses.

There will be a chair and four deputy chairs (not two as at present), plus four members representing employers and four members representing employees and all will be full-time. It will sit in four divisions, not three as at present to cope with the expansion of employment rights appeals. In 2011 the Labour Court received 449 employment rights appeals and it will receive an estimated 500–540 appeals a year under the new appellate provisions according to an interviewee, with appeals at the upper end of the range initially as the new system beds down. The Minister, however, has estimated 'a possible 56 per cent increase' (Bruton, 2012a: 27).

Appointments of the chair and the deputy chairs will be carried out transparently through the Public Appointments Service and the present thinking, according to an interviewee for this study, is that they will not be required to be legally qualified. Ordinary members (lay judges) will be appointed after a selection process based on merit from a panel of candidates put forward by employer representative groups and a panel of candidates put forward by the trade unions, so ending the social partners' one-for-one nomination without any further selection (Bruton, 2012b).

Like the WRC, the Labour Court will be an Office of the DJEI and be required to produce an annual report. The two bodies will share administrative facilities and corporate services, for instance financial, training and human resources services and a common internet/computer system, but unlike the WRC the Labour Court will not have an advisory board.

If an award by a WRC adjudicator or the Labour Court is not implemented the complainant will be able to apply to the relevant body for a Determination Order. If this Order is still not implemented, it may be enforced by civil proceedings or criminal proceedings (or both) in the District Court by either an employee or a trade union. In addition, the Director of the WRC will have discretion to launch civil or criminal proceedings in the District Court in respect of Labour Court Determination Orders.

Appeals from the Labour Court will go to the High Court on a point of law only and then, with leave to appeal, to the Supreme Court. At the time of writing there is a proposal to insert a Court of Appeal between the High Court and the Supreme Court, but this constitutional change will require a referendum (Mac Cormaic, 2013).

Common law employment claims, for instance breach of contract, restraint of trade, personal injury, will still go to the 'ordinary' courts. As noted above, unlike New Zealand, Ireland's new workplace resolution adjudication bodies will not have exclusive jurisdiction over all employment matters.

Criticisms and counter-criticisms

On the whole stakeholders are generally supportive of the changes, welcoming the much needed simplification. Nevertheless, criticisms have been made particularly in response to the consultation (DJEI, 2011). Many of these criticisms have since been answered or have evaporated, so here we concentrate on the more important criticisms that are outstanding.

A key criticism from IBEC centres on the compliance division. First, an IBEC interviewee was critical of the plan to house the labour inspectorate in the same body as the adjudication service. She said: 'it would be a bit like having the *Garda*, our police service, firmly embedded in the court service... It's a perception thing'. Secondly, she was concerned about labour inspectors being given the power to issue fixed charge notices. The model is the fixed charge notices that can be issued for parking infringements; however she maintained that compliance with employment rights is more complex and open to interpretation than parking violations and thus not suitable for fixed charge penalties.

In addition, the IBEC interviewee was of the view that an opportunity had been missed to charge a fee for adjudication and appeal. IBEC had wanted 'a modest fee', in line with the fee charged at the Small Claims Court. In contrast, ICTU was wary of the fact that the Minister had not altogether ruled out the imposition of fees for complaints to the WRC or appeals to the Labour Court in the future (Bruton, 2012a).

The Irish Employment Bar Association (EBA) has made several trenchant criticisms. It considers that the proposed system has serious flaws and that it will not be the 'World-Class Workplace Relations Service' that the Minister has dubbed it. The main flaw, according to both the past and current chairs of EBA, is 'the failure to recognise that the mass of employment law requires fair adjudication by people who know the law'.

First they argued[19] that there should be separate bodies, one dealing with industrial relations disputes and the other hearing appeals on individual employment rights which often raise complex issues of law. This was because the approach required in acting as a third party seeking to resolve a collective dispute and the approach required in adjudicating a legal dispute were very different. The current workload of the Labour Court was primarily in respect of industrial relations matters (see above), unlike the EAT which only deals with individual legal rights (Mallon, 2012).

Against that the current Labour Court chair has contended that the Labour Court currently deals with both industrial relations and employment rights issues. It 'is demonstrably capable of differentiating between the approach that must be adopted in exercising these different roles' and has done so for many decades. Moreover, an understanding of the workplace context is important both for industrial relations disputes and employment rights disputes (Duffy, 2012: 82).

EBA interviewees admitted that the EAT was 'badly managed, badly run and does a disservice by creating appalling delays', unlike the Labour Court, but that this could be remedied given more resources.

Furthermore, EBA interviewees said, whereas the EAT has a legally qualified chair and two wing members, there is no provision for the chairs and deputy chairs of the Labour Court now or in the future to be legally qualified and currently the Labour Court is populated by people nominated from 'the industrial relations industry'.

Under the proposed system, however, chairs and deputy chairs will be appointed through the Public Appointments Service and, as an interviewee pointed out, Labour Court members are not alone in not being required to be legally qualified; appeals commissioners who hear appeals on tax matters are not required to be legally qualified. Moreover, the employment rights adjudication system was 'never intended to replicate the procedural formalities of the ordinary courts' and any requirement to have a legally qualified chair and deputies of the Labour Court would 'undermine the very reason for their existence' (Duffy, 2012: 81).

The EBA interviewees agreed with the IBEC interviewee that the standard of EAT decisions varied and admitted that at present the Minister appoints legally qualified chairs to the EAT 'who have no [employment law] practice as solicitors or barristers but they're politically well connected... That can be resolved'.

The EBA interviewees also criticised the fact that WRC adjudicators will hold their hearings in private. Only at the second stage, the Labour Court, will the parties obtain their rights under the European Convention on Human Rights (ECHR) and their constitutional rights. Against this, it has been pointed out that at present hearings of the Rights Commissioners and the Equality Tribunal are in private and there has not been a challenge under the ECHR so far. Furthermore, it is unlikely that there will be one, given the provision for a rehearing in public by the Labour Court.[20] Moreover, the Attorney General is of the view that the proposal to hold hearings in private is not contrary to Article 34.1 of the Constitution (DJEI, 2013).

The EBA interviewees also criticised the fact that WRC adjudicators will not be required to be legally qualified, although perhaps dealing with a complex issue of unfair dismissal, for instance unfair dismissal when there is sub-contracting and a transfer of an undertaking. As the former chair of EBA said:

> Not only will individuals have their disputes determined by persons who are not trained or qualified in law, they will also, in truth, be denied, in the vast majority of cases, the opportunity to have their issues determined by a judge even on appeal.
>
> (Mallon, 2012: 79)

Timetable

Despite these criticisms the proposed new system is being brought into being, with some steps already having been taken. These include a new online contact portal, The Workplace Relations Customer Services, replacing five separate entry points; a single complaint form in place of 30 forms previously in use; and a pilot Early Resolution Service (Bruton, 2012b).The exact shape and format of the Early Resolution Service will be influenced by an independent evaluation being carried out at the time of writing. Legislation, however, will be necessary including amendments to existing legislation and the government's aim is to have the proposed new structures in place from 2014 (DJEI, 2013).

Conclusions

There is no doubt that the current Irish employment adjudicatory system is forbiddingly complex and in need of a radical overhaul. Radical overhaul is rare however. More often countries introduce incremental and ad hoc changes. Nevertheless, this book contains two other examples of radical overhaul: South Africa, Chapter 10, after apartheid ended in 1994 and in New Zealand, Chapter 9, after a change of government in 2000. Both conciliation in South Africa and mediation in New Zealand are conducted mainly face-to-face and high levels of settlement are reported. It remains to be seen whether Ireland's Early Resolution Service, which will normally operate by telephone and email, will be equally effective. Furthermore, in the Employment Courts both of South Africa and New Zealand, a hearing is before a professional judge sitting alone. In contrast, in Ireland's Labour Court the chair and deputies will not be required to be legally qualified. It will be interesting to examine Labour Court judgments in future, especially when the current chair of the Labour Court, who commands much respect personally, retires.

These questions apart, the proposed Irish system is to be welcomed. It will enable the state to achieve economies of scale and users will no longer be confronted with a confusing array of institutions, making the adjudication of employment rights simpler and easier.

7
Italy

Daniela Comandè

Introduction

Unlike many other countries in this study, Italy does not have labour courts. There are, however, specialist chambers within the civil court system. Moreover, the process of adjudicating substantive employment rights is supported not only by such specialist chambers but also by special procedural rules that are intended to provide workers with speedy and effective protection where employment law has been breached. Although the roots of this go back many years (Taruffo, 1980), the most important reforms date from the 1970s (in particular to law 533/1973 for individual hearings and to art. 28 of law 300/1970 for cases involving trade unions). Since then the system for individual employment rights claims has been amended, but not radically altered, several times.

In Italy, as in other countries, there are a number of reasons why special provisions exist for the adjudication of workers' individual legal rights: to redress the balance between often powerful employers and individually vulnerable workers, but also because collective rights are often intertwined with individual rights. In Italy, however, perhaps the most important reason is the need to have special procedures for employment rights disputes that take less time than is required to pursue 'ordinary' civil cases (Ministero della Giustizia, Direzione Generale di Statistica, 2011: 1–2). As will be shown, however, despite special procedures and recent measures to relieve the courts by providing extra-judicial dispute resolution mechanisms, employment litigation in Italy cannot be described as speedy.

The plan of this chapter is as follows: first the industrial relations background is examined followed by an overview of the development of the court system from its beginnings to the present day. We divide this into three periods: up to 1945, 1945–2000, and the current position. Then we look at extra-judicial provisions: conciliation, arbitration and labour inspection, before concluding.

Industrial relations background

Industrial relations in Italy have been characterised in recent history by close interconnections between trade unions and political parties (see Treu, 2007 for a full discussion). This resulted in a monolithic structure for trade union/employer contracts and collective bargaining during the fascist regime[1] and a plurality of actors and outcomes in the post-Second World War period.

Today, Italian industrial relations are characterised by a high level of voluntarism and a minimal degree of legal intervention. Freedom of association, provided for under Article 39 of the Italian Constitution, is implemented through law 300/1970, which was inspired by U.S. labour legislation adopted during the New Deal (Kahn-Freund, 1977). It includes a number of union rights relating both to the individual worker and to trade unions. Surrounding this core of legal rights, regulation is effected through collective agreements, bipartite and tripartite accords, joint opinions, and specific items of employment legislation. As we note below, over the course of the evolution of the Italian industrial relations model there have been repeated initiatives to redraw the boundaries between different levels of bargaining as well as efforts to achieve a degree of consensus between the main actors over the structure and rhythm of bargaining and employee representation.

During the period 1968–73, a 'bi-polar' model of bargaining emerged that was almost unique in Europe, characterised by a high level of autonomy between different levels of bargaining. Beginning in 1975, this was succeeded by a trend towards the centralisation of bargaining, culminating in the first tripartite agreement concluded in 1983 (*Protocollo Scotti*), which aimed at setting up a 'neo-corporatist' industrial relations system. During this period, and following the 'Hot Autumn' of the late-1960s, the 1970s and 1980s saw a relatively stable phase in terms of the constitution of the principal actors, as the major union confederations were affiliated with corresponding political parties: the CGIL with the Italian Communist Party, the CSIL with the Christian Democrats and UIL with the Social Democrats. Despite political differences, there was a fairly high level of practical cooperation both at workplace level in terms of employee representation and in concluding sectoral collective agreements. These political alignments came under strain in the immediate wake of the end of the Cold War, and the subsequent implosion of the political landscape in Italy – fuelled, in addition, by the exposure of political corruption. Since then, the union confederations have been nominally politically independent, although with continuing alignments to political groupings sympathetic to their aims and policies.

The most significant framework agreement on collective bargaining was agreed in 1993 between government, the main trade union confederations, and the employers. This abolished the system of wage indexation and created a new structure and rhythm for collective bargaining that led to a fairly high level of bargaining centralisation, in which sectoral bargaining was to be guided by official inflation predictions with scope for workplace bargaining on issues such as productivity or performance. In addition the agreement provided for a reform intended to add more coherence to unions' workplace organisational structures with the aim of promoting internal democracy and grass-roots participation.

Cracks in this system of moderate concertation began to appear in the early-2000s, when an agreement ('Pact for Italy') was struck between the Berlusconi government and two of the large union confederations (CISL and UIL), but which CGIL, the largest federation, refused to sign. While the previous model of tripartite concertation had involved some reciprocity between all the actors, including the government and its budgetary policy, this latter period of social dialogue was aimed at obtaining social partners' prior consent to legislative proposals, but without entailing any financial commitment on the part of the state. However, this method of social dialogue was seen as unsuccessful and was followed by numerous calls for a return to the concertation route by both the trade unions and Confindustria (Giugni, 2007). Even if there was a perception of a general need to reform the structure of collective bargaining, no important outcomes had been achieved, in particular because of disagreements amongst trade unions.

Despite agreement on a common platform for revising the structure of collective bargaining in 2008, the period 2009–11 was a time of intense inter-union conflict. The main cause was a 2009 agreement between the main employer organisation, Confindustria, and CISL and UIL to reform collective bargaining and revise the 1993 arrangements. CGIL refused to sign, in particular due to the scope for local 'opening clauses' that would allow for derogation from sectoral agreements (EIRO, 2009b). However, the growing intensity of the economic crisis led to improved relations among the main trade union confederations during mid-2011, when a joint agreement on bargaining and representativeness was signed between all three main unions and Confindustria. This provided for a new negotiating structure and regulated the issue of opening clauses, allowing for 'temporary and experimental' derogation from sectoral provisions. This agreement, and some of its consequences, together with Fiat's decision to leave Confindustria have generated a new model of bargaining, the so-called Fiat Model (according to which company-level agreements are considered as being at the same level as national ones). It has also led to a high level of litigation, the main litigant being Fiom-Cgil, the metalworking section of CGIL, which has found itself excluded from representation at FIAT due to its refusal to sign a company-level agreement.

Despite the ongoing evolution in the structure of Italian collective bargaining, it continues to take place at three levels. Firstly, there are inter-sectoral agreements, which may take the form of a tripartite policy accord or a bipartite agreement between the social partners, depending on whether or not the outcome is also signed by the government. Secondly, there is sectoral-level collective bargaining. This was the keystone of the industrial relations system until June 2011; it aimed to safeguard a minimum income and a range of matters regarding working conditions, such as hours, information rights and work organisation. Finally, there are decentralised agreements, which may be signed on a company, district or regional basis and which enable the parties to agree detailed arrangements for such matters as productivity, innovation and work organisation that reflect the immediate context.

Furthermore, in recent years, a good deal of conflict between government and trade unions, and in particular the CGIL, has turned on proposals to relax the law on dismissals and allow scope for local workplace agreements. In 2011, a new set of provisions were introduced permitting further negotiated derogation (known as 'proximity bargaining', Art. 8, Decree Law 138/2011) both from the provisions of sectoral agreements and from certain aspects of statute law, provided the changes accord with the Italian constitution, EU-level requirements, and international obligations (EIRO, 2012).

As a result of collective provisions in the most recent inter-sectoral agreements and the new legal provision allowing company and district collective agreements to have an *erga omnes* effect ('proximity bargaining'), decentralised collective bargaining has become increasingly important.[2]

Nevertheless, national agreements have also recently been given a boost. On 31 May 2013 all three main trade union confederations and Confindustria signed a cross-industry agreement. This aimed to identify the bodies that can legitimately negotiate national collective agreements and to define the parameters of national agreements, thereby setting out what appears to be the first step towards making national agreements apply *erga omnes* as originally envisaged in the Italian Constitution, but never formally implemented.

Although in Italy there are no official data, a (perhaps optimistic) EIRO report in (EIRO, 2009a; Visser, 2008) estimated that collective bargaining coverage at industry level was around 80 per cent, while decentralised collective bargaining coverage was much lower at around 30–40 per cent (Cella and Treu, 2009: 139). OECD data (2013), updated to the third quarter of 2012, showed that the employment rate in Italy was 44.1 per cent seasonally adjusted, with almost 23 million employed workers and almost 26 million economically active in the population, including unemployed workers. As to trade union density (Pedersini, 2010), this stood at 49.7 per cent 20 years ago in the trade unions' golden age. Since then the OECD (OECD and Visser, 2011)[3] indicates that it was 35.4 per cent in 1999, fell to 33.2 per cent in 2006 and rose to 35.1 per cent in 2010.[4] This slight increase in trade union density in recent years is perhaps a response by workers to the economic crisis (Treu, 2011).

The courts: 1893–1945

The first step towards a labour judicial system was taken in 1893. Inspired by the *conseil des prud'hommes* in France (see Chapter 3), the so-called *Collegi dei probiviri* were established by law 295/1893 (Chiovenda, 1923; Napoletano, 1960).

These courts were tripartite: for each case there were two lay judges, one representing employers and the other employees. The court was chaired by an experienced lawyer appointed by the President by means of a royal decree following nominations from the Ministries of Justice and Industry. The establishment of these *Collegi* was not mandatory for the whole country or for all industries and, as a consequence, their coverage was patchy (Calamandrei, 1968; Romagnoli, 1973; Segni, 1927). Although collective issues remained beyond the *probiviri's* jurisdiction, they had jurisdiction in respect of individual employment contracts (Redenti, 1905) and thus were able to fill in gaps in the civil code and provide equity. Moreover, certain features of the old *Collegi* are still to be found today in law 533/1973: these include the investigative powers of the judge to collect evidence before the hearing, the provision of oral evidence, and the issuing of a judgment where the facts of a dispute are evaluated and the reasoning shown.

From 1926 Italy had a totalitarian fascist regime that eradicated workers' rights through legislation introduced in 1926 (law 563/1926); for instance, strikes attracted criminal sanctions and only fascist trade unions were recognised. At the same time a special labour court for adjudicating collective rights and for appealing *probiviri* decisions was established. This was a special branch of the Appeal Court and at each hearing it was composed of three judges and two citizens with expertise in employment problems appointed by the President from 'untarnished' people listed in a special register.

In 1928 a Royal Decree (no. 471), replaced in 1934 by a further Royal Decree (no. 1,037), formally abolished the tripartite *Collegi dei probiviri* and jurisdiction passed to the ordinary civil courts presided over by a single judge, but with employer and employee representatives as advisers. This also introduced a special fast-track procedure (Mortara, 1934; Proto Pisani, 1987) and gave a major role to the fascist trade unions (Preti, 1977). This was because before workers could bring a case they were required to notify their trade union and request conciliation (Grassetti, 1950; Jäeger, 1935). This so-called trade union gangway enabled unions to exert control and monitor litigation (Nascosi, 2007; Trisorio Liuzzi, 2001). As noted above, however, these Decrees also provided for conciliation to resolve employment disputes. If a matter was not settled and litigation ensued, there were special procedures within the civil courts. Further reform in 1942 again restructured employment disputes, removing employer/employee advisers and treating both individual and collective labour disputes as 'ordinary' civil disputes.

The courts: 1945 to the end of the century

The system of worker protection after the Second World War was based first on the Constitution, promulgated in 1948, which contains fundamental principles relating to workers, such as freedom of association, the right to work and equality before the law irrespective of distinctions such as gender, race and language; and secondly on three statutes:

- law 604/1966 on individual dismissals;
- law 300/1970, the so-called Workers' Statute;
- and law 533/1973 on individual employment rights disputes, the most important law procedurally.

This latter law extended the principle of the single judge to all individual employment rights disputes, as with Italy's civil court system, but established special procedures to make the adjudicatory process speedier, aiming to remedy the 'scandalous duration of the proceedings' (Ciocchetti, 1999: 113).

To that end the district (first-instance) judge was given wide powers of investigation, the so-called *principio inquisitorio* (Tarzia, 2008), and could gather evidence independently of the parties. For instance, he/she could 'call additional witnesses, order "free interrogation" of the parties, order inspection of the workplace and ask for written or oral evidence from union representatives' (Hepple, 1987: 61).

Other measures aimed at speeding up proceedings included oral evidence during the hearing, the reading out of the decision at the close of the judicial hearing, and enforcement of the first-level decision if it provided for pecuniary compensation in favour of the worker (Art. 420 ff. Code of Civil Procedure). The major limitation of the 1973 reform was that these new-style hearings only had the power to award monetary compensation to workers, and could not issue injunctions for specific performance (for instance, if they had found discrimination against trade union activists).

At this time there was a new generation of judges, the so-called *pretori d'assalto* (literally 'storming magistrates'), chosen from among the judges who worked as *pretori,* who were district judges with jurisdiction over small claims and petty offences. According to Hepple (1988: 173), 'the national average of decisions *in favour* of the worker by the *pretori* was three to one, compared to about four to one *against* the worker in British employment tribunals' (our emphasis). In short, the *pretori* applied the legislation in a manner sympathetic to workers (De Luca Tamajo, 2008).

The changes outlined above, however, were not totally effective (Picardi, 1979; Proto Pisani, 1983), given the socio-economic differences between regions in Italy. While in some courts, usually medium-sized ones and those in the industrialised centre-north of Italy, court hearings were speeded up, in others, especially the larger ones and in the centre-south of Italy, with the exception of Naples, hearings were often delayed because employers procrastinated (Sgroi, 1989: 74).

Furthermore, the trade unions criticised these judicial proceedings, essentially because of their lack of involvement in them (Ghera, 1973; Romagnoli, 1974; Treu, 1975). Indeed, one reason for this was because the *pretori* rarely used their powers to order union access to the workplace or requested information from trade unions.

In the 1990s, far from any speeding up of court proceedings in respect of individual employment rights disputes, such proceedings became more protracted with delay becoming common almost everywhere in the country, possibly partly as a result of a new round of legislation, in particular law 51/1998 which introduced a number of reforms to civil procedures. Meanwhile, a judge replaced the *pretore* and the Tribunal (the first-instance court in the civil court system) replaced the *Pretura,* with a special labour branch constituted within the civil court. The same framework was also applied to the upper level, with a labour branch established within the Court of Appeal.

During that period, as a result of laws 80/1998 and 387/1998, proceedings became even lengthier when the same courts that had adjudicated private sector workers' individual employment rights disputes were given the additional responsibility of adjudicating civil servants' individual employment rights disputes, replacing the administrative courts which had until then had jurisdiction over those matters (Garofalo, 1993). This brought an influx of new cases, which inevitably increased the already heavy case-load in the courts (AA. VV., 2004; Ciocchetti, 1999).

The judges and the courts today

The judges

Judges in Italy are career judges, as in Sweden (Chapter 11) and Germany (Chapter 4). This contrasts with the position in common law countries, such as Great Britain and South Africa, where judges are only first appointed in mid-career after previously serving as lawyers (or a legally related job such as in academia) and acquiring significant legal experience (see Chapters 5 and 10).

All Italian judges are assigned and appointed for life by the Ministry of Justice according to their rankings in competitive examinations which are open to all who have a law degree (European Commission for the Efficiency of Justice, 2012).[5] After success in these competitive examinations and a brief period of training, the President of the Tribunal decides on the posting, which could be labour, bankruptcy or another civil branch if the successful candidate has opted for the civil area. Subsequently judges may be moved from one branch to another, or if they have some years of service, they may be promoted from a first-instance court to a higher court.

The courts

There are three levels in the court system: the Tribunal, the Court of Appeal and the Supreme Court, each of which has a special chamber exclusively for employment jurisdiction, although, as noted above, these employment chambers do not have specialised judges. Usually, individual employment law cases, after having been heard at first instance, are then appealed because an appeal can be lodged both on fact and law. In 2012, the number of employment law appeals to the Court of Appeal increased by 1.1 per cent compared to the previous year, but distinguishing between private sector and public sector cases, the latter increased by 20.7 per cent (Relazione sull'amministrazione della Giustizia, 2012: 74). The Court of Appeal has almost the same powers as the first-instance court, but the provision of new evidence is limited by the principle of necessity. In theory one can only appeal to the Supreme Court on a point of law, but in practice the number of disputes at this level shows that most judgments are appealed (Rapporto Statistico del settore civile, 2012).

The size of the panel of judges increases according to the level of the hearing: from a single judge at first instance, to five judges in the Court of Appeal, and to five or nine judges at the Supreme Court.[6] Where several judges sit together (Court of Appeal and the Supreme Court) there is just one judgment and dissent is not announced, so the parties never know whether there is unanimity or not. Interestingly, unlike German judges, Italian judges do not usually wear robes, apart from at the highest level in the Supreme Court.

As noted above, although one long-standing concern has been to speed up the Italian adjudication process, data concerning the length of proceedings make gloomy reading. According to the European Commission for the Efficiency of Justice (2012), the average length of proceedings for employment dismissal cases at first instance was 619 days in Italy in 2006 compared to 80 days in the Netherlands and 369 days in France. The Ministry of Justice, with data updated to 2011,[7] distinguishes between the public and private sectors and provides data for all employment law cases. It gives a slightly lower figure: the average length of time an employment law case took was 536 days for private sector disputes and 604 days for public sector ones. This increased to 971 days (private sector) and 944 days (public sector) from filing a claim at first instance to the Court of Appeal judgment, and 1,105.8 days for the Supreme Court's judgment including both the public and private sectors. Only with regard to the highest level of hearing (Supreme Court) has this decreased, falling to 1,004.4 days in 2012.[8]

In theory, no more than 60 days should elapse between the date of initially lodging a claim and the first hearing, and after that there should be a very limited number of hearings, all of them strictly regulated by the need to gather evidence that the judge considers important. However, in practice this does not happen and, although the special employment rights procedure takes about half the time of ordinary civil proceedings (1,602 days in the Court of Appeal and 1,127 days in the Tribunal), the aspiration to speed up proceedings that was part of the 1973 reforms has never been realised.

Until recently there was no fee for lodging or hearing employment rights disputes, but this free-of-charge principle was abrogated in 2011 and now a fee has to be paid to lodge a claim, except where a claimant has a gross income of less than €21,256.32. Where a claimant has a gross income of less than €32,298.99 the fees to file an employment claim before Tribunals and the Court of Appeal are reduced by half in comparison to the other civil cases and are related to the value of the claim: for example, this stands at €225 (£192; $291) to file a claim in a case of individual dismissal. This does not apply in the Supreme Court, where there is no distinction between employment cases and other civil cases.

It is mandatory for employers and also for workers to have legal representation and each side bears its own costs. Even if a worker is eligible for legal aid because of his/her income level, she/he generally has to cover the costs related to the lawyer (except below a very low threshold of income), and eventually, if the case is lost, is required to pay the winner's costs according to an amount decided by the court: this applies at all three court levels. Despite this, the unions do not provide their members with a lawyer, although they sometimes provide pre-judicial legal advice in order to evaluate the prospects for success.

In spite of the fact that fees were imposed in 2011, in 2012 there was an increase in the number of claims, both in absolute terms in comparison with employment rights hearings in 2011, and in relative terms when compared to civil claims generally, which decreased by 6.1 per cent. Considering first-instance proceedings, public sector employment cases increased significantly: in 2011 they rose by 21.5 per cent compared to 2010, with a further increase in 2012 of 8.7 per cent compared to 2011. Private employment sector employment cases also increased although to a lesser extent than public sector employment cases: in 2011 there was an increase of 8.7 per cent compared to 2010, and in 2012 there was a rise of 2.8 per cent compared to 2011.

Looking solely at new employment claims (that is, not all employment claims currently before the courts) the increasing number of employment rights disputes is a cause for concern: these were up 34.9 per cent for the public sector and 15.7 per cent for the private sector, compared with a fall for other new civil hearings (in 2011 a fall of 8.3 per cent; and in 2012 a fall of 6.1 per cent). Indeed, in the light of these developments, the Supreme Court has interpreted the increase as a symptom of Italy's economic crisis (Relazione sull'amministrazione della Giustizia, 2012: 77, *passim*).

Unfortunately in Italy there are no available statistics on the success rate of employment dispute hearings in the courts. Ichino and Pinotti (2012), looking at economic dismissal cases heard in some specific courts, have suggested that the results suggest a form of 'Russian roulette'. Judges are often influenced by local labour market conditions, which are very different across Italy, and will often decide in favour of workers where there is a high level of unemployment (Ichino et al., 2003).

Extra-judicial dispute resolution

So far, this chapter has focussed on the court system and adjudication by judges, but extra-judicial dispute resolution mechanisms are becoming increasingly important in Italy, both in the form of conciliation and arbitration.

Conciliation

There are two types of conciliation: first, so-called administrative conciliation, where conciliation is carried out by a special board at the Area Labour Directorates, which are sub-regional units of the Labour Inspectorate; and second, conciliation carried out according to the provisions of a collective agreement. There can also be *ad hoc* conciliation, provided by the *Collegio di Conciliazione e Arbitrato.*

Administrative conciliation occurs when a labour inspector has detected an infringement of a worker's rights or where an alleged infringement has been reported by an employee or a trade union. Such conciliation is carried out by a tripartite panel established at each Area Labour Directorate. Typically the panel is composed of the local labour inspector (or his/her substitute) in the chair and four representatives (or their substitutes), consisting of two representatives of employers and two representatives of employees, nominated by the most representative organisations at national level. The attempt at conciliation can lead to a settlement in the form of a legally enforceable agreement signed by a labour inspector or the settlement can be enforced by a court order at the request of a single party. In 2012 (law 92/2012), mandatory administrative conciliation, as a precondition for initiating court procedures, was only required for cases of individual dismissal for economic reasons (*giustificato motivo oggettivo*).

Alternatively, conciliation can be carried out according to the provisions of a collective agreement. (For an example regarding the commerce sector, see Lucchetti, 2011.) A report must be filed with the Area Labour Directorate if conciliation is successful. If it is not, extra-judicial administrative conciliation can, and usually is attempted.

Between 1998 and 2010, the judge was required to ascertain at the beginning of the hearing that an attempt at conciliation between employer and employee had been made; otherwise the case could not be heard. In 2010 (law 183/2010, so-called *Collegato Lavoro*), such conciliation became discretionary and as a result failing to engage in conciliation no longer precluded the filing of an employment claim. This change was made possibly because few settlements were reached through conciliation (De Cristofaro, 2011; Vallebona, 2011).

There is, however, an exception. The judge is still required to ascertain at the beginning of the hearing whether conciliation has been attempted where an employment contract has been 'certified'. This certification procedure was introduced in 2003 to prevent future disputes about the type of employment contract (such as whether the worker was a temporary worker or an employee) and such certification is carried out by a Commission.[9] Commissions can be found in a variety of places: at the Area Labour Directorates, the provinces, the bilateral bodies established by national collective agreements, or universities. Furthermore the composition of the Commission varies: for example Commissions at the Area Labour Directorates include a labour inspector (or substitute), together with officials from INAIL (Istituto Nazionale Infortuni sul Lavoro), which deals with occupational illness and accidents, and INPS (Istituto Nazionale di Previdenza Sociale), which manages the social security system; at universities the Commission is composed of labour law professors, researchers and lawyers who specialise in labour law.

Data on conciliation is collected by the Ministry of Labour only in respect of administrative conciliation and indicates that the conciliation process usually ends without a settlement, particularly in the public sector. For example, in 2012, out of 1,758 public sector disputes, including new and pending claims, only 58 were settled through administrative conciliation, while in the private sector, out of 69,647 disputes 32,423 were settled through administrative conciliation. Conciliation in both sectors was not even started in many cases, for instance because of the absence of a party (Ministero del Lavoro e delle Politiche Sociali, 2013). Looking specifically at individual dismissals for economic reasons (*giustificato motivo oggettivo*) in the private sector, out of 10,675 attempts at conciliation 4,023 were settled; 3,667 failed; 1,848 were abandoned; and 1,137 were still in progress.

Arbitration

Individual employment rights disputes in Italy can also be resolved through arbitration, with a third party who is not a judge, making the decision. There are two kinds of arbitration, both regulated by law, but the main difference is the effect of the award because only one kind is legally enforceable. This latter kind is called *arbitrato rituale* (or arbitration by law, otherwise known as *arbitrato di diritto*) and the decision of the arbitrator can, if necessary, be enforced by a judicial order (*exequatur*). This kind of arbitration, however, applies only if certain conditions are met: first it has to be provided for by law or by a collective agreement (Art. 806 ff. Code of Civil Procedure); second, both parties have to agree to go to arbitration; third, it does not cover all statutory rights (for instance some constitutional rights cannot be adjudicated by arbitration). It does, however, cover not only employees, but also workers who are neither employees nor genuinely self-employed.

Whereas the award emanating from *arbitrato rituale* can be judicially enforced, this does not apply to the other kind of arbitration known as *arbitrato irrituale* (literally 'non-ritual arbitration'), where any award is akin to a gentleman's agreement. Otherwise both kinds of arbitration are virtually indistinguishable: in respect of the type of dispute that can be arbitrated, the fact that arbitration is only available if it conforms to a specific law or to a collective agreement, and the parties to the dispute have to agree to go to arbitration.

Non-legally enforceable arbitration (*arbitrato irrituale*) has been enhanced by recent legislation, the *Collegato lavoro* law 183/2010. As a result there are now four ways that non-legally enforceable arbitration can be conducted:

1. Arbitration can be conducted by a panel composed on a tripartite basis during, or immediately following, administrative conciliation with the same panel (a district labour inspector plus two employee and two employer representatives), if the parties agree (essentially con/arb as in South Africa – see Chapter 10 below).

2. Arbitration can be carried out according to the provisions of a collective agreement (Art. 412 ter).

3. Arbitration can be carried out by the 'Certification Commission', as mentioned above (Zoppoli, 2010).

4. Arbitration can be carried out by a tripartite panel (*Collegio di Conciliazione e Arbitrato*) composed of a member for each side (employer and union) and an arbitrator jointly appointed by them from law professors at universities or lawyers able to plead at the Supreme Court (Art. 412 quarter). Usually both the employer and the employee are represented by a lawyer.

Only in this fourth type of *arbitrato irrituale* are the fees set out: these depend on the value of the claim and have to be paid in advance (five days before the arbitration hearing). They are calculated as 2 per cent of the value of the claim to be paid to the chairperson and 1 per cent to the other arbitrators. The parties share the cost of the fee for the chairperson, and each side reimburses the arbitrator who is on their 'side', although workers can sometimes be refunded by the union.

Non-legally enforceable arbitration (*arbitrato irrituale)* represents a missed opportunity because it is so limited. As noted above, it can only be conducted when it is specifically provided for by law or by a collective agreement; the parties' own wishes are not a sufficient trigger (Ichino 2010; Treu, 2010).

There is, however, an important exception. Under law 183/2010 the parties can agree in advance to go to arbitration rather than the courts, signing a clause to that effect in the individual employee's contract of employment (*clausola compromissoria*). There are, however, a few safeguards (unlike pre-mandatory employment arbitration agreements in the United States; see Chapter 12). This is because the clause cannot be signed before 30 days' employment; it has to be approved by a certifying Commission; and it has to be provided for by a collective agreement. Nevertheless, this takes little or no account of the fact that normally the employee is in a much weaker position than the employer, especially at the beginning of the employment relationship (Licci, 2011).[10]

Finally, mediation has never been used in civil cases according to the latest data from the Ministry of Justice from June 2012.[11] This is perhaps because there is uncertainty over its legitimacy, given art. 2113 Civil Code (Stipo, 2012), and the most recent judgment of the Italian Constitutional Court (6 December 2012, no. 272) which rejected the mandatory nature of mediation.[12] Given that mediation is essentially indistinguishable from conciliation, however, as both leave the decision about whether or not to settle firmly in the hands of the disputing parties, unlike arbitration, and conciliation is already provided for in employment rights cases (see above), this is unlikely to have any practical import in the employment arena.

Labour inspection

Last but not least, this chapter deals briefly with labour inspectors, a separate arm of regulation and distinct from health and safety inspectors, who come under *Aziende Sanitarie Locali*.

Although labour inspection goes back over a century, it is currently based on law 124/2004 and law 183/2010 (*Collego Lavoro*).These statutes give labour inspectors both administrative and criminal powers to promote compliance with labour law, collective agreements and social security provisions and the right to visit a workplace at any time.

Among labour inspectors' powers is the power to issue warnings, make orders, and impose a range of sanctions. If, for instance, the labour inspector finds that the employer has contravened certain hiring rules, he/she can require the employer not only to remedy the situation, but also to pay a civil penalty; and if a labour inspector finds that a worker has been paid less than the amount specified in the collective agreement, he/she can order the employer to pay the amount due. If the employer chooses not to pay, he has 30 days to apply for conciliation held at the area office of the labour inspectorate. If conciliation has not been sought or is unsuccessful and the amount has still not been paid, the order becomes tantamount to a court order. Labour inspectors also have the power to close down a business temporarily where an employer has been employing workers covertly, for instance to avoid paying tax and social security.

If the labour inspector finds that there has been a major violation, such as the employment of child labour, the labour inspector is obliged to submit the case to the competent judicial authorities. In respect of a minor violation, the labour inspector can require the employer to carry out certain actions and to pay a fine within a time limit. If the employer does not comply, penal proceedings ensue.

There were 3,156 labour inspectors in 2012 (Ministero del Lavoro e delle Politiche Sociali, Divisione generale per l'attività ispettiva, 2012a: 6). These come under the aegis of the Ministry of Labour and Social Policy and are organised into regions, further sub-divided into areas. Although labour inspectors can inspect in the public and private sectors, in practice their focus is on the private sector and their activities have recently been made easier as there is now a single register of workplaces, replacing a variety of listings (see Rausei, 2012 for a full description).

Each year the Directorate General for the Co-ordination of the Inspection Activities (DGCIA), which is part of the Ministry of Labour, identifies specific sectors (for example the construction industry, agriculture, tourism) and specific types of potential violations (such as the use of undocumented workers) and decides where to focus labour inspectors' activities according to the particular circumstances of each region (Ministero del Lavoro e delle Politiche Sociali, Divisione generale per l'attività ispettiva, 2012b: 9–18). Irrespective of whether an industry is to be targeted for inspection, a labour inspector will respond to a worker's or a trade union's complaint.

In Italy, as in other countries in this book (see for instance Chapter 5), the number of labour inspectors has declined recently. For instance in 2012 there were 169 fewer labour inspectors than in 2011 and only a small proportion (15 per cent) of all enterprises were inspected (243,847 out of 1.6 million) according to INPS.

Conclusions

In Italy, there are special chambers in the civil courts for the adjudication of disputes concerning employment rights, but paradoxically the judges themselves do not specialise and may, or may not, remain in the employment chambers.

Outside the civil court system there are labyrinthine provisions, making it difficult for workers to know how to enforce their rights. For instance there are two types of conciliation (administrative conciliation and conciliation as a result of collective agreements), in addition to ad hoc commissions and a maze of certifying commissions; then two kinds of arbitration (legally enforceable arbitration and non-legally enforceable arbitration), the boundaries of which are not completely clear because of their similarities in function and structure (see Bove, 2010 for a full discussion). This complexity may be because the trade unions and government do not share a common approach; for example, they could, but do not, collaborate in order to create a cadre of labour disputes arbitrators (Borghesi, 2010). Importantly, trade unions are also wary of arbitration.

Another long-standing problem in Italian employment rights adjudication is the time taken for a case to go through the court system from filing the claim to the handing down of the judgment. Despite the reforms carried out in 1973 (Ianniruberto, 1999; Montesano and Mazziotti, 1974; Perone, 1975), the ever growing number of disputes and inadequate financial resources have led to delays in the system year after year. Yet despite this evidence of delay in the judicial system, there is still a strong cultural resistance to alternative dispute resolution (Ichino, 1996) and a preference by the parties for litigation, with trade unions being unwilling to take labour disputes away from judges as they seem to consider that only the courts can adequately protect workers' rights (Canale, 2011). There is an old English adage: justice delayed is justice denied and certainly in Italy's employment rights adjudication in the civil courts there is much delay.

8
The Netherlands

Introduction

The Netherlands does not have a separate system of labour courts, and individual employment disputes are heard by the civil courts. When terminating employment, employers have historically had a choice either to have the contract ended by official authorisation in a procedure that has some bipartite lay involvement or have the contract annulled by a civil court. In recent years, this has been added to by termination by mutual consent at the instigation of the employer. Under proposals outlined in spring 2013, employers will no longer be able to choose which dismissal track to take: all economic, technical and organisational dismissals, as well as those for long-term incapacity, will be routed down the administrative procedure and all other dismissals will go before the courts.

After outlining the context for the current system, we look at the procedures for employer termination. We then consider the process for resolving disputes arising out of alleged discrimination on one or more of the grounds specified in Dutch equal treatment legislation. Finally, we look at the changes intended to come into force from 2016 in the procedures for dealing with termination of contract.

Background and context

Industrial relations context

The Netherlands has a broadly dualist structure of industrial relations, in which collective bargaining is overwhelmingly conducted by trade unions and workplace information and consultation, with some scope for negotiation on a narrow range of issues, by elected works councils (*ondernemingsraad*). Employers must establish a works council in any establishment with 50 or more employees, with a compliance rate of some 70 per cent. These have rights to information, consultation on economic matters, and, on some social issues, their consent is required before employer decisions can be implemented. Subject to a requirement for mediation, an employer may resort to the courts to overrule a works council veto on workplace social issues and, for their part, the works council may apply to the courts to have an employer's economic decision set aside in some circumstances. There is no requirement to inform works councils about individual dismissals, although any change in policy on dismissal would require works council consent. Works councils act as an important filter for dealing with individual grievances and disputes, even on issues for which they might lack formal competence.

There are three main trade union confederations, the Federation of Dutch Trade Unions (FNV), the Christian Trade Union Federation (CNV), and a union for professional and managerial staffs (MHP). Each has sectoral affiliates, with the FNV, with 16 affiliates and 1.2 million members, being the largest with just under two-thirds of all union members.[1] Net union density is 19 per cent, with a gentle decline, interspersed with short periods of stability, over the past three decades (Visser, 2011).

Employers are well organised and centrally represented by the VNO-NCW, which embraces more than 60 per cent of medium-sized firms and almost all larger ones. The AWVN employer association, which is affiliated to the VNO-NCW, is a long-standing general employers' association that organises across the economy and coordinates collective bargaining together with company and sectoral-level policies on social matters.

There are two important national bipartite organisations. The Social and Economic Council (SER) has a consultative role on all major economic and social issues. It includes a number of Commodity and Industrial Boards that have an administrative role under public law, sometimes dubbed 'co-governance', in enforcing and implementing official regulations. The Labour Foundation (STAR) is a bipartite body constituted under private law comprising the three main union confederations and three main employer associations. It is a discussion forum for policy between the social partners and can also advise the government if requested.

Collective bargaining covers just over 80 per cent of the workforce (Visser, 2011). The dominant form is at industry level, with some company bargaining in large firms that straddle industry boundaries. Bargaining coverage is high, partly because employers must offer agreed terms to all employees, whether union members or not, and partly due to the formal extension of agreements to non-signatory employers. Collective agreements often contain procedures for resolving individual grievances.

There is a statutory minimum wage, subject to control by the Labour Inspectorate (see 'Public law' below). The rate is set by the Minister of Labour after consultation with the Social and Economic Council.

Legal context

The Dutch legal system was profoundly influenced by the Napoleonic Civil Code as a consequence of French occupation between 1794 and 1813. The

Dutch system was assigned to the 'Romanistic' legal family by Zweigert and Kötz (1977: 101–2), for example, although other commentators have noted that this should be qualified by the extent to which the Dutch Civil Code has also drawn on German legal principles (Taekema, 2011: 20), including Dutch practice on codetermination and in the social field. Although there is no formal doctrine of precedent, decisions that deviate from judgments of the Supreme Court may be appealed. There is no separate system of labour courts. First-instance employment cases are heard in the cantonal sections of district courts (*Kantongerechten*), presided over by a cantonal judge (*Kantonrechter*), usually in chambers for small claims (up to €5,000). Following graduation in law, individuals may be appointed as judges either after a six-year judicial training programme or six years of practice as an admitted lawyer. There is a policy of trying to achieve a 50/50 balance of judicially trained and external appointments (Ijzermans and de Roo, 2011: 78).

There are three levels in the general (civil and criminal) law system:

- First instance consists of the cantonal sections of district courts (*Rechtbank*) and there are 11 district courts, subdivided into 53 local (canton) courts (de Rechtspraak, 2013).
- Appeal to a Court of Appeal (*Gerechtshof*), of which there are five – although the right to appeal is restricted in termination cases to procedural matters.
- Final appeal on points of law only at the Supreme Court (*Hoge Raad*).

The courts have separate chambers for civil and criminal cases.

There is no lay participation in the court system.

Public law and labour inspection

The Ministry of Labour and Social Affairs operates an inspectorate system ('Inspectorate SZW'), with a number of teams, which replaced the previous Labour Inspectorate in 2012. One team deals with working conditions, a further with labour market fraud, and another is responsible for hazards. Accordingly, there is no longer a unified 'Labour Inspectorate',[2] although many of its former roles are now exercised by the relevant team.

The fraud inspection team is responsible for oversight of the employment of foreign nationals, the minimum wage and holiday allowance, and agency employment and placement. This team is also responsible for ensuring that extended collective agreements are complied with, which also means checking that the employer complies with hour and wage provisions. The team may be instructed by the Ministry to investigate any alleged breaches of a collective agreement, following a request from trade unions and employee representatives, in particular on the underpayment of posted workers. It may make unannounced visits for this purpose and interview employees as witnesses.

The working conditions team deals with health and safety, including hours and rest periods. Employees, together with trade unions, social workers, or legal advisers, may notify the inspectorate if they consider that an employer has breached any statutory provisions in these areas.

Labour jurisdiction – termination

As noted above, there is no separate system of labour jurisdiction in the Netherlands, with disputes over the application of employment laws heard in the civil courts.

Before terminating a contract of employment an employer must obtain either official authorisation or judicial permission, unless the employee is on a probationary contract, or their conduct warrants summary dismissal,[3] or the employee consents. Consensual termination was introduced in 2006 and usually involves the payment of an agreed sum in compensation. This was predicated on a change in social security rules that allowed unemployment benefit to be paid despite 'voluntary' entry into unemployment. This is now the preferred option for employers, as it avoids lengthy procedures.

The employer can choose whether to apply for judicial permission or official authorisation as follows:

- *Judicial permission*: dissolution of the contract by a cantonal court for an 'important reason': this can cover dismissal on grounds of the person or conduct and for economic, technical or organisational reasons. This route is preferred by large firms.
- *Official authorisation*: termination of contract with authorisation from the official employment service, UWV WERKbedrijf.[4] This option is used more by small and medium sized enterprises (SMEs), and also for economic terminations, including collective dismissals.

With some fluctuations, the two routes deal with approximately the same number of cases each year.

Official authorisation can be advantageous for employers as there is no *legal* requirement to pay severance compensation unless provided for in a collectively agreed 'social plan'.[5] UWV WERKbedrijf may, however, require an employer to rehire an employee terminated on economic grounds if work of a similar nature becomes available within 26 weeks of previous employment ending.

The court route may be faster as cases must begin within four weeks of application and the court may set aside the contractual notice period. There is also no appeal from a cantonal court, except on a procedural issue. However, a judge may simply sit to set a hearing date within this deadline, with the full hearing typically beginning within two months. The court option is more expensive for employers as judges typically award a severance payment based on a standard formula, the *Kantonrechtersformula* ('judges' formula') (see 'Court procedures' below). The ability to impose a severance payment also allows the judge to draw a balance between the interests of the parties and assess their 'culpability'. In contrast, the UWV WERKBedrijf procedure is not concerned with assigning culpability or ordering compensation and is more focused on whether the termination is objectively warranted.

Larger firms tend to opt for the court route, in the belief that it is quicker (not always the case) and are less deterred by the prospect of severance compensation. Some interviewees for this study felt that large international employers had a 'cultural bias' towards the courts and against the official procedure, with some noting that this might be due to the presence of trade union members on the dismissal advisory panel. Employers may employ both procedures simultaneously, although this is rare; more commonly, an employer will turn to the courts if official authorisation has been refused. For their part, an employee may apply to the courts to have an authorisation overturned (see 'Court procedures' below).

Official authorisation

The administrative procedure for employer-instigated dismissals is unique in Western Europe, in particular as it deals with individual dismissals.[6] The procedure emerged during the Second World War in the wake of the German invasion of the Netherlands in May 1940 (van Arkel, 2007: 171ff.). After the withdrawal of the government to London, the Commander in Chief of the Dutch Armed Forces was given authority to take decisions in the public interest. One measure intended to prevent mass unemployment was that employers were prohibited from dismissing workers without official permission. This was maintained under the Occupation as a means of controlling the labour market, supplemented by a requirement for employees to obtain permission to leave an employer. In 1944, fearing labour market disruption after the war, the government-in-exile issued a decree that continued to require official authorisation for employer and *employee* termination (Windmuller, 1969: 267ff): in the latter case, this was seen as a means to curb inter-employer competition for skilled labour. However, control over employee freedom of movement was limited and could not be invoked to thwart career development.[7]

The official procedure came into force under the 1945 Special Decree on Labour Relations (*Buitengewoon Besluit Arbeidsverhoudingen*). As well as wage controls, this included limits on public interest grounds both on employer and employee freedom to terminate.[8] The procedure was intended to be temporary but became permanent in 1953 (with the addition of a provision that courts could overturn a 'manifestly unreasonable' termination, even if authorised). Initially, this was the only means by which employment could be terminated without employee consent. However, in 1959, the Supreme Court confirmed that an employer could apply to a Cantonal

Court to dissolve the contract, creating the dual system (van Arkel, 2007: 163). One significant change in the 1950s was the creation of a process under which officials were provided with an opinion on the validity of the dismissal by a committee of one employee member and one employer member, the 'dismissal advisory panel' (see Dismissal advisory panel' below).

Procedure

In order to obtain a dismissal permit, the employer must detail the reasons for the termination, and set out any steps taken to warn employees (in the event of a disciplinary dismissal) or to avert it (for an economic dismissal, both individual and collective).

If UWV WERKbedrijf officials consider that the application does not contain sufficient information, the employer is given eight days to submit more details. Information submitted to the UWV WERKbedrijf is also sent to the employee, who may contest the application and normally has two weeks to respond: they may consult a lawyer or their union for advice. The official procedure is based on written documents only, with up to two rounds of submissions, and the parties will only be invited to attend in person in exceptional circumstances and if requested, and justified, by one of the parties.[9] Where this happens, a senior UWV WERKbedrijf official will conduct the hearing in a generally inquisitorial style.

Dismissal advisory panel

All applications for authorisation are referred to a 'dismissal advisory panel' (*Ontslag Adviescommissie*) based at the local UWV WERKbedrijf office. This comprises one employee and one employer representative, plus a 'technical' chair who is an employee of the WERKbedrijf and who manages the agenda and may clarify the regulations and facilitate the discussion; however, they do not 'preside'. The official handling the application, that is the case manager, will also usually attend. The employer and employee members issue an opinion as to whether the application should be granted, rejected or the decision delayed.

Members of the panel are appointed by the UWV for four years on nominations from employee and employer organisations deemed to be representative by the Labour Foundation. In practice, members are selected by their organisations and appointment is a formality. However, there are exchanges between the parties; for example, UWV WERKbedrijf expressed concerns about the proportion of retired employees and had doubts about their active involvement in the labour market, after which the age profile of advisors changed. There is no formal obligation for nominating organisations to pursue diversity, and moves towards greater participation by women have been through informal encouragement.

The members must meet statutory criteria such as being familiar with the labour market and employment in the broadest sense combined with knowledge of a number of specific sectors; knowledge of employment law in general and dismissal law in particular; capacity for financial analysis and 'concrete and abstract reasoning'; and 'social competence'.

Each organisation tends to meet these criteria in different ways, in some cases, for the employer side, appointing legal specialists from their own organisations, while the unions tend to select those with workplace experience. UWV WERKbedrijf has also set up an informal mechanism by which nominating bodies can ascertain from local UWV managers how their members are performing.

There is no attempt to match cases to members' experience, with cases assigned as they fall due. Members' names are not published. However, if a party requests it, the names of panel members in their case are disclosed. It was emphasised to us by officials that the process is transparent inasmuch as the actual *decision-makers* – that is, the officials concerned – are named.

The procedure is not a hearing of the two sides but a closed meeting that considers documentary material. Interviewees for this study reported that the procedure was rigorous but open and informal, and that evidence was judged on its merits and not in line with members' organisational affiliation. The panel's opinion is formally presented by the 'technical' chair of the panel. As noted above, in theory the chair does not have a vote and has not previously been involved in the case and the decision is taken de jure by the head of the local UWV WERKbedrijf office. In practice, especially in larger UWV offices, the decision is made by the chair, aided by notes taken by the case manager, who drafts the overall arguments for the decision, and the panel's opinion.

In the overwhelming majority of cases the panel is unanimous. If it is not unanimous, the official *may* seek the advice of the manager of the local Labour Law Service, a department of UWV WERKbedrijf. If the opinion is unanimous, but the official does not wish to follow it, the official *must* consult the UWV WERKbedrijf centre, which will issue a 'reasoned decision'. Regulations and guidance are set out in a handbook (UWV WERKbedrijf, 2010), originally introduced to ensure consistency between local offices. One interviewee for this study noted that the guidance is also used by the courts as it details criteria for different types of dismissal, selection criteria and other matters, leading to some convergence of approach between the two systems. Ultimately the decision is an administrative one, and the panel's opinion is not binding. The decision is communicated in writing to each side, and their representatives, with the main reasoning.

Authorisation can be granted subject to certain conditions. For example, in the event of economic dismissal, the UWV WERKbedrijf can require that at least 26 weeks should elapse from authorisation before any new employees can be hired to perform the same work as an employee who has been made redundant.

Obtaining authorisation normally takes four to six weeks, with a maximum of two months from application. If authorisation is not granted, the employer can apply to the courts for the contract to be dissolved, re-apply for a permit, or try to gain the consent of the employee. There is no internal appeal system for employees after the initial challenge; however, as noted above, employees may go the courts to have the authorisation set aside on the grounds that it is 'manifestly unreasonable' and can seek severance compensation even if the dismissal is then upheld.

In 2011, there were 59 per cent of applications through the official procedure that were granted and 8 per cent was refused. The rest were either withdrawn or deemed incomplete.

Assessment

There have been a number of assessments of the dismissal system in recent years (see van Arkel, 2007: 209–14), and the entire termination regime remains one of great political sensitivity. The National Ombudsman (Nationale Ombudsman, 2007) conducted a survey in 2007, and investigated the views of participants through a survey and direct observation. Employers felt the authorisation procedure could be improved, but that overall it represented a fair process. By contrast, and perhaps ironically given the desire of employer associations to remove the process, it was employees who considered that they were disadvantaged. There was a perception that employers were the 'the client' of the employment service, not employees, and the flow of information was felt to favour the employer side. Moreover, the chair was seen to have disproportionate influence because of their role in managing the procedure and the flow of information to the advisory panel.

The lack of oral presentation and scope for challenge was also seen as a problem, as there was no scope for parties to argue out their respective cases. This also touched on the issue of the anonymity of the panel members for particular cases. Although prior to the study it had been argued that disclosing names would deter people from becoming panel members, a majority of respondents stated that they would not object to their identity being disclosed. However, this suggestion was rejected by UWV WERKbedrijf, as was the recommendation for an oral hearing.

Court procedures

The most common first instance for individual employment disputes is to go a Cantonal Court (*Kantongerecht*), the first-instance civil chamber. In addition to applications to have an employment contract terminated or employee claims for unreasonable dismissal, courts also deal with enforcement of restrictive covenants, disputes over bonus payments, social compensation plans in redundancy situations, and issues such as fraud at work.

Complaints may also be lodged with a full district court using employment law procedures, and employees will nearly always seek an injunction to obtain not only re-instatement but also a return to work. In addition, there is an accelerated procedure, in which an interim ruling may be given pending a full hearing. Using such procedures, the president of the court may order an employer to reinstate a dismissed employee until a formal hearing is possible.

Unless an employment relationship has been ended by mutual consent or official authorisation, the only other option for an employer is to apply to have the employment contract dissolved by a court order for reasons specified under Section 7: 685 of the Civil Code. This allows for termination for 'urgent reasons', such as would warrant summary dismissal, or if the basis for the employment relationship has changed in a way rendering it fair for it to be terminated. An employer may also go to the court if official authorisation has been refused.

The court is not bound by the contractual notice period, as it rescinds the contract (possibly relevant for employers seeking to dismiss long-service staff). There is no requirement for pre-hearing conciliation, although a judge may recommend that the parties attempt this in some cases (such as lack of compatibility or in the event of long-term illness).[10]

Court proceedings are governed by the code of civil procedure although the degree of formality, in terms of dress and procedural style, may vary between Cantons, with the south of the country tending to be less formal. The procedure is as for other civil cases, but with the proviso that there is always only one presiding judge in employment cases, unless the matter involves a managing director (*statutair directeur*), where both employment and commercial law are involved. There will also be a court clerk. Cantonal Court judges dealing with employment matters will be highly specialised in this field and are generally seen as capable and competent by participants in the system, and enjoy high esteem.

The parties can be formally legally represented, but the form of representation is not specified for employment proceedings, and employees may be represented either by a solicitor or their trade union.[11] An oral hearing is mandatory and the procedure is inquisitorial, with no cross-examination. It is rare for witnesses to be called, and submissions will usually be in writing. Each party will be allowed two rounds of presentations, and then the judge will end the proceedings. The judgment will be issued in writing within two weeks (except in rare cases where there might be public interest).

As already noted, there is no scope for appeal on matters of fact or law, but only in the event of breach of procedure (including any conflicts of interest).

There is no statutory severance payment. Since 1997, compensation for termination of employment has generally been based on the 'Cantonal Court Formula', developed by the Association of Cantonal Court Judges. According to research by the University of Amsterdam (von Bergh et al., 2009), around 87 per cent of termination cases heard by the courts culminated in payment of severance compensation where they found for the employee. The formula consists of multiplying three elements: A (weighted years of service) × B (monthly salary) ×C (an 'adjustment factor' to reflect the contribution of each party to the dismissal: if neither party is culpable, it is set at 1). Changes were introduced in 2009 to reflect the employer's financial situation, their investment in employee skills, and the employee's employability.

Subject to a six months' time limit, employees may also go to the courts if they consider the termination was 'manifestly unreasonable', even if officially authorised, in part because the UWV WERKBedrijf does not award compensation: this can cover a variety of grounds, including disproportionality of the termination and the seriousness of the consequences for the employee compared with the employer, or a breach of agreed selection criteria. In such cases, the courts are unlikely to enforce reinstatement but will order compensation: this is not subject to the cantonal judges' formula and must be based on the merits of each case.

A court may also order reinstatement if a termination is deemed 'irregular' (Civil Code, Art. 7: 677). In most cases, reinstatement is refused by the employer and the court will allow the contract to end subject to payment of damages and/or 'redemption money' (*afkoopsom*). There is no right of appeal, unless a party can establish a procedural error or argue that vital evidence was not heard.

Employees may apply to the courts if the employer has breached a fundamental term of the contract and there are 'compelling reasons' not to expect the employee to continue to perform their contractual duties. The award will be as for a 'manifestly unreasonable' dismissal.

In general, Dutch trade unions have not argued for the establishment of separate labour courts to deal with individual disputes, although there have been a range of views in response to proposed changes in the overall system (see below). Court procedures are seen as speedy and also as a last resort, given the scope for filtering disputes through workplace and collectively agreed mechanisms.

Proposed changes

Under a government proposal issued in June 2012, the dual pre-emptive procedure of either courts or administrative authorisation was to be replaced by a single-track process in which the employer would give notice to terminate the contract, with the employee then having to challenge the termination in the courts, as is customary in most other jurisdictions. This was to be tied to a number of conditions, such as payment of a 'transition budget' to the employee to raise their employability. The proposal was supported by employer organisations. As well as easing the procedure, compensation awarded to the employee was also likely to be lower than the cantonal court formula for long-service employees and could, therefore, be attractive for the large employers that tend to use the courts. One associated argument in favour of the change was that it would encourage employee mobility as the potential gain from long-service in the court formula would be removed. Conversely, it could be considerably more expensive for SMEs that currently use the administrative procedure.

Following the change of government in September 2012, which saw the formation of a coalition between the Liberals (VVD) and Labour Party (PvdA), a shift in approach took place. In the course of tripartite negotiations over a new 'social pact' in April 2013, the Labour and Social Affairs Minister proposed fresh options for employers contemplating termination (Ministry of Labour, 2013). This pact, in which the proposed changes to the dismissal procedures was one of the most sensitive issues, was only possible because the FNV union confederation was able to obtain a mandate from its affiliates to engage in national level negotiation and exchange, something that had previously proved very difficult. Under the proposed change, the courts and UWV procedures will be retained but employers will no longer be able to choose which to take, and will face a single procedure, albeit with two institutional tracks. The government, as well as the trade union side, argued that the existing position meant that high- and low-income employees were often treated unequally when facing dismissal and that the existing system did not contribute to sustaining employability. Should the procedure be implemented, as intended from 1 January 2016, the UWV procedure would be compulsory if employment was terminated on economic, technical or organisational grounds or in the case of long-term incapacity.

Subject to further specification by the government, not finalised at the time of writing, the signatories to collective agreements will also be able to establish bipartite sectoral committees that, on request from the UWV, will be able to check whether any economic dismissals comply with the law – in effect, replacing the more general bipartite dismissal advisory panel. The UWV would retain the right to make the decision, and would do so in the event of a disagreement between the members of the committee. The court procedure would be compulsory for individual dismissal on other grounds, such as for misconduct and poor performance and for instances where the employment relation has broken down or encountered difficulties. Either party would be able to appeal against these decisions. One aim will be to steer the parties towards the option for termination by mutual consent.

One further effect is that trade unions and employee representatives are likely to become more actively involved in the early stages of the dismissal process through the new scope for negotiating alternative exit terms and procedures in collective agreements or social compensation plans. Such procedures could be significant for small and medium-sized firms covered by industry agreements.

The proposal for a 'transition payment' to employees will be implemented, both on fixed-term contracts and indefinite contracts, with at least two years' service of one-third of a month's pay for each year of service up to ten years, or half a month's pay for each year thereafter with a maximum of € 75,000, or one year's salary, with details still to be confirmed at the time of writing. This is effectively a form of compulsory severance payment that will also apply for the administrative procedure, where no compensation has been required in the past. It is intended to be spent on outplacement, training and finding fresh employment. Although an individual employee could not be compelled to buy such services, the aim is to channel payments collectively into employability schemes where procedures are established on a collective basis. Should a case of dismissal go to a Cantonal Court, the court will be able to add extra compensation to the transition payment if the employer is highly culpable in the dismissal or reduce it to zero if the employee is seriously culpable. The existing Cantonal Court formula would be abolished.

Discrimination and equal treatment

Individuals who wish to challenge discriminatory actions or policies may either bring a criminal prosecution in some instances, such as racial harassment, or approach the statutory quasi-judicial body with competence in this area. Prior to 2012 this was the Equal Treatment Commission. In 2012, the Commission was merged with the newly founded Institute of Human Rights (College voor de Rechten van de Mens), and will operate as a separate division within the Institute. The substantive procedures outlined below are those that apply specifically to discrimination within the ambit of the (former) Commission and its successor unit in the Institute.

In terms of discrimination and equal treatment, including discrimination at the workplace, the Institute's aim is to offer an informal and free service, and there is a focus on its skill in fact-finding.

There is no scope for the imposition of sanctions or any other penalty, and it is up to a claimant to pursue claims through the civil courts either for damages or for an order to cease or withdraw discriminatory conduct, policies or procedures. There are also local Antidiscrimination Bureaus, some of which were established by local authorities and others by NGOs (Havinga, 2002). These are often claimants' first port of call and can help in dealing with procedures.

Around 80 per cent of the workload of the Equal Treatment Commission prior to the merger was concerned with employment-related cases, where the main activity has consisted in carrying out investigations and issuing an opinion following an application from an individual(s) claiming discrimination at work (including an allegedly discriminatory policy) and providing an opinion if an employee wished to challenge an employer application for dissolution of the employment contract in the courts. It is very rare for an employee to approach the Commission if a dismissal is being processed through the official authorisation route.

Court proceedings can be initiated by a claimant without an opinion and, in principle, claimants may rely on their legal representative to advance their case. The opinion does not have any special legal standing, but is persuasive. If an opinion is not accepted, the cantonal judge would need to justify the grounds for rejecting it in the judgment. The Commission/Institute cannot state whether a dismissal is invalid, which will depend on the judge applying the law, but can indicate whether the situation prima facie appears to involve an act of discrimination.

The Commission/Institute, as an agency, is not called to attend proceedings, nor can it be subject to questioning by the judge.[12] Rather, the opinion is part of the evidence and may be contrasted with arguments from one or other party. In principle, a cantonal court judge could request an opinion, but this appears to be an extreme rarity. Judges hearing such cases will be employment specialists, but not necessarily discrimination specialists.

If the Commission/Institute has been approached by employees over allegations of discriminatory policies and practices, it will conduct an investigation and hold its own hearing. It has extensive right of access and an organisation could be fined for failing to comply with a request for information. All investigations conclude with a hearing, intended to air the issues, explore positions and establish a conclusion to the process. Prior to the hearing, parties are asked for written submissions.

Hearings are generally informal. Parties may be represented: employees are usually not represented, but larger firms tend to be.[13] The aim is mainly to facilitate a discussion between the parties to elucidate the issues and extract relevant information rather than act as an intermediary between professional representatives. Usually, both parties attend.

Hearings are presided over by a Commissioner, who may be, but is not required to be legally qualified, but must have a high level of legal competence although they are not members of the bench. In complex cases, a Commissioner may be assisted by a Substitute Commissioner, with a maximum of three Commissioners in a hearing. Commission/Institute legal advisers will draft a preliminary statement and identify the questions to be addressed, and also clerk the meeting.

After the hearing, the Commission will issue an opinion and possibly recommendations. These will be drafted by its internal legal advisers, including the clerk to the hearing. The opinion is signed by the commissioners and by the adviser, whose relationship is key to the operation of the procedure. The parties will be asked to respond, usually within a month. Recommendations cannot be enforced, but there is a formal follow-up procedure and in 2011 the Commission had a 70 per cent compliance rate, according to a Commission official. In addition, a claimant can approach the court as noted above.

Summary and conclusions

The Dutch system has a number of notable features. While there is no separate system of labour courts, there are official procedures to deal with termination of contract, in which lay members representing the social partners deliver an opinion on an application that is likely to determine the official decision, but is not binding. There have been concerns that the official route favours the employers as there is no scope for a formal challenge through an adversarial encounter. Despite this, employer organisations were in favour of abolishing this procedure, leaving all dismissals subject to the civil courts. However, the dual structure for termination is to be retained, but in future with no employer choice over which to use. Economic, technical and organisational dismissals will continue to require official authorisation, with dismissals for cause going before the courts. There is a developed and distinct set of arrangements for dealing with discrimination cases. Although these do not conclude with enforceable decisions, they allow a full investigation of the circumstances, are linked to the development of public policy, and constitute the basis for judicial deliberations should individuals resort to the civil courts.

9
New Zealand

Introduction

New Zealand's statutory duty of good faith[1] and its emphasis on mediation to resolve what are statutorily termed 'employment relationship problems' mark New Zealand out from all the other countries in this book. The good faith duty requires the parties to the employment relationship to be active, constructive, responsive and communicative. The emphasis on mediation as the primary problem-solving mechanism reduces the need for judicial intervention. If mediation fails, first-instance adjudication is conducted by the Employment Relations Authority, where a case is heard by a single adjudicator adopting an investigative approach. A decision of the Authority can be challenged through an appeal de novo, heard normally by a judge sitting alone in the Employment Court; further rights of appeal to the Court of Appeal and the Supreme Court are on points of law only.

This chapter first looks at the background to today's institutions and next at the institutions themselves, how they are constituted and how they operate. It then turns to the Human Rights Commission/Human Rights Review Tribunal and the Labour Inspectorate, ending with a discussion and summary.

Background

When New Zealand was colonised in 1840 by the British, common law formed the basis of its fledgling legal and industrial relations systems. From 1894, however, industrial relations in Great Britain and New Zealand diverged significantly when the New Zealand legislature enacted the Industrial Conciliation and Arbitration Act 'with the objectives of ensuring socially acceptable conditions of employment for most workers while at the same time limiting destructive industrial conflict' (Anderson, 2011: 689). This Act established the Court of Arbitration to make and interpret legally binding awards for specific industries and in so doing to determine the terms and conditions of employment and resolve disputes over the terms of employment or dismissal. The Court was tripartite, consisting of a judge, a union representative, and an employers' representative.

The Act also provided for union registration. Although not compelled to do so, unions could only gain certain benefits if they registered: the right of access to arbitration, monopoly rights to represent workers in an industry or occupation for which the union was registered and, after 1936, compulsory union membership for all workers bound by an award (Anderson, 2001).

According to Anderson (2011: 689), this system was never fully comprehensive; it only covered the private sector and even within the private sector essentially only blue collar workers. Managerial and white collar employees in the private sector continued to be regulated by the common law, while there was a comprehensive employment relations system for public servants, including rules for recruitment, promotion and discipline and procedures for rights of appeal against disputed decisions, which dated back to 1912.

In 1973 the Industrial Relations Act was passed. It required awards and collective agreements to include a procedure for dealing with personal grievances partly with the aim of minimising strikes as a response to dismissals (McAndrew, 1995: 37). A personal grievance, then and now, includes not only unjustified dismissal, but also any unjustified action that disadvantages the employee during employment. A disadvantage may arise as the result of the employer's exercise of discretionary powers and need not be monetary, nor need it relate to a contractual term.

A new body, the Industrial Court, was established to adjudicate on those personal grievances and also on disputes relating to an award or a collective agreement. Tripartism in this new body continued: worker/employer involvement was provided through direct nominees of the New Zealand Federation of Labour and the Employers' Federation who adjudicated alongside a professional judge.

This structure was reformed again in 1978 when the Industrial Court and the Industrial Commission, set up in 1974 to determine disputes of interest, were merged into the Arbitration Court. This also included direct nominees from the national union federation and the employers.

The arbitration system started to collapse from the mid-1960s, giving way to direct collective bargaining at the industry/occupation level. Compulsory arbitration was abolished in 1984 (Anderson, 2001) and the remit of the Arbitration Court was reduced to disputes of interest under the Labour Relations Act, 1987. This Act then established a new body, the Labour Court, to hear personal grievances, demarcation disputes and injunctions and damages arising from industrial action. Like its predecessors, it was tripartite, but unlike its predecessors its remit was extended from the private sector to the state sector, with the separate provisions for public servants being abolished (Ministry of Justice, 2013a).

From 1973, when a personal grievance adjudicatory procedure was established, up until 1991, access to adjudication was confined to union members, so unions were the gate-keepers and acted as advocates for those members whom they chose to support. Union membership, however, was in effect compulsory by law essentially for workers below managerial level in the private sector (Corby, 1999) as noted above and union density peaked at 53.3 per cent in 1989 (Charlwood and Haynes, 2008).

Alongside these specific adjudicatory institutions, from which there was an appeal to the Court of Appeal on a point of law, mediation services were established by government: one body for disputes of interest and the other, the Industrial Mediation Service, for disputes of rights. Before reaching the Industrial Mediation Service, there was first a joint in-house committee containing equal numbers of union and employer representatives and if the parties wished, which they usually did, they appointed a member of the Industrial Mediation Service to act as chairperson (Corby, 1999, 2000). These two mediation bodies were merged in 1987.

The Employment Contracts Act 1991

In 1990 the National Party was elected to government with a commitment to labour market restructuring and deregulation, building on the radical economic reforms that had commenced in the 1980s. A key plank of the government's policy was the Employment Contracts Act (ECA) 1991, which has had an enduring impact. It individualised the employment relationship, triggering a major decline in union density from 44.7 per cent in 1990 to 21 per cent in 1999 (Charlwood and Haynes, 2008). This was because under the Act, compulsory union membership was outlawed and employees and employers negotiated legally binding contracts, which could be either individual or collective. In either case an employee could authorise someone to negotiate on his/her behalf, such as a lawyer, employment advocate or a trade union, with trade unions becoming incorporated societies and losing their monopoly rights of representation and their privileged position in the workplace.

The ECA, while giving pride of place to contracts of employment, essentially incorporated the previous personal grievance provisions, albeit now applying them irrespective of union membership. It abolished the Labour Court and the Industrial Mediation Service and in their place it established two new bodies: the Employment Tribunal (ET) and the Employment Court. The former was given first-instance jurisdiction in both mediating and adjudicating personal grievances: ET members were warranted for mediation and/or adjudication, but the member did not mediate *and* adjudicate the same case. ET members presided alone as nomination by social partner bodies was abolished and were not required to be legally qualified (although many in fact were). When adjudicating, ET members mostly operated on adversarial principles in line with the procedures prescribed in Regulations.[2]

The Employment Court was given appellate jurisdiction to hear appeals against ET decisions on fact and law based on a transcribed record. It was also given first-instance jurisdiction including injunctive relief, plus the common law remedy of wrongful dismissal. It comprised a judge sitting alone, although at the direction of the Chief Judge three judges could hear a case.

The Employment Relations Act 2000

When a Labour/Alliance government replaced the National government in 1999, it enacted the Employment Relations Act (ERA), 2000, amended in 2004 and 2010. The aim was to stem individualisation in the labour market by promoting collective bargaining and giving unions, once registered, certain exclusive and privileged legal rights, most importantly the exclusive right to negotiate collective agreements. Nevertheless, under the ERA, as with the preceding ECA, a union is empowered to negotiate only for its members and cannot win majority legal rights in a workplace. The outlawing of compulsory union membership has also been maintained (Anderson, 2001). In fact union density as a percentage of the employed labour force has essentially flat-lined since the introduction of the ERA 2000. In 2012 it was 21 per cent of wage/salary earners.[3] See also Table 1.1 p. 2.

The Act has sought to redress the inequality of power between employer and employee by requiring all collective agreements and contracts of employment to contain a 'plain language' explanation of the processes and services available for resolving 'employment relationship problems' (ERPs). An employment relationship problem is a statutory concept and 'includes anything that harms or that might harm an employment relationship' and might be the basis of a personal grievance (Department of Labour, 2011a: 17). To support the requirements for plain language agreements, the Ministry of Business, Innovation and Employment (MBIE) has an 'Employment Agreement Builder'.[4]

Another way the government sought to redress the inequality of power in the employment relationship was by imposing a good faith obligation on the parties. The duty of good faith (s.4(1) ERA 2000):

(a) is wider in scope than the implied mutual obligations of trust and confidence; and

(b) requires the parties to an employment relationship to be active and constructive in establishing and maintaining a productive employment relationship in which the parties are, among other things, responsive and communicative.

Under s.4A a party to an employment relationship who fails to comply with the duty of good faith is liable to a penalty (see Anderson (2011) for a full discussion).

The ECA's employment tribunal was abolished by the ERA and there is currently a three-stage process for resolving disputes outside organisations' internal procedures: mediation by the Mediation Service, adjudication by the Employment Relations Authority and adjudication by the Employment Court. In addition there are appeals on points of law to the Court of Appeal and Supreme Court. We deal with each of these stages in turn (Figure 9.1).

Mediation

The New Zealand workplace dispute resolution system gives precedence to mediation, as noted above. To that end the Employment Relations Act, 2000, replaced Employment Tribunals, which conducted both mediation and adjudication, with two separate institutions, one for mediation called The Mediation Service, the other for adjudication, called the Employment Relations Authority. The Mediation Service was originally part of the Department of Labour but since 2012 has been absorbed into a bigger ministry, the Ministry of Business, Innovation and Employment (MBIE). Mediators are employed by the MBIE, but act independently when mediating disputes and indeed sometimes mediate disputes within MBIE itself. Their mediation is based on the principles of impartiality and confidentiality, while anything said in mediation is without prejudice to any future adjudication.

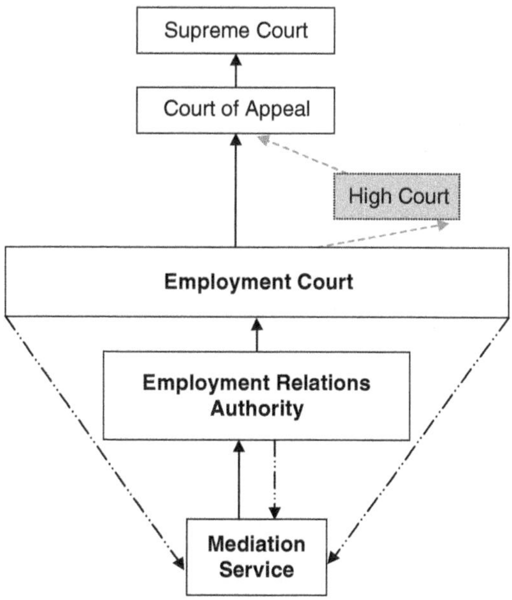

Figure 9.1 Adjudication in New Zealand
Note: Rumoured structure shaded.

Mediator posts are advertised through the government jobs service and the criteria for appointment include a mediator's personality; experience of, and passion for, mediation; and knowledge of employment legislation. In addition, those recruited are either already accredited by the Association of Dispute Resolvers (LEADR) or, if not, are expected to go through the accreditation process. In 2009/10 there were 34 mediators, based in seven regional offices, of whom 21 were interviewed by Risak and McAndrew (2010). They found that nine of the 21 had been employed by social partner organisations at some point in their careers (six by unions and three by employers) and two were lawyers, with most of the others having been civil servants formerly.

The Mediation Service mediates in both collective and individual issues. Where an employee considers that a personal grievance has arisen, he/she has 90 days to inform the employer,[5] after which a case may be referred for mediation. Initial enquiries to the Mediation Service are filtered through a Contact Office, staffed with information officers who can provide both information on employment rights and make 'common sense suggestions' (Department of Labour, 2011b: 7). As to the mediation itself, it is normally conducted in one of the Service's seven offices, is face-to-face (not telephone or email) and typically lasts some four hours.

Mediators deploy different styles depending on their personality and the nature of the case; some are more settlement focused and some are more facilitative focused. The parties may also agree that the mediator can decide the issue (s.150, ERA 2000), and hence act in an adjudicative capacity. The advantage of such a mediator's decision is that it is free, unlike a determination by the Employment Relations Authority, but the disadvantage is that there is no appeal. According to the Chief of the Mediation Service, it is not used much.

From 1 April 2011, mediators (and Authority members – see below) may make recommendations for resolving a dispute if requested by the parties. The parties will be given an agreed period in which to decide whether they will accept the recommendation. If neither party objects within this timeframe, this becomes final and enforceable. If a party rejects the recommendation, further mediation may be provided and either party may request that mediation be conducted by a different mediator than the one who made the recommendation. According to the Chief Mediator 'it's happened quite a bit, more in the Auckland office than round the country'. Both decisions and recommendations entail evaluative mediation, which some commentators have dubbed an oxymoron (Kovach and Love, 1996). Mediators, however, consider that in practice decisions and recommendations can occasionally be useful tools and they do not find it problematic to move from a facilitative to an evaluative style according to two interviewees.

Another useful tool is the provision of early assistance mediation where the mediator seeks to resolve an ERP at an early stage: this typically covers personal issues between colleagues or between an employee and manager. In such cases the mediator may go into the workplace, rather than require the parties to attend a Mediation Service office.

In the majority of cases, the parties attend mediation (except early assistance mediation) with a paid representative, a lawyer, an employment advocate, a HR manager, a union organiser or a union lawyer.[6] A paid representative is normally not as emotionally involved as a party and can take a detached view of the situation. Although a mediator is statutorily empowered to speak to the parties on their own, in practice mediators only speak to the parties on their own with the representative's permission.

In theory, mediation can be carried out by a private sector mediator as the ERA 2000 does not require that only The Mediation Service is to be used. The latter, however, is free, unlike private sector mediation. Moreover, only a settlement that has been signed by a mediator employed by MBIE can be enforced by the Employment Relations Authority, although in practice most settlements are complied with voluntarily according to an interviewee for this study. Accordingly, the Mediation Service carries out the lion's share of mediation. Risak and McAndrew (2010) found that private mediation seemed to exist only in some niches, such as the tertiary education sector. Those employers that opted for private mediation stated that they valued being able to choose a mediator, and that the service was more discrete as they preferred not to be seen in the offices of the Mediation Service of the Department of Labour[7] (ibid.).

In 2011/12 the Mediation Service completed 5,850 mediations, settling 81 per cent, with settlement defined as a case where a written agreement is recorded. In the previous five years the number of mediations settled was either slightly below, or slightly above this figure (Department of Labour, 2012). Cases that remain unsettled do not always proceed to the Employment Relations Authority as sometimes a case is dropped, though data on this are not available.

According to Woodhams (2007, cited in McAndrew, 2010), the median direct cost to the employer of a dispute resolved through the Mediation Service was NZ$7,275 (approximately $5,680; £3,650; €4,246): almost 80 per cent were below NZ$5,000 and 44 per cent below NZ$2,000 (approximately $1,562; £1,003; €1,167). The bulk of claims were for unjustified dismissal, and the costs to the employer were mainly in respect of compensation for hurt feelings.

Employment Relations Authority

Procedure

The Authority (and the Employment Court, see below) have exclusive jurisdiction over personal grievances, which are very widely defined (see above). Unlike other common law jurisdictions (see Great Britain, Chapter 5;

Ireland, Chapter 6; and South Africa, Chapter 10) there are no alternative remedies, such as wrongful dismissal or actions against restraint of trade, available in the 'ordinary' civil courts.

If agreement through mediation has not been reached, a party can then refer the ERP to the Employment Relations Authority. The Employment Relations Act does not require expressly that mediation be attempted before an ERP can be lodged with the Authority, but the thrust of the Act is to encourage the parties themselves to try to resolve matters, albeit with the help of a mediator. Thus the Authority is obliged to consider whether mediation has been attempted and if not, it has the discretion to direct mediation or further mediation.[8] If the parties fail to comply with the direction, this could be a breach of the good faith obligation and influence the judicial outcome. Furthermore, from 1 April 2011 the Authority is obliged to prioritise cases where mediation has been attempted.

A party has three years from the date that the ERP occurred, or knowledge of it, to file a case at the Authority; a party lodges a statement of the problem and pays NZ$71.56 (approximately £38, €44.81, $57.88) and the respondent, after being contacted by the Authority, provides a statement in reply. Forms are available, but are not mandatory. If necessary a Support Officer will seek clarification or additional information. This is followed by a preliminary case management conference, normally a conference telephone call between the Authority member, that is the Authority adjudicator, and the parties or their representatives. The case management conference includes identification of the issues and relevant witnesses, and agreement on the date and length of time of the investigation meeting.

Meetings (hearings) are normally public (unless specifically excluded by the member, a rare event) and, in contrast to New Zealand's common law tradition of adversarialism, the Authority is an investigative body. According to the Act, the Authority is not inhibited by strict procedural requirements (s.143(f) ERA 2000) and resolves grievances 'by establishing the facts and making a determination according to the substantial merits of the case, without regard to technicalities' (s.157 ERA 2000). In practice, whereas some members of the Authority are very investigative, taking charge of the proceedings and requiring answers from both parties to a host of questions, other members, particularly if both sides are legally represented, allow the lawyers essentially to present their case and witnesses and to make submissions.

In complex cases evidence is almost always based on the written statements of witnesses lodged in advance of the investigation meeting in accordance with the timetable set at the case management conference. Witnesses are not asked to read their statements out at the investigation meeting, although the content is taken into account as part of the evidence and forms the basis for questioning.

In addition, the Authority has wide powers. It can conduct further enquiries and seek further evidence either at the request of a party or on its own motion and can even ask the Inland Revenue to disclose any taxpayers' files that might be relevant. Each side may sum up their case and cite appropriate case law and/or the member may ask for written submissions to be made after the investigation meeting. The first day of the investigation meeting is free, after which fees are payable by applicants for each subsequent half day at NZ $153.33 (£82.00, €96, $122).

Whatever the approach adopted, the member is required to make clear to the parties in advance during the telephone case management conference what the format will be. Moreover, at the start of the investigation meeting, the member sets out the procedure to be followed in the particular case.

Authority investigations take place in meeting rooms with the member and the parties sitting on the same level. There is not a dais as in a court, nor is there a witness box although evidence is given on oath or affirmation. To curtail legalism, cross-examination originally was allowed only if permitted by the member and, after a legal challenge, this was put on a statutory basis in 2002. Controversy continued, however, and the Act was amended in 2010 enabling cross-examination to be conducted as of right from 1 April 2011. According to the Chief of the Authority (interviewed for this study), the controversy over cross-examination was overblown. In practice, both originally and now, lawyers cross-question.

The Authority member can make a recommendation where requested to do so by the parties, but in practice this seldom occurs and the Authority adjudicates. The member's determination is usually reserved and given in writing, after which it is displayed on a publicly accessible website. At the time of writing, in an attempt to limit delay, an amendment to the ERA is being considered under which the member would have to give an oral determination at the end of the investigation meeting or alternatively preliminary findings of fact to be followed by a written record of that determination and reasons within three months.

The Authority member has the power to award a range of remedies including reinstatement, reimbursement of lost wages, compliance (for instance with the terms of the employment or settlement agreement) and compensation for hurt and humiliation caused by dismissal or unjustified action. In addition, the member normally awards costs to be paid by the losing party. As a rule of thumb the Authority awards costs of NZ$3,500 per day of investigation meeting (approximately £1,777; €2,091; $2,712).

Before making a determination the Authority may refer an issue to the Employment Court for an opinion on a matter of law, if it is an important question of law likely to arise in the case other than incidentally. In practice this occurs once or twice a year, according to an interviewee. Alternatively the Authority has the power to remove the case from the Authority to the Employment Court (s.178 ERA), although in practice this is not done unless a party has asked for this. According to the Chief Judge of the Employment Court there are some 50 removals a year.

Other matters

On average an investigation meeting lasts less than two days, according to an estimate by the Chief of the Authority. Although the Authority deals with both collective and individual matters, the bulk of its work is personal grievances. Roughly three-quarters of personal grievances are cases of alleged unjustified dismissal. The bulk of the remainder of personal grievances are cases of unjustified action to the disadvantage of the employee, such as failure to pay the correct wage or withdrawing/altering a condition of employment.[9] Unusually when compared to many other countries, the number of cases being adjudicated at first instance in New Zealand is falling, not rising. For instance in 2009, the Authority received 2,587 applications, but this had fallen to 1,989 in 2012 (Rasmussen and Greenwood, 2014).

At the time of writing (July 2013) the Authority had 17 members (including the Chief) with offices in Auckland, Wellington and Christchurch. Members are salaried employees appointed by the Governor General on a recommendation from the Minister on a four-year term and may be re-appointed. When there is a vacancy there is an advertisement, short-listing of applications and a panel interview. The interview panel then puts forward those who are eligible for appointment, from whom the Minister selects to fill the vacancy. The process of this ministerial selection is not transparent, but it is thought that the Minister consults certain stakeholders. Members are not statutorily required to be legally qualified and when the Authority was first established, the number of lawyers and non-lawyers was broadly equal (McAndrew, 2010). Now legal qualifications and experience are a *de facto* requirement according to the Chief of the Authority.

Parties may be supported or represented by a third party (lawyer, union official, family member, friend or 'whanau').[10] At a rough estimate, according to the Chief of the Authority, 70 per cent of those who come to the Authority are represented by somebody who is receiving a fee for a professional service. Such a person may be a solicitor, or a barrister, or a lay advocate, as New Zealand has a strong tradition of lay advocacy.

The Employment Court

The Employment Court of New Zealand, although originally established under the Employment Contracts Act 1991, was retained by the ERA. The Employment Court has exclusive jurisdiction to hear appeals relating to employment disputes, and in particular challenges to determinations of the Employment Relations Authority, questions concerned with the interpretation of law, and jurisdiction as a court of first instance in the case of strikes or lockouts. It is a court of record and the bulk of its work is individual not collective (some 80 per cent according to an interviewee). One interviewee for this study opined that having a Court with a conventional, adversarial approach was the quid pro quo for establishing the investigative, informal Authority.

The Employment Court currently comprises the Chief Judge and four other judges. Normally a case is heard by a judge sitting alone, although six or seven times a year a case will be heard by three judges, a so-called full court. A decision by a full court is no more binding than a single judge's decision, but it may be more persuasive in the higher courts. Whether or not a full court is convened is at the discretion of the Chief Judge. There are no stipulated grounds for this, but informally his criteria are where there is a new legislative provision that will have widespread effect, where existing law needs to be revisited, or where a party indicates that it wishes to challenge a decision of an existing judge.

Judges must be legally qualified, with at least seven years' experience as a practising lawyer. They are appointed until they reach the retirement age of 70, after which they can be temporarily reappointed. Judges wear gowns and the layout is the traditional court layout with the judge(s) on a raised dais.

Although pre-1991 adjudicatory bodies (the Arbitration Court, the Industrial Court and the Labour Court) were tripartite, the Employment Court is unipartite. On the face of it, this was a major change. Reactions, however, appear to have been muted. According to an interviewee for this study, when the employment institutions were recast in 2000, no stakeholder argued for tripartism to be reintroduced. He speculated that perhaps the unions felt that some of their erstwhile panel members had been captured by the court and virtually become judges. Moreover, he said, the issue of tripartism/unipartism was probably not at the forefront of stakeholders' concerns because there were many more significant changes being considered at that time.

Procedures

The bulk of the cases that come before the Employment Court are challenges, that is, appeals against a determination of the Employment Relations Authority. Roughly 10 per cent of Authority determinations are challenged, according to an interviewee and a challenge must be lodged in the Employment Court within 28 days of the issue of the decision. A challenge may be confined to a specific aspect of a determination (such as an alleged error of law or fact, which must be specified in the statement of claim). More commonly, however, the challenge follows from blanket dissatisfaction and results in the matter being heard de novo without any particular ground being cited. In such a case the Authority's determination is set aside, all documents are resubmitted and witness evidence is given again. There is a filing fee that varies according to the application. For challenges to a determination by the Authority the filing fee at the time of writing is NZ$204.44, although there is a proposal to double this to NZ$500 (approximately $391, €304, £261).

The Court must direct that mediation or further mediation, as the case may require, be used before the Court hears the matter, unless the Court considers that the use of mediation or further mediation will not contribute constructively to resolving the matter; be in the public interest; or undermine the urgent or interim nature of the proceedings (s.188 (2) ERA 2000). The Court has expanded its remit to direct that mediation be used to include judicial settlement conferences as an alternative to referring the parties back to the Mediation Service. This alternative has proved popular. The Chief Judge estimates that over three quarters of the cases lodged are resolved in a judicial settlement conference. If the parties do not reach a settlement, the hearing must be conducted by a different judge. Any documents submitted to this conference are confidential and will not be part of the Court's record, unless agreed by both parties.

Representation is not confined to lawyers. Anyone can act as a paid representative, for instance a union official, HR manager, employment advocate. It is possible for a litigant to represent themselves, which 'can be a scary prospect', albeit there is an advice sheet provided by the Ministry of Justice (Ministry of Justice, n.d.a). There is a *pro bono* legal advice service only in Auckland and because of restrictions on legal aid there is an increasing number of self-represented litigants, about 20–25 per cent according to the Chief Judge. Evidence is given on oath, with cross-examination of witnesses.

A hearing normally takes place six to nine months after an application has been lodged, unless a matter is urgent. The average length of hearing is one to two days. As a rule of thumb, according to an interviewee, where there is a challenge, the Employment Court's hearing lasts twice as long as the Authority's determination. The first day of hearing is free, but then it is NZ$245 per half day at the time of writing. There is a proposal, however, to increase this to NZ$350 (approximately $224, €213, £183) per half day.

Judgments are usually reserved and may not be delivered for some months, except where urgent action is required. Costs often, but not invariably, follow the event as the Court has a broad discretion on costs and there are no scales. Accordingly, for instance, the Court might not award costs where the case concerns the interpretation of a collective agreement that is going to have widespread effect.

There were 183 new cases filed with the Employment Court in 2012, with a disposal rate of 228 cases. The 2012 caseload was slightly higher (12.7 per cent) than the 163 cases filed in 2011 (Ministry of Justice, 2013b). There is a right of appeal to the Court of Appeal on a point of law only. In about 10 per cent of cases such an appeal is sought, but the Court of Appeal grants leave to appeal in only about half of the cases where it is sought, according to the Chief Judge. There can be a further appeal to the Supreme Court on a point of law, if leave is granted.

According to several interviewees, the Employment Court might be downgraded to District Court status. This would bring it into line with another specialist court, the Environment Court, adding another level of appeal. A party would have to appeal first to the High Court on a point of law, before any further appeals on a point of law to the Court of Appeal and Supreme Court (see Figure 9.1).

Where a plaintiff files a statement of claim challenging on a de novo basis a determination of the Authority, the Court may ask the Authority for a good faith report (s.181 ERA 2000), that is an assessment as to whether the parties facilitated the Authority's investigation and behaved in good faith towards each other. The Chief Judge estimates that this is done in some 5 per cent of cases, normally where the Authority's determination arouses the Court's suspicion that a plaintiff has not acted in good faith. For instance, the Authority will note whether or not the plaintiff attended mediation, attended the investigation meeting and assisted in resolving the ERP in a timely and efficient way. Both the plaintiff and the defendant can comment in writing on this assessment of good faith. Then there is normally a hearing where the Court gives an interlocutory judgment, directing whether or not the case can proceed in full or in part to a full hearing (s.182 ERA 2000). If the Court finds that the plaintiff has breached the good faith obligation it might, for instance, restrict the issues that may be the subject of a challenge and it might award costs to the defendant in respect of the costs of representation in the good faith process.

Human rights claims

New Zealanders have a considerable number of statutory employment rights including provisions on unjustified dismissal and unjustified action to the disadvantage of the employee. Moreover, both the ERA 2000 and the Human Rights Act 1993 (HRA) prohibit discrimination on the grounds of sex, marital status, religious belief, ethical belief, colour, race, ethnic or national origins, disability, age, political opinion, employment status, family status and sexual orientation, as well as sexual and racial harassment.

Complaints based on the HRA go to the Human Rights Commission (HRC). They can be made by phone, fax or email (they do not have to be in writing) and if the HRC accepts the complaint it seeks to mediate, either by written correspondence, telephone calls or more typically by a face-to-face meeting. Where the complaint involves matters within the jurisdiction of both the HRA and the ERA, that is if the complaint emanates from the employment relationship, a complainant may either go to the Mediation Service (see above) or to the Human Rights Commission (HRC). In such an event there is a co-mediation protocol agreed between the two bodies irrespective of whether the claim was lodged with the Mediation Service or the HRC. Otherwise, in employment-related matters where no employment relationship exists, the complainant can only go to the Human Rights Commission, for instance where a complaint is about discrimination during selection or the provision of a reference from a previous employer.

Up to 2001 the HRC carried out an investigation into a complaint. Now complaints are mediated and there is a high level of settlement. Since then, up to 30 June 2012, of 1,156 unlawful discrimination complaints, 77 per cent 'recorded a resolved or partially resolved result through the provision of information, self-help strategies and dispute resolution' (Human Rights Commission, 2012: 28).

If a complaint is not settled through mediation, or if a settlement is not honoured, a complaint can be made to an adjudicatory body, the Human Rights Review Tribunal (HRRT), or if the matter falls within the jurisdiction of the ERA to the Authority; but a complainant cannot go to the HRRT and the Authority on the same matter (s.79A, HRA).

There are distinct advantages in following the HRRT route: it is free, unlike the Authority and the Office of Human Rights Proceedings can agree to provide representation irrespective of the complainant's income, if there is a real prospect of success and the matter is of public interest. In practice, the Office rarely does so: in the year to 30 June 2012 the Director of the Office made 52 decisions concerning representation and agreed to provide representation to only one applicant. Seven matters were referred back to the HRC (s.91(2) HRA) and in one of those cases the Director agreed to provide the complainant with legal representation at mediation (Human Rights Commission, 2012).

In the year to 30 June 2012, the largest category of complaints (30 per cent) to the HRC related to unlawful discrimination in employment (Human Rights Commission, 2012). Where complaints are not settled through mediation, as noted above, they can be taken further, but the HRRT rarely considers employment cases, around one every couple of years, and neither does the Authority. This might be because the Authority adjudicates where a complaint of unjustified action has been made and unjustified action is broader and easier to demonstrate than discrimination.

Where a case goes to the HRRT it is usually heard by the chairperson and two panel members and witnesses can be called, evidence is given on oath and a decision can be made by a majority. The HRRT's remedies include declarations and compensatory damages for losses suffered and/or lost benefits – although typically awards are for injury to feelings, humiliation and/or loss of dignity. The HRRT has the same monetary limit as the District Court: NZ$200,000 (approximately $157,174; €120,000). In some situations the HRRT passes cases to the High Court if a greater award is indicated. It can also issue a declaration of inconsistency in legislation.

The HRRT may seek the opinion of the High Court on any question of law or can transfer a case to the High Court on an important matter of law, or if the High Court is already hearing a case of a similar nature. Determinations of the HRRT can be appealed through the civil court system.

In addition, the HRC can intervene in a human rights matter at any level in the civil courts, but in practice it does not intervene at first instance. Because of cost constraints, the HRC reserves its interventions where it is likely to influence the jurisprudence. For instance, at the time of writing the HRC was intervening at the Employment Court on a case under the Equal Pay Act 1972 (whether a comparator can be notional).

At the time of writing there are 11 Tribunal members, including four who have legal qualifications, plus the Chairperson who must be a solicitor or barrister of the High Court with at least five years' practice, with appropriate experience in dispute resolution and who is appointed for five years (Ministry of Justice, n.d.b).

Labour Inspectorate

Until 1990, unions monitored awards and collective agreements to ensure that their terms were observed. There was a hiatus in the 1990s and New Zealand's labour inspection system was established by the Employment Relations Act, 2000 to monitor and enforce certain minimum employment standards including those concerning employment agreements, time records, annual leave, sick pay, parental leave, public holidays, holiday pay and wages as set out in various Acts of Parliament. Since the beginning of 2013, the Labour Inspectorate has become a stand-alone entity, rather than operating in a local office together with other public servants. According to an interviewee this has helped generate a sense of identity and culture among labour inspectors.

Although a stand-alone entity, the Labour Inspectorate often operates with other enforcement agencies such as the Immigration compliance officers and investigators from the Inland Revenue Department and/or the local authority liquor licensing inspectors.

There are 35 labour inspectors in four regions and the numbers have increased slowly but steadily in the last decade. At the time of writing over half are female and there is an ethnic mix including those of Fijian, Indian and Chinese origin. Of these 35 inspectors, three are dedicated to auditing the Recognised Seasonal Employer (RSE) scheme, an arrangement for bringing in workers seasonally to work for accredited employers in horticulture and viticulture and for providing pastoral care to RSE employers and employees.

Once selected, a labour inspector has online and face-to-face training and three months mentoring, known by the Maori word *Kaiarahi*. Only after these three months is the new recruit warranted as a labour inspector.

An inspector's role is to manage complaints and support business in achieving compliance with minimum employment rights (ERA s.223A). To this end the labour inspector has various powers. At one end of the scale is the self-resolution approach, where the inspector explains the issues to the employer and the employer agrees to resolve the issues. If the labour inspector is not entirely confident that the employer will do this, he/she can ask the employer to enter into an enforceable undertaking: this is a written voluntary agreement usually three to four pages in length, under which the employer agrees to take certain steps within an agreed timeframe.

Towards the other end of the scale is the issuing of an improvement notice, whereby the labour inspector can require the employer to correct the breach and/or take certain steps to address any systemic practices that could lead to a future breach and finally a demand notice. A demand notice can be served after an employee has complained and the employer has seven days to comment on it. In addition, the employer has 28 days to challenge the improvement notice or the demand notice at the Employment Relations Authority. If there is non-compliance, the labour inspector can seek a compliance order from the Employment Relations Authority and a civil penalty of up to NZ$20,000 (approximately $15,620; £10,032; €11,672) for failing to comply with the enforceable undertaking, the improvement notice or the demand notice. The determination of the Authority can be challenged in the Employment Court (see above); (also see ERA 2000, Part XI for full details). Further appeals are permitted only with leave on points of law to the Court of Appeal and the Supreme Court.

There is a separate health and safety inspectorate and health and safety prosecutions are taken in the District Court.

Discussion and conclusions

The procedures for resolving employment disputes in New Zealand give primacy to mediation. It is virtually mandatory in almost all circumstances before other forums may be approached and can also be resorted to at later stages (at the Authority and the Employment Court). One of the claimed positive outcomes of mediation is the achievement of agreement on issues such as references, permitted 'resignations' (instead of dismissal), apologies and severance packages, as well as compensation for hurt and humiliation, reinstatement and reengagement. In contrast, the range of remedies available through adjudication is more limited.

Furthermore, the New Zealand system is not costly for employers – in the thousands, not the tens of thousands according to research by Woodhams (2007) (see above), although costs increase if a case goes to the Authority and then to the Employment Court. Nevertheless, there are drawbacks to this emphasis on mediation. Because mediation is carried out in private and any settlement is confidential to the parties, legal norms are not generated and case law is not developed (see Dolder (2004) for a full discussion).

In a review of the system, however, prior to some recent reforms, the Department of Labour (2010) found that what little evidence there was suggested that the majority of employers were satisfied with the process and outcomes of the entire personal grievance system and this was echoed by Business New Zealand who considered that the system was as fair as it could be (Cabinet Economic Development Committee, nd: 37). There was, however, some indicative evidence that some employers and employees found that the system was not efficient and effective (Department of Labour, 2010). This led to minor amendments to the system, including the recent strengthening of the role of mediators to make recommendations, with the agreement of the parties. These developments suggest that there might be a growth in the role of evaluative mediation over facilitative mediation in future.

A live issue at the time of writing is the role of the Employment Court. This includes its rumoured downgrading which would insert an extra level of appeal on a point of law and whether complex legal issues should be allowed to bypass the Authority and go straight to the Court, as some have argued (McAndrew, 2010: 90).

Nevertheless, there is a generally high level of user satisfaction with the service. Furthermore, McAndrew (2010: 92) maintains that:

> New Zealand enjoys the advantages of a very effective network of employment institutions, delivering broad job and social protections to the workforce at a minimal level of intrusion on the rights that attend free enterprise.

Rasmussen and Greenwood (2014) echo this. Moreover, McAndrew (2010) points out that New Zealand's employment institutions are much studied, admired and copied. For instance, New Zealand's mediation system was praised in a review of the British employment dispute resolution system by Gibbons (2007: 39) and Ireland's proposed system has many similarities with that of New Zealand.

10
South Africa

Introduction

When a democratic South Africa was established in 1994, a new labour relations regime was conceived – tripartism at national level, centralised bargaining mainly at sectoral level, and participation and joint decision-making at the workplace level to address inequality, unemployment and poverty (Everett, 2012). To prevent and resolve collective and individual disputes, new institutions were formed, in particular the Commission for Conciliation, Mediation and Arbitration (CCMA), which was charged with providing speedy and informal arbitration for certain employment rights, primarily conduct and capability dismissals, and the Labour Court (LC), which was given the power to adjudicate in respect of a wide range of other individual employment rights matters. Importantly also, the Labour Court was given the power to review CCMA arbitration awards with appeals going to the Labour Appeal Court (Donnelly and Dunn, 2006). Nearly two decades later, these institutions have bedded in and, as will be shown below, are on the whole working efficiently in the field of individual dispute resolution, even though the broader industrial relations environment is increasingly problematic because of growing, and often violent strike activity and collective conflict.

Background

South Africa today has a workforce of some 13.1 million of whom almost a quarter are employed in the informal sector. Unemployment is high; about a quarter of the working age population is unemployed, but these figures disguise differences based on age and ethnicity. Unemployment is significantly higher amongst blacks than whites and just over half of all youths aged 15–24 of African origin are unemployed (Benjamin, 2013).

From the discovery of gold and diamonds in South Africa in the nineteenth century and the ensuing colonisation and industrialisation, South

African employment relations were characterised by gross racial disparities, with white South Africans being given certain employment rights under Acts passed in 1924 and 1937. After the Nationalist Party came to power in 1948 with its policy of separate development/apartheid, disparities between white and black workers became more deeply entrenched with the adoption of the Industrial Conciliation Act in 1956. This Act banned multiracial trade unions and barred non-white workers from working in certain occupations (van Niekerk et al., 2012). This legal segregation by race (white, black, coloured and Indian) led to the creation of a white labour aristocracy in reserved jobs who had employment rights and who were institutionally separated from black workers who were excluded from such rights. The latter essentially were unskilled migrants, transient workers or the urban poor often in precarious employment (Donnelly and Dunn, 2006).

In the 1970s the apartheid regime was increasingly challenged by strike action. In response the government first set up a Commission of Inquiry headed by Professor Wiehahn and then passed legislation on the basis of the Commission's recommendations. This legislation provided certain employment and trade union rights to all employees (white or black), allowed mixed-race trade unions and established an Industrial Court with an unfair labour practice jurisdiction.

That Court, however, was understaffed with cases often taking several years, so increasingly disputing parties shunned it and resorted to private dispute resolution, particularly the Independent Mediation Service of South Africa (IMSSA) (Benjamin, 2013). Moreover, although as a result of such changes, black workers began broadly to enjoy formal equality in the workplace, it was not until the apartheid regime ended in 1994, that they became enfranchised and racial segregation became unlawful (Venter and Levy, 2009).

The apartheid regime left a legacy of profound inequality: black unemployment and poverty and skills shortages as a result of apartheid's Bantu education system, while in the last decade the spread of HIV/AIDS has been rampant. It also left a legacy of strong and vocal employers' organisations and trade unions, with the Congress of South African Trade Unions (COSATU) linked to the African National Congress which has been in government since apartheid ended and a tradition of private arbitration to resolve individual employment rights disputes.

Against that background a new system of labour relations conforming to South Africa's new constitution and bill of rights was erected from 1994. The centre piece is the Labour Relations Act (LRA) 66 of 1995, amended in 1996, 1998 and 2002, which established key labour dispute resolution institutions (see below). Another seminal statute was the National Economic Development and Labour Council (NEDLAC) Act 34 of 1994, which created a body to promote social dialogue between key economic and social interests. NEDLAC has four chambers, one of which is the tripartite Labour Market Chamber, whose brief includes considering labour legislation before it is submitted to parliament (van Niekerk et al., 2012). Other important statutes in the 1990s in the employment sphere included the Basic Conditions of Employment Act 75 of 1997 regulating terms and conditions of employment and the Employment Equity Act 55 of 1998 (Donnelly and Dunn, 2006).

Nevertheless, despite new labour dispute resolution institutions and new laws, industrial relations have become increasingly conflictual in the past ten years. Since 2003 there has been an increase both in the number of strikes and the number of working days lost each year accompanied by 'a growth in violence and intimidation, as well as damage to property in strike situations' (Levy, 2013: 18), This violence became headline news across the world when over 34 striking miners were killed at Marikana in 2012.

Conciliation and arbitration

The CCMA and BCs

A primary objective of the new labour law system is the provision of cost effective, speedy and user friendly dispute resolution mechanisms. As a result, central to South African labour relations are conciliation and arbitration, provided either by the Commission for Conciliation, Mediation and Arbitration (CCMA)[1] or by bargaining councils (BCs) or through private arrangements.

The CCMA is governed by a nine-person tripartite body approved by the tripartite NEDLAC (representatives of government and the social partners). This governing body is both advisory and executive; for instance, it makes the final decision on the appointment and termination of office of CCMA commissioners – that is, those individuals who conciliate and arbitrate (Benjamin, 2013).

CCMA commissioners, who are not required to be legally qualified, although many are, are predominantly part-time (60 per cent) (CCMA, 2012a) and half are female (CCMA, 2011). Full-time commissioners are appointed for six years and part-time commissioners for three years. The CCMA has 18 offices (plus the head office) and many satellite offices throughout the country. In addition, in order to make conciliation and arbitration more geographically accessible, commissioners regularly travel to outlying areas and use school halls, community centres, churches and Labour Centres (CCMA, 2012a).

One or more registered trade unions and employers' organisations may register a bargaining council (BC) which may be set up in any sector, whether private or public. At the time of writing there were 47 BCs covering 2½ million workers, that is, over a quarter of the formal workforce (Benjamin, 2013). Consistent with South Africa's tradition of private mediation (see above) and the LRA's philosophy of autonomy and self-regulation within organised sectors, they not only provide sectoral collective bargaining; they also offer dispute resolution including arrangements for conciliation and/or mediation and/or arbitration in respect of individual employment rights (van Niekerk et al., 2012).

BCs can, but do not have to be accredited by the CCMA to carry out dispute resolution. If accredited, they can obtain a subsidy (Benjamin, 2013). Usually accredited BCs use part-time commissioners, but two BCs, metal and engineering (the largest private sector BC) and rail/port transport (Transnet, a parastatal), use the leading private sector dispute resolution agency, Tokiso, whose conciliators and arbitrators known as panellists, are all accredited by the CCMA and may also be part-time CCMA commissioners.

Conciliation

Any worker in the formal or informal sector, for instance a manager or a sex worker, can use the CCMA currently. There are no fees and no service qualifications. All that is required is a simple claim form, with the claimant attaching proof that a copy of the referral form has been served on the respondent (such as a facsimile transmission report).

There are short time limits in which to make a claim. For instance in dismissal disputes the employee must refer the matter to the CCMA within 30 days of the final decision to dismiss, unless the employee shows good cause. In cases of discrimination, the time limit is six months after the claimant became aware of the discriminatory event. Where there is an unfair labour practice an employee has 90 days from the act or omission or when he/she becomes aware of it to apply to the CCMA. If a time limit is not met, a party can apply for condonation of the late referral. This occurs in 10 per cent of cases (Benjamin, 2013) and about three quarters of condonation applications are successful (Venter and Levy, 2013: 26).

In 2011–12 there were 161,588 referrals to the CCMA, with business/professional services being the highest referring sector, followed by retail (CCMA, 2012b: 93). In addition, there are referrals to BCs as well as those referred privately for mediation and arbitration. In total, according to estimates by Venter and Levy (2013), this amounts to some 200,000 referrals each year.

Over the six years from 2006–7 by far the largest category of referrals to the CCMA (around 80 per cent) were dismissals, 'a statistic reflected in all BCs with the exception of the Public Sector Bargaining Council' (Venter and Levy, 2013: 36). There is compulsory conciliation for all CCMA referrals, but first they are screened by administrative staff to ascertain whether the dispute should instead be referred to another institution (for instance a BC or the 'ordinary' courts). Just over a fifth of referrals (22 per cent) were screened out in 2011–12 (Venter and Levy, 2013). According to Benjamin (2009: 28), 'The high number of mis-referrals indicates the extent to which the CCMA is better known and more accessible than the other dispute resolution institutions.' In addition in a minority of cases administrative staff carry out pre-conciliation by telephone and may arrange settlements, although in such cases a commissioner has to step in and issue a certificate. In 2011–12, 20,578 pre-conciliations were initiated, of which just over half resulted in a settlement (Benjamin, 2013).

A CCMA commissioner has 30 days from the date on which the CCMA received the referral to resolve the dispute through conciliation,[2] unless the parties jointly agree to extend the 30 days' period, but the average time taken is 28 days (Benjamin et al., 2010). As to the format of conciliation, the commissioner normally has a round table, face-to-face meeting with all the parties together: the claimant and respondent and the parties' representatives (if there is representation). Furthermore, the commissioner acts as a fact-finder and may also make recommendations. In the interests, however, of keeping the conciliation meeting informal, neither legal representation nor representation by family nor friends are allowed, only representation by registered trade unions and employers' associations. To circumvent this, labour consultancies have registered as employers' organisations or trade unions in order to gain representational rights at the CCMA, although sporadically the Department of Labour deregisters these organisations as it is entitled to do (Venter and Levy, 2012).[3]

At the end of the relevant period for conciliation, the commissioner issues a certificate, specifying whether or not the dispute has been resolved through conciliation. The CCMA's final settlement rate was 72 per cent in 2011–12 (CCMA, 2012a: 43). This figure includes cases that were withdrawn or settled by the parties themselves. Benjamin (2009: 35) calculates that if such cases are excluded, the settlement rate is 'in the vicinity of 50 per cent'.

Where a case is not settled in conciliation, it is often because a party does not attend. The Labour Appeal Court has ruled that a commissioner may not dismiss a case due to non-attendance of a party at the conciliation stage.[4]

Arbitration

If a dispute remains unresolved by conciliation, it can then only be resolved by arbitration (not by the Labour Court), if it concerns unfair dismissal for misconduct or incapacity, dismissal of employees of small employers (less than ten employees) for an operational reason (known as retrenchment),[5] an unfair labour practice related to probation and certain provisions relating to the treatment of part-time and fixed term employees.

At the CCMA the arbitrator can be the same commissioner who conducted the conciliation, or a different one if any of the parties object to using the same commissioner as before. This contrasts with the position in Great Britain (see Chapter 5) where Acas conciliators never arbitrate on any case, never mind the one where they have previously conciliated.

CCMA arbitration is more formal than conciliation: commissioners who are arbitrating have the power to subpoena witnesses (who can be cross-examined by the other side), require witnesses to testify under oath or affirmation, and even enter premises and seize documents.

Nevertheless, the LRA gives the commissioner a wide margin of discretion; for instance he/she may dispense with oral evidence or concluding arguments. As a result the procedure may be investigative rather than adversarial, although this varies according to the personalities of the commissioner and the parties.

As in conciliation parties can self-represent or be represented by an official of a trade union or employers' organisation. Similarly up to now, in the interests of resolving the dispute with a minimum of legal formalities, CCMA rules have provided that legal representation has not normally been allowed in the most common category of arbitration cases (unfair dismissal for misconduct or incapacity), although the arbitrator has discretion to allow it, for example if the case is legally complex. Benjamin (2009) says that there was legal representation in 15 per cent of cases. This restriction on legal representation has recently (October 2012) been successfully challenged in the High Court, which has issued a declaration of constitutional invalidity, but suspending its application for 36 months to enable the CCMA to reframe its rules.[6]

Commissioners have to give their arbitration award in writing along with reasons for their decision within 14 days of the hearing, although some 7 per cent of all awards did not meet this statutory requirement in 2011–12 (CCMA, 2012a: 44). Where the commissioner finds that a dismissal is procedurally unfair, in theory the CCMA may require the employer to pay the arbitration fee, but in practice has rarely done so.[7] In addition, a commissioner is empowered to award costs against a party who has behaved frivolously or vexatiously. Again that is rare: costs were awarded in only one in every 2,000 awards (Venter and Levy, 2013: 26).

Con-Arb

The CCMA is now promoting con-arb, which was introduced by a legislative amendment in 2002. Since then the number of cases finalised through con-arb has been rising and now comprises 41 per cent of all jurisdictional cases (CCMA, 2012b). Con-arb is a one-stop process which is speedier than separate conciliation and arbitration proceedings as the conciliator then morphs into an arbitrator often on the same day. Con-arb can be used for several individual statutory employment rights including unfair dismissal relating to conduct or capacity and unfair labour practices during probation. Normally a con-arb is conducted some four months after referral to the CCMA and almost three quarters are finalised by conciliation, with only a minority being finalised through arbitration (CCMA, 2012b). BCs also provide con-arb.

Nevertheless, the con-arb practice has a high rejection rate from employers 'at around one in three and... nearly one in two of the con-arbs that begin are not finished on the same day largely due to objections' (Venter and Levy, 2012: 31). One view is that con-arb is suitable for small employers, but not for larger employers who have formal and well-structured disciplinary processes and who want separate conciliation and arbitration processes so that they can have time post-conciliation to assess the other side's case (Venter and Levy, 2012).

Inquiry by an arbitrator

Arbitration can be held before termination, as well as after it. This is because there can be an inquiry by an arbitrator[8] (formerly called pre-dismissal arbitration) by the CCMA, a Bargaining Council or an accredited agency such as Tokiso at the request of an employer and with the employee's consent. It is thus voluntary, is not free (with the employer normally paying) and is final as an employee may not apply to the CCMA after dismissal. In the six months until 30 September 2012 the CCMA conducted 51 such arbitrations (CCMA, 2012b). This number has been rising from a low base, albeit slowly and may gather pace. This is because an amendment, being put into effect at the time of writing, enables such so-called inquiries to be provided for in collective agreements, while high paid employees (the amount yet to be set by the Minister) will be able to agree in their contract of employment to such an inquiry (see amendment to s.188A LRA 1995).

Default awards

The CCMA/ BCs can issue what is known as a default award if the employer is not present at the arbitration hearing and there is a high number of default awards. Research by Venter and Levy (2013), looking at all awards issued in the four years from April 2008 found that 35 per cent of CCMA arbitration awards were default awards, compared to 22 per cent of awards by BCs, but default awards rose to 60 per cent in CCMA con-arbs, as opposed to 24 per cent where the CCMA had held an arbitration hearing separately from a previous conciliation meeting.

An employer against whom a default award was made can apply for rescission, a procedure which allows a commissioner to withdraw an award on a range of technical grounds, including where the employer has shown that the notification of the hearing had not been received. A further arbitration hearing is held if a rescission application is granted, thus causing duplication of work and further pressure on CCMA resources. According to Benjamin (2009) in 2007–8, rescission applications were made in over four-fifths of default awards and of these the majority (62 per cent) were granted.

Enforcement of awards

The failure of a substantial number of employers to comply with arbitration awards is the Achilles heel of the system. If an employer fails to comply with an award providing for compensation/reinstatement, the worker must first apply to the institution that carried out the arbitration to get the award certified, that is, declared bona fide. If the award is for compensation, the worker must then apply to the Labour Court whose registrar will issue a writ of execution enabling the worker to approach a sheriff to seize the goods of the non-complying party. The sheriff normally only does so after the worker has paid a deposit to cover the costs that may be incurred by the sheriff, for instance if the company has moved, or has since closed down. Many cannot afford a deposit. Where there is non-compliance of an award providing for reinstatement or reengagement,[9] the worker has to institute contempt proceedings at the Labour Court.

According to Venter and Levy (2012: 53), '[Enforcement] is a messy and protracted process that only the most persistent person can endure'. As a result many awards are at best seriously delayed and at worst denied to the worker. At the time of writing, the enforcement provisions are being simplified by amendments to LRA 1995 s.143: first, certification will no longer be required in the case of awards which are enforced by contempt proceedings in the Labour Court (e.g. reinstatement); second, where awards are for compensation, a party will not be required to obtain a writ from the Labour Court; third, costs after service will be taxed at the Magistrate Court's scale which is lower than the High Court's scale which previously applied.

CCMA achievements

The CCMA has been a victim of its own success in conciliating and arbitrating. It receives over 600 referrals for each working day. As noted above, at least half of all conciliations end in a settlement, while only a small percentage of CCMA awards are reviewed by the Labour Court – 10–15 per cent (Benjamin, 2013). In its first 15 years the CCMA has had to establish and equip offices, recruit and train commissioners, interpreters and staff and develop and implement policies, procedures and a case management system. Accordingly '[u]ntil recently the focus in dispute management and prevention services have been awareness raising and capacity building by developing and sharing best practice' (Everett, 2012: 15). Now the CCMA is taking a more proactive approach, for example proposing alternatives to large-scale retrenchments in partnership with other organisations (Everett and Daphne, 2012).

Private arbitration

Last but not least is private arbitration. As noted above, private arbitration has a long history in South African industrial relations, mainly because there was distrust of the apartheid courts, and it still remains an important component of the system of labour dispute resolution, especially in relation to dismissal. For example, Anglogold Ashanti has a longstanding agreement with the National Union of Mineworkers which provides for conciliation by mine-based bodies, with unresolved cases being referred to arbitration by an arbitrator drawn from an agreed panel. Private arbitration has probably declined in popularity in recent years because it carries a cost, unlike the CCMA which is free. Nevertheless, for those, albeit a minority, who wish to avoid the statutory route, it remains a significant institution, while some senior executives have clauses in their contract requiring them to resort to binding private arbitration in the event of a dispute.

The courts

The Labour Court

The 'ordinary' common law courts in South Africa do not deal with employment rights adjudication routinely because, in addition to the CCMA, another key institution established under the LRA 1995 is the Labour Court. This is a single first-instance court of High Court status, with national jurisdiction in respect of both collective issues and individual issues. The latter include, for instance, if a dismissal is alleged to be automatically unfair (e.g. because of pregnancy or an unfair labour practice), if a dismissal is because of retrenchments for operational reasons and involves more than one employee, or if there has been employment discrimination (see Figure 10.1). Surprisingly the Labour Court hears very few cases of discrimination, which accounted for just 2 per cent of its caseload in 2011 (Bosch,

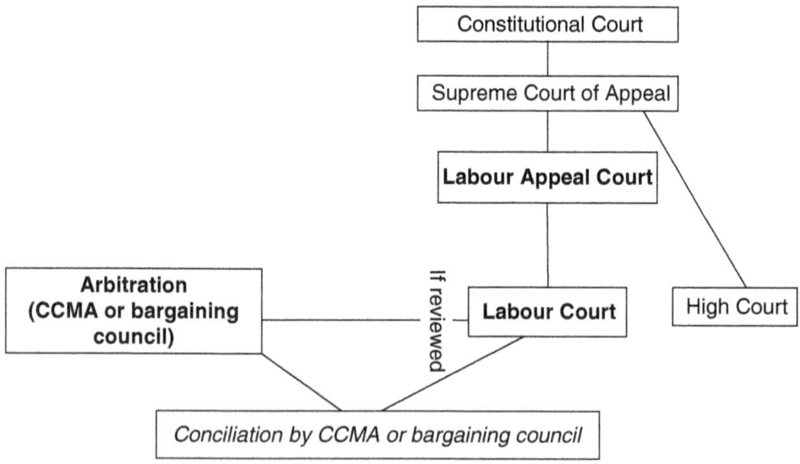

Figure 10.1 Adjudication in South Africa

Notes:

1. The bulk of employment rights cases go to the bodies shown in bold type.
2. The Labour Relations Act specifies which cases are to be resolved through arbitration (primarily dismissal for conduct or capability) and which cases go to the Labour Court.
3. The Labour Court has the power to review arbitration awards.
4. A case can go straight to the Constitutional Court from a lower court.

2013: 71), even though South Africa has very detailed and well-developed discrimination legislation and a legacy of discrimination.

Labour Court judges are appointed currently for ten years. A legislative amendment (Superior Courts Bill) that had not yet reached the statute book at the time of writing will provide for judicial appointment until retirement or appointment to another superior court (the current position for High Court judges). NEDLAC has an input into the appointment of Labour Court judges; this takes the form of having NEDLAC personnel sitting alongside personnel from the Judicial Services Commission when interviews are held for the selection of labour court judges, who are drawn from experienced legal practitioners (advocates or attorneys). There are no career judges as in much of continental Europe. Once appointed, a judge sits alone.

There is no filing fee and a party can self-represent, be represented by an advocate or attorney, or by an official of a registered trade union or a registered employers' association. Representation by a friend/family member is not permitted. Of course legal representation can be costly, and to meet this, there is legal aid, while the Society of Labour Lawyers of South Africa has established a *pro bono* scheme. Under it, over 4,000 clients were assisted in the 18 months up to 5 October 2012.[10] The Court has discretion to award costs taking into account the requirements of law and fairness. In practice, costs are not routinely awarded, as they are in the common law courts, where costs follow the result.

The Labour Court has overlapping jurisdiction with the High Court on certain matters. Although the extent of overlap was recently narrowed by the Constitutional Court,[11] there is still potential for forum shopping. For instance, both the Labour Court and the High Court have jurisdiction on contract of employment matters.[12] Moreover, the High Court recently gave judgment on CCMA rules,[13] so it occasionally has a significant role in individual employment rights adjudication (van Niekerk et al., 2012).

Reviews of arbitration awards

The Labour Court also serves as a forum for reviewing arbitration awards as noted above and nearly half (44 per cent) of its decisions are in respect of reviews. Examining the Labour Court's activity on reviews in 2011, 54 per cent of its judgments related to reviews of CCMA awards, 44 per cent to reviews of BC awards and the remainder to reviews of awards by other institutions (Bosch, 2013: 72).

A review application has to be filed at the Labour Court within six weeks of the award (although there are procedures for the condonation of late filing), but thereafter the process is driven by the parties who have to supply to the Court in advance of the hearing not only affidavits and heads of argument, but also a transcript of the arbitration award. (Arbitration awards are always recorded and this recording is provided to the parties, but the applicant then has to transcribe the recording.) According to Bosch (2013), the average time elapsing from the date of issue of the arbitration award to the date of the review judgment was 936 days in 2011 and an application for a review can be used strategically as a delaying tactic, as the Labour Court often receives an application to stay the enforcement of an award pending the outcome of the review. In such a case, a judge considers a wide range of factors, including and importantly the interests of justice (Savage, 2013).

These delaying tactics are now being restricted. First, the applicant must file the transcript of the record of the arbitration hearing within 60 days of being informed that it may be obtained from the registrar and will be deemed to have withdrawn the application if the transcript is not filed within the prescribed period (Labour Court, 2013: 19–20). Second, amendments to the LRA (not yet promulgated at the time of writing) provide that applicants will be required to apply for a hearing date within six months of their application and a review application will not normally have the effect of suspending an arbitration award unless the applicant furnishes some security.

Looking at the outcome of reviews in the Labour Court in 2011, half of applications succeeded, and of those that succeeded, the Labour Court replaced the outcome of the award with their own decision in 62 per cent of cases. Otherwise the parties were required to have a de novo arbitration hearing (Bosch, 2013). When the LRA was formulated, it was decided not to allow appeals against arbitration awards, but instead to have the narrower test of a review. As the Explanatory Memorandum of the Department of Labour (1995: 142) said: 'The absence of an appeal from the arbitrator's award speeds up the process and frees it from the legalism that accompanies appeal proceedings... [A]ppeals lead to records, lengthy proceedings, lawyers, legalism, inordinate delays and high costs.'

In practice, however, the test for a review and the test for an appeal have become blurred. In the leading case of *Sidumo*,[14] the Constitutional Court said the test for review 'Is the decision reached by the commissioner one that a reasonable decision maker could not reach?' This was fleshed out by the Supreme Court of Appeal in *Herholdt v Nedbank Ltd* where it was held (para. 25) that for the courts to set aside a CCMA arbitration award:[15]

> the arbitrator must have misconceived the nature of the inquiry or arrived at an unreasonable result. A result will only be unreasonable if it is one that a reasonable arbitrator could not reach on all the material that was before the arbitrator. Material errors of fact are not in and of themselves sufficient for an award to be set aside, but are only of any consequence if their effect is to render the outcome unreasonable.

The *Sidumo* test of reasonableness, however, does not apply where the Labour Court reviews private arbitration awards where they concern employment matters. Here the test is narrower (such as bias or corruption of the arbitrator) as set out in s.33 of the Arbitration Act and not the wider test under the LRA.

Labour Appeal Court

The Labour Appeal Court (LAC) hears appeals from the Labour Court. They are not limited to points of law, but leave has to be granted by the LC or, failing that, the LAC can be petitioned. There were 80 appeals in 2010 (Rycroft, 2012) and appeals can be brought on fact and/or law. In theory, at the request of a party, the Labour Appeal Court can sit as a court of first instance, if the judge-president agrees. In practice this has only happened twice in 17 years.[16]

There are a number of similarities between the LC and the LAC. First, the appointment process for LAC judges involving NEDLAC is similar to that of the LC (see above) and similarly judicial appointment is for ten years.[17] Second, representation in the LAC follows that in the LC: a party can self-represent, be represented by an advocate or attorney or by an official of a registered trade union or a registered employers' association. Representation by a friend/family member is not permitted. Third there is no filing fee and costs are not normally awarded to the successful party.

Nevertheless there are important differences between these two courts in terms of composition and procedure. First, an appeal in the LAC is heard by three judges, not a judge alone as in the LC. The decision can be either unanimous or by a majority and, if the latter, the judgment records both the majority's reasons and the minority's reasons. Second, whereas most of the judges in the LC are full-time, in the LAC only the Judge President and the Deputy Judge President are full-time and other LAC judges are drawn from other divisions of the High Court and, pursuant to an amendment to LRA 1995 s.168, from the Labour Court.

The LAC existed before the LRA. (It heard appeals from an Industrial Court which was abolished after apartheid ended.) Between 1988 and 1996 the LAC was constituted with a Supreme Court judge and two lay assessors, one representing workers and one representing employers. This was consistent with South Africa's High Court composition at the time, which also used assessors. These assessors were not limited to questions of fact and could in theory (but rarely in practice) overrule the judge as each person had an equal vote. In practice, most of those who were then LAC assessors were practising lawyers who sat on a *pro bono* basis.

The drafters of the LRA, according to one drafter interviewed, considered retaining assessors and thus emulating the wing members in the Employment Appeal Tribunal in Great Britain. Their main concern, however, was to make the LAC like the Supreme Court of Appeal. Accordingly, when the LAC was reconstituted by the LRA, it was established with three judges (not one judge and two assessors).

Supreme Court of Appeal

When the Labour Relations Act (LRA) was drafted in 1994, the Interim Constitution (promulgated in 1993) was in force and the drafters of the LRA designed a specialist and separate labour adjudication system, with the LAC as the final appeal court except on constitutional matters. In 1996 the final Constitution was adopted and s.168 states: 'The Supreme Court of Appeal may decide appeals in any matter. It is the highest court of appeal except in constitutional matters.'

Probably as a result of an oversight by the drafters of the Constitution, the LRA became inconsistent with the Constitution and the latter trumped the former. The Superior Courts Bill (before parliament at the time of writing) will remove the SCA from the appellate chain in most matters dealt with by the LC, but for the time being appeals can be made from the LAC to the non-specialist SCA. In practice, however, this occurs only rarely. For instance in the calendar year 2011 the SCA heard only six appeals from the LAC, comprising less than 0.1 per cent of its work and in the first six months of 2012 it heard no appeals from the LAC at all.[18]

Appeals can be made on fact and/or law but there is no automatic right of appeal to the SCA. Leave has to be granted by the SCA. Furthermore, appeals have to be made within a month of the date of the LAC judgment, although appeals made after that date may perhaps be condoned. The appellant has a further three months from the date of appeal to provide a record of the proceedings in the court below.

When hearing appeals, the SCA sits in panels of five or three judges, depending on the nature of the appeal and a party can self-represent, or be represented by an advocate or senior attorney. Officials of trade unions or employers' associations cannot appear. The decision can be either unanimous or by a majority and in the latter case the judgment records both the majority and minority reasons (Supreme Court of Appeal South Africa, 2012). There is no filing fee and costs generally follow the result.

The Constitutional Court

The South African constitution provides a unique constitutional right. S.23(1) states: 'Everyone has the right to fair labour practices.' The constitution also provides in s.33(1) that: 'Everyone has the right to administrative action that is lawful, reasonable and procedurally fair' and the Constitutional Court has held that the CCMA is an administrative body. Against that background, the Constitutional Court has developed a significant jurisprudence in respect of employment matters (van Niekerk et al., 2012); see, for instance, the test for the review of arbitration awards (*Sidumo* above); whether HIV positive status is grounds for refusal of the offer of employment,[19] and rights on the transfer of undertakings.[20]

The Constitutional Court consists of 11 judges appointed for a non-renewable term of between 12 and 15 years depending on the age of the judge when first appointed. Although the quorum is eight judges, in practice normally all 11 judges hear a case and decisions are by a majority. Each judge has two law clerks, who essentially act as researchers. They are appointed for one year, and generally hold, or are about to be awarded, a law degree.

There is no automatic right of appeal. It is for the judges of the constitutional Court to decide if an important principle relating to the constitution has been raised. In theory a person can bring a matter directly to the Constitutional Court but in practice a constitutional matter in relation to employment rights reaches the Constitutional Court from the SCA or the LAC.

There is virtually no filing fee, just a revenue stamp of 75 rand[21] is required on the original initiating document, and private litigants who bring constitutional claims, including non-governmental organisations, are given some measure of protection against exposure to adverse costs awards (Constitutional Court of South Africa, 2012).

Labour Inspectorate

A Labour Inspectorate, part of the Department of Labour, enforces labour legislation including the Basic Conditions of Employment Act (BCEA), the Employment Equity Act and sectoral determinations of minimum wages for low-paid workers who are not covered by collective agreements. This Inspectorate carries out both proactive and reactive inspections but there are several shortcomings. First, there is an acute shortage of labour inspectors owing to a high turnover leading to a vacancy rate of 14.2 per cent in 2010; second, there are concerns about the quality of inspectors as two-thirds do not have a university degree; third, there are poor data gathering and record keeping systems (Benjamin, 2011).

Labour inspectors have extensive powers to enter workplaces, question persons and inspect documents. Enforcement, which is cumbersome, in practice is through administrative and civil procedures as criminal prosecutions are extremely rare. Inspectors must first endeavour to secure a written undertaking from the employer if the provisions of the BCEA have been flouted.[22] Then if the employer does not commit to a written undertaking or fails to honour one, inspectors can issue compliance orders, against which the employer can appeal to the Director-General, who can confirm, modify or cancel the compliance order. An employer may appeal to the Labour Court against an order of the Director-General, while if the employer continues not to comply with the compliance order, the Department can apply to the Labour Court for the compliance order to be made a court order. If the employer fails to comply with the court order a writ can be issued and the sheriff is instructed to seize the assets of the employer (Benjamin, 2011). In short, according to Savage (2013: 52):

> This lengthy process is not only time-consuming and costly to the state but allows the employer to raise a host of technical points along the way... [I]f employers do not pay, the Department of Labour regularly does not proceed to enforce against the employer.

Employers are concerned about corruption issues within the Inspectorate, while trade unions are critical of the low level of enforcement and both employers and trade unions favour the establishment of a tripartite advisory body to have oversight of the Labour Inspectorate (Benjamin, 2011), but there has been no legislative change up to the time of writing.

Conclusions

There are noticeable strains in South African labour relations at the time of writing, as discrimination persists yet appears to be largely unreported, let alone a basis for litigation, and adversarialism in industrial relations has increased.[23] The latter development has been reflected in an increasing number of strikes and a resort to violence. Moreover, nearly 20 years after apartheid ended there remain high levels of inequality, low skills, unemployment and a large informal sector, particularly among the black population (Everett, 2012).

This provides a challenging background for the work of the institutions for resolving disputes. Additionally, there are in-house challenges in respect of recruiting and training CCMA commissioners, the enforcement of arbitration awards and the looming requirement for legal representation at CCMA arbitration hearings (see above), which is likely to lead to greater formality. Nevertheless, and perhaps paradoxically, given the industrial relations environment, the CCMA has essentially provided a speedy and relatively informal system of adjudication for conduct and capability dismissals, with only a minority of its arbitration awards being reviewed by the Labour Court. Moreover, the CCMA is increasingly playing a proactive role in job-saving strategies (Benjamin, 2013). At the same time, the judgments of the Labour Court and the Labour Appeal Court continue to command respect from a wide range of commentators.

11
Sweden

Introduction

Sweden has a unique system for the referral of employment rights disputes to judicial adjudication, both individual and collective, under which cases cannot be brought to the Labour Court by a worker, although he/she can go to the District Court. Only trade unions, the Discrimination Ombudsman, an employers' association, or an employer who has entered into a collective agreement can lodge claims. The Labour Court itself has a mixed composition of legally qualified presiding members, expert members drawn from government departments or public agencies and nominees of the main labour market actors.

Both the composition of the Labour Court and the access provisions for the parties reflect the high level of collective bargaining coverage and the role of collective agreements in employment regulation. There is no appeal from Labour Court decisions. The District (civil Courts deal with any employment cases that fall outside of the scope of the Labour Court, but appeals from the District Courts go to the Labour Court. Thus the Labour Court, unusually, is both a court of first instance and a court of last instance.

After sketching in the background, we first look at the provisions relating to the Labour Court, including the steps necessary to bring a claim and the Labour Court's composition, procedures and judgments. We then turn to the District Courts and quasi-judicial bodies, before making some concluding observations.

Background and origins

Collective agreements have effective primacy in many aspects of labour jurisdiction and there are some 60 unions and 50 employers' associations and they negotiate some 600 collective agreements (Diskrimineringsombudsmannen, 2009). Bargaining takes place at various levels: the most important is the national level at which nationwide collective agreements are negotiated for whole sectors, but there are also single employer collective agreements and, in addition, there may be supplementary workplace agreements. These collective agreements cover many areas of working life, not just pay, hours and holidays and the provisions of collective agreements are legally binding on signatories and members of signatory organisations. The strength of collective bargaining as a central regulatory instrument is illustrated by the fact that there are no statutory extension mechanisms for collective agreements and nor is there a statutory minimum wage, an issue highlighted by the *Laval* case (Woolfson et al., 2010).

Almost 70 per cent of the labour force and 85 per cent of companies are members of their respective social partner organisations, and collective agreements cover some 90 per cent of the labour force. Levels of union density amongst white-collar and professional employees are as high as for manual workers (European Commission, 2011; Scheuer, 2011)[1] and the main route for enforcement of individual statutory rights, for instance because of a dismissal or discrimination, is through a collective procedure and a claim to the Labour Court. Accordingly the Labour Court both develops case-law on the application and interpretation of collective agreements (such as the scope for employer prerogative or implicit non-written terms) and on the application and interpretation of employment legislation, for instance legislation governing employment protection, parental leave and discrimination in employment on grounds of gender, ethnicity, religion or other belief, age, sexual orientation, transgender identity and expression, disability.

Sweden's prioritisation of collectivism as a criterion for accessing its Labour Court has a long history. The Swedish Labour Court (*Arbetsdomstolen*) was created in 1929 in the wake of the 1928 Collective Agreements Act that had marked a further step in the consolidation of the 'Swedish model' of industrial relations. The Court's primary task was to deal with disputes on the interpretation and application of collective agreements and disputes relating to the non-strike requirements of the 1928 Act. In 1947 collective agreements covering salaried employees were brought within the Labour Court's scope and from 1966 public sector employees could be covered by collective agreements, like their private sector counterparts.

The jurisdiction of the Labour Court was widened in 1974 by the Labour Disputes (Judicial Procedure) Act, 1974 (LDA), to cover virtually all aspects of employment law, in addition to all aspects of collective agreements, to enable trade unions to bring all cases on behalf of their members, including those concerning individual rights. In 1977, the LDA was amended to prevent trade union members not supported by their union from bringing claims to the Labour Court. As a result, today any 'labour dispute' – collective or individual – to use the term in the LDA, which affects the relationship between employer(s) and employee(s) is within the Labour Court's scope, but only trade unions, the Discrimination Ombudsman, employers' associations and employers can bring claims (Arbetsdomstolen, n.d.).

Before a claim to the Labour Court

When a labour dispute arises and if the worker(s) is a member of the union and covered by a collective agreement there are initially formal local negotiations between the most senior workplace manager and the local union representative. These negotiations may involve several meetings and most issues are settled locally, providing a significant filter.

If there is no resolution, however, the next stage is central negotiations between the trade union official and the employers' association official. According to interviewees, these negotiations are more formal, often with the parties' lawyers providing advice and most cases which reach this stage are settled, so providing a further filter.

Where a worker(s) complains to the Discrimination Ombudsman[2] (DO), and there were 700 complaints in 2011 to the DO that were related to employment, the DO advises the worker to approach his/her union. If the worker is not a union member, or if the union does not wish to take the complaint further, the DO will investigate. After investigation, it takes no further action in the vast majority of cases. For instance in 2011 it settled 23 cases and brought seven to the Labour Court.

Bringing a claim to the Labour Court

As noted above, a worker cannot make a claim directly to the Labour Court. Such a claim has to be made on their behalf by a trade union or the Discrimination Ombudsman. This distinguishes the Swedish system from the employment rights adjudication systems in all the other countries in this book.

A trade union can only bring a claim on behalf of a worker if the worker is a member of the trade union, supported by the union and covered by a relevant collective agreement. In other words, the case must either directly involve a dispute arising out of a collective agreement or the Codetermination Act (sometimes called the 'Joint Regulation Act' to distinguish it from German legislation with the same name), or a dispute between parties who are subject to a collective agreement. For example, provided the employee and employer are within the scope of a collective agreement, a dispute over termination of contract under the Employment Protection Act 1982 will be dealt with on the worker's behalf by the trade union and before the Labour Court. In turn, many of the provisions of this Act, such as seniority rules for redundancies, will have been derogated from by collective agreement. Redundancy payments are provided solely through collective agreements.

The Codetermination Act 1976 (*Medbestämmandelagen*) is a wide-ranging piece of legislation that regulates employee involvement in working life in a variety of ways, including the right of trade unions to negotiate on any aspect of the employment relationship. Employers are required to consult local trade unions before implementing major changes, such as transfers of undertaking and redundancies. Employers are liable for damages if they fail to consult. However, employer prerogatives remain intact, provided consultation takes place. The Act also stipulates whose interests should prevail while a dispute is being resolved, which varies depending on the issue. The 1976 Act also includes provisions on freedom of association.

The Discrimination Ombudsman (DO) can bring a case to the Labour Court on behalf of a worker if the case concerns an employment matter, whether or not the worker is a trade union member and/or covered by a collective agreement.[3]

As to employers and their associations, an employers' association may bring a claim in its own right or on behalf of an employer who is a member of that association either in relation to a sectoral agreement or in relation to a single-employer agreement: this could deal with a collective matter, such as the timing of industrial action, or an individual issue such as recovery of a worker's wages because of inadvertent overpayment. Similarly an employer who has a collective agreement can also bring a claim to the Labour Court.

There is no pro forma claim form; a party lodging a claim must apply in writing setting out the particulars of the claim and providing an account of the disputed issue. There is no fee required and the time limit for bringing a claim is set out in the collective agreement. It is usually four months after the matter in dispute has come to light. Where a case involves a dismissal, an employee remains in employment until the case is determined by the Labour Court, except for summary dismissals or if the Labour Court has decided otherwise.

After receiving the claim, the Labour Court issues a notice of appearance to the respondent. If a union has brought a claim on behalf of the worker, the respondent may be both the employers' association and the company.

The Labour Court has only one location, Stockholm, but as the parties bringing the claim are in the main national organisations, they generally have national headquarters in Stockholm.

Pre-hearings

The Labour Court follows largely the same judicial processes and procedures as the civil courts and, in particular, the Code of Judicial Procedure. Initial case management normally takes place through written communication but in all Swedish first-instance courts there is normally an oral pre-hearing and the Labour Court is no exception. Accordingly, some six months after a Labour Court claim has been lodged, there is a pre-hearing both for case management and for an attempt at settlement.

The pre-hearing is held by a chair alone (LDA, s.7) or by a so-called secretary, where the case is thought not to be significant. These secretaries are legally trained and are in essence trainee or apprentice judges who are on the first rungs of the professional judicial career ladder. They are often very experienced as all Swedish courts have secretaries and often the Labour Court's secretaries have previously been secretaries in another court. The Labour Court has four secretaries and four assistant secretaries. Accompanying the pre-hearing chair is a secretary who takes notes and does not speak. (If a secretary is in the chair, another more junior secretary takes notes).

The chair has a duty to explore the scope for a settlement at the pre-hearing. Normally one side (e.g. the union's attorney accompanied by the union official and the worker(s) involved) has one room and the other side (e.g. the employers' association attorney and the chief executive of the company concerned) has the other room and the chair shuttles between the two rooms, seeking to conciliate.

Some 400–425 claims per annum are made to the Labour Court and about half were settled before a full hearing in 2010–11, according to the then Chief Judge. If they are not, the full hearing follows some six months after the pre-hearing. The same judge will conduct both the pre-hearing and the full hearing, so he/she never gives an opinion on the prospect of success if the case were to proceed to a full hearing. If a secretary chairs the pre-hearing, then he/she will normally act as the secretary at the full hearing.

Labour Court membership

The Labour Court has had a tripartite composition since its formation in 1929 and now consists of 25 people. Of the 11 official/neutral members four are professional judges serving as chairs (one for each of the Labour Court's departments of whom one is the Chief Judge), four are vice-chairs, and three are labour market experts, that is persons with 'insight into labour market conditions', who are not required to be legally qualified (LDA, 1974). These experts are, for instance, a senior person in a relevant government agency or an official with responsibility for a standing parliamentary committee on employment. In addition to these official/neutral judges there are 14 employer/employee side members who serve as judges.

The four chairs are full-time and are appointed until retirement, but the vice-chairs are part-time, typically working in other courts. The non-professional judges are also part-time in the Labour Court and are otherwise working in, or have retired from social partner organisations, or in the case of the labour market experts a government department or agency. Both the professional and lay judges are required to take the judicial oath. Lay judges are appointed by the government for a period of three years, usually renewed, with many serving for a considerable period.

The employer side and the trade union side nominate ('recommend') seven members each to the Ministry of Employment and in practice all these 'recommendations' are accepted automatically. The union side members in Sweden tend to be national officials or retired national officials as opposed to those in Great Britain, where local union representatives commonly are lay judges at the first-instance labour court, not national union officials. There is an organised arrangement set out under statute under which both the employer and employee side comprise nominees from a range of bodies representing the spectrum of economic life, including separate representation for private and public employers, white-collar workers and the graduate professions.

Of the 14 members, 13 are appointed on the recommendation of the main social partner organisations as follows:

- Four members are nominated by the Confederation of Swedish Enterprises *(Svenskt Näringsliv, SN)*.
- One member is nominated by the Swedish Association of Local Authorities (*Sveriges Kommuner och Landsting*).
- One member is nominated by the Swedish Federation of County Councils.
- Four members are nominated by the Swedish Trade Union Confederation (LO), which represents a range of occupations, including manual and technical, and which has 1.7 million members, and is linked to, but independent of the Social Democrats.
- Two members are nominated by the Swedish Confederation of Professional Employees (TCO), which primarily represents professional and qualified employees. It has roughly 50/50 public/private split so traditionally draws one of its nominees from the public sector and one from the private sector. It has 1.2 million members, of which 60 per cent are women. It has no political affiliation.
- One member is nominated by the Swedish Confederation of Professional Associations (SACO), which represents a range of graduate professions through a number of professional affiliates (teachers, academics, engineers etc.).

The 14th member is appointed by the Ministry as a representative of the state as an employer.

The nominating organisations may receive guidance from the Ministry, for instance on securing a gender balance when nominating, but the Ministry does not set rules on retirement for the non-professional judges. Indeed, the nominating organisations have different policies on the retirement of their nominees. For instance the LO does not re-nominate a lay judge after retirement from union employment, while the TCO has now decided that it will recommend re-nomination only twice after retirement, having previously allowed TCO nominees to determine when they no longer wished to sit.

Also 'recommended' to the Ministry and then appointed are the stand-ins or deputies. The vice-chairs deputise for the chairs, but everyone else, the vice-chairs, the labour market experts and the social partner nominees, each have three stand-ins or deputies. So, for instance, when an 'ordinary' social partner nominee cannot sit, she/he contacts the office of the president of the nominating organisation and an administrator will then seek one of the three stand-ins as a replacement. Occasionally, when neither the 'ordinary' member nor one of his/her three stand-ins is available, a temporary stand-in can be appointed on an *ad hoc* basis by the chair. Typically a temporary stand-in is a person who has previously served in the Labour Court.

All those selected for nomination by the social partner organisations are chosen by informal means. There is no formal system of self-nomination. Those nominated by the employers' organisations often are legally trained (although that is not a requirement), but trade union side members are generally not legally trained.

The third or neutral persons, that is, the labour market experts, are appointed by the government, but there is no formal application process. As, however, Sweden is a comparatively small country (population 9.5 million) the Employment Ministry is aware of potentially suitable people with insight into labour market conditions.

The employee and employer side members and the neutral expert received 1,500 Swedish kroner per hearing day[4] at the time of writing, but nothing extra for reading the papers in advance or reading/amending the draft judgment. An 'ordinary' member typically sits up to 30 or 40 times a year and a stand-in may sit about five or six times a year.

The full hearing

The chair can only sit alone on certain procedural matters, such as staying a case or issuing a default judgment, while for other procedural matters there is a so-called lawyers' composition, typically two professional judges and a secretary such as whether new evidence can be submitted for an appeal. Otherwise the Labour Court must include non-legal/lay judges.

In practice, the number of professional and lay judges hearing a case is tailored to the nature of the dispute: however, for the most part a full hearing normally comprises seven people, three of whom are neutral members. Of these three neutral members, two must be legally qualified professional judges (the chair and vice chair), and the third is a labour market expert. These three people sit with two members each from the employer-side and the employee-side. No one wears robes.

At the chair's discretion, the Labour Court may sit with a reduced composition, but only if an equal number of employer and employee representatives are present. For instance a chair may sit with one employee side member and one employer side member on cases that the chair considers to be not very complicated.

In cases brought by the DO, however, the Labour Court normally is composed of five people for a full hearing: three neutral members and only one each from the employer and worker side. The rationale is that the employer side and the employee side member have a mutual interest in defending their agreements and thus preserving the status quo at the workplace to the detriment of those from a minority group and thus the neutral members in discrimination cases should be able to outvote the employer/employee members. This provision was brought in from 1 January 2009 after the then gender equality Ombudsman had lost many cases on wage discrimination to the consternation of female Members of Parliament.[5,6]

The chair designates a case as 'general' or 'special' and the split is about 50/50. The former concerns the application of employment legislation. The latter concerns the application of a collective agreement and the employer/employee members are chosen from the sector of the labour market in which the dispute arises, provided there are no conflicts of interest. For instance if it is a 'special' case in the TCO area, the two union side judges are generally from the TCO union confederation, either a union side judge who had retired some time ago or an employed person who is not from the union that was a party to the collective agreement. For a 'general' case the two employee side members will not be from the same union confederation as a party.

A full hearing normally takes place eight to ten months after the claim has been lodged. All those who will hear the case receive the papers several days in advance. A full hearing normally lasts at least a day and often a day and a half, and the procedure is adversarial with both sides legally represented. The employers' associations normally have their own legal departments, while the largest trade union confederations (the LO and the TCO) jointly own a legal services company which only takes LO/TCO cases.

Witnesses attend and give evidence on oath and do not draw up written witness statements in advance. Proceedings are recorded normally just as an aide-memoire, not an official record and a secretary is present taking notes, again as an aide-memoire and not an official record. The recordings and notes are normally destroyed after the judgment has been sent to the parties.

Judgments

Decisions are always reserved and sent to the parties about seven weeks from the date of the hearing. The judgments are detailed, generally about

25 pages. Normally a secretary will provide the first draft for the chair, who will then redraft and send to all the others who heard the case who, after perusing the draft and amending where appropriate, sign the judgment.

Judgments of the Labour Court are subject to a vote and each member of the Court has one vote with any dissent announced. In principle, the non-legal members can outvote the professional judges and experts, although this has only reportedly happened once (in 1947).[7] According to former Chief Judge Michaël Koch (Koch, 2002: 3) 'about 85 per cent of all judgments of the Labour Court are unanimous. In the remaining 15 per cent of the cases, it is mostly one or two of the lay members who disagree'. He comments that 'lay members certainly do not see their role as that of representative of "their" side of the industry. On the contrary, they obviously act as independent judges' (ibid.) In 2012 Judge Koch, when interviewed, estimated that the proportion of unanimous judgments had risen in the ten years since he had made that comment.

If there is dissent, it is recorded in the judgment. In a typical year the Labour Court issued 224 judgments of which 96 (43 per cent) were published. The chair asks the other members whether the judgment should be published or not.

Costs normally follow the event, that is, the losing party has to pay the winning party's costs in addition to their own costs. Very occasionally the Court decides that both parties should bear their own costs, for instance if both parties have a mutual desire to establish legal clarity on a point. There is no further appeal from the Labour Court's judgment, and judgments can be enforced through the auspices of public bodies in the same way as judgments in other Swedish courts (Arbetsdomstolen, n.d.).[8]

Training

There is now an introductory day for new lay judges, but otherwise no regular training is provided by the State or the Labour Court. According to the Chief Judge of the Labour Court, Michael Koch (2002: 2), 'It is up to the professional judges, primarily the chairman, to explain matters of law and procedure'. He added that 'in practice, the lay members are highly knowledgeable in labour law matters'. He distinguished between the lay members that sit as assessors in Swedish courts and the special nature of the lay members on the Labour Court, whom he preferred to designate 'specialist members'.

In fact most employer-side members and a few employee-side members are legally trained and one neutral labour market expert interviewed had formerly been a secretary in the Labour Court. Furthermore a few nominating bodies may hold meetings for their lay judges, including the stand-ins. For instance the TCO lay judges meet about once a year and they invite the Labour Court's Chief Judge and secretaries to attend and provide information on the latest statistics or pending legislation.

The District Court

Where a worker is not a member of a trade union and not covered by a collective agreement, but wishes to bring a case against their employer the worker must lodge a claim with a District Court (*tingsrätt*), of which there are about 60 in Sweden. Occasionally a large union may have a member at the workplace but no collective agreement with the employer, so a worker goes to the District Court with the support of the union. Similarly an employer who does not have a relevant collective agreement and/or is not a member of an employers' association must lodge a claim with the District Court, although the employer is much more likely to be the respondent at the District Court, than the claimant. There are normally no local or central negotiations prior to a District Court claim, so an employer may only hear about a dispute after the worker has lodged a claim.

The fee for lodging a claim was 450 kroner[9] at the time of writing (unlike the Labour Court where there is no fee). Although the District Court has a pre-hearing, there is less likelihood of a settlement prior to a full hearing. According to an interviewee, this is because discussions between lawyers are less likely to result in a deal than those between an employers' association and a trade union, as lawyers are less accustomed to deal making than are the social partners.

In addition the District Court is normally slower than the Labour Court. It is generally two years before there is a full hearing in the District Court compared to less than one year in the Labour Court. Employment cases are usually heard by three professional judges, with a secretary taking notes, and the standard of judging varies. Stockholm's District Court has a department dealing with employment law, but a judge in some of the rural District Courts may only hear an employment case once every two or three years or even less frequently. Moreover, the approach of the judges in the District Court and in the Labour Court differ, according to an interviewee. The former tend to look at the contract and the latter tend to consider the implications of the decision for the workplace.

As in the Labour Court, costs normally are awarded to the winner, but whereas in the Labour Court the trade union or the DO take the case on behalf of the worker and bear the costs, if a worker loses in the District Court (unless supported by a union) he/she can be saddled with a big bill of perhaps 100,000 kroner for the other side's costs as well as their own costs. Furthermore, the costs can be doubled if there is an unsuccessful appeal (see below). There is legal aid for claims in the District Court, but it only covers those with very low earnings so very few workers qualify for legal aid.

No statistics of the number of employment cases handled by the civil courts have been uncovered but anecdotal evidence suggests that the number is low as the fees, and the fact that costs are normally awarded to the winner serve to discourage putative claimants. Nevertheless, it has become increasingly common in the last few years, albeit from a low base, that individuals are taking cases to the District Court according to two interviewees.[10]

Appeals

As noted above there are no appeals from a first-instance decision in the Labour Court and the Labour Court hears appeals from the District Court, but only if permission to appeal is granted. Normally it takes about three months for permission to appeal to be granted or refused and the decision as to whether to allow an appeal in full or in part is taken by 'lawyer composition', which consists of three professional judges. Typically this means two of the chairmen and a secretary who have perused the papers, the appellant's submissions, the District Court's judgment and, as the District Court's hearing has been videoed from start to finish, they sometimes watch at least part of that video. Appeals are granted both on a point of law and on the facts, and permission is granted in about a third of all cases with no reason given either for acceptance or rejection of an appeal.

There is no pre-hearing before an appeal and normally the Labour Court is composed of seven members (chair and vice chair plus the expert and two employer side and two employee side members) for an appeal hearing. The Labour Court watches the video and thus rehears the case in the District Court completely, as well as hearing submissions from the parties' representatives. A witness cannot give evidence 'live' at an appeal unless permission has been granted and that is very rare. The Labour Court's judgment on an appeal is shorter than its first-instance judgments because it just attaches its judgment at the front of the District Court's judgment. A third of all cases before the Labour Court are appeals from the District Court (Labour Court, 2010).

Quasi-judicial bodies

Apart from the Labour Court and the District Court, employment disputes can be resolved through arbitration. If specified in the contract or the collective agreement recourse to the Labour Court and the District Court can be barred with arbitration in its place. In practice, arbitration on employment matters is limited to certain types of employees: the chief executive of the company and perhaps a few other senior managers, professional footballers and their trainers and those employed by a trade union. In addition, there is arbitration where a worker has a dispute with his/her union. Arbitration can be carried out by a single arbitrator or a panel of three or even five arbitrators and, as with any arbitration, the proceedings and the decision are secret.

There is also a board of arbitration for personal injury at work. A collective agreement normally prescribes that no-fault personal injury insurance is purchased by the employer, the amount typically set as a percentage of the wage bill. If a worker is injured his/her case is against the insurance company and the arbitrators decide whether the injury took place at work and, if so, what compensation should be awarded to the worker. Normally only the parties' representatives attend and any witnesses submit statements, but do not give oral evidence.

There is also a quasi-judicial board to determine cases where a public authority has refused employment and the individual alleges that this has been done unconstitutionally. This covers all public bodies except the courts, education and the military and its decisions are published.

Although there is the National Mediation Office, a government agency, which provides mediators for collective disputes between employers and employees either at the request of the parties or on its own, its remit does not extend to individual rights. Accordingly it is outside the scope of this chapter.

Conclusions

The collective mechanisms that underpin access to the Labour Court for upholding individual rights have their foundation in the continuing high levels of union density and membership by employers of employers' associations and the high coverage of the workforce by collective agreements. In effect, individual disputes are 'collectivised', either through the actors involved (representation by a union) or through the fact that many terms and conditions are directly regulated by collective agreements (in some cases derogating from statute).[11]

Moreover, Sweden is known for its industrial peace and the Labour Court contributes to this: it enjoys the confidence of the social partners and its judgments benefit from the input of the lay judges. The former Chief Judge of the Labour Court (Michaël Koch) highlighted two key contributions made by the lay judges. One was the interpretation of collective agreements based on a knowledge of how agreements are concluded in practice; the second, was the need to interpret labour law, such as an 'objective reason' to warrant termination, where knowledge of workplace practice is important in determining what is reasonable and fair. Indeed a recent government inquiry into the courts attested to the high level of confidence in the Labour Court by stakeholders and concluded that labour disputes should continue to be heard by the Labour Court and not be transferred to the civil courts (Mål och medel, 2010).

Furthermore, the Swedish system is a low cost one for both the public purse and the parties for two reasons. First, the majority of labour disputes are settled through local or central negotiations without the need to go further and lodge a claim with the Labour Court. Second, the Labour Court provides finality as Sweden does not have several appeal stages unlike labour courts in other countries (see for instance France, Germany, Great Britain, New Zealand and South Africa in this book).

Finally, some interviewees considered that the number of cases to the District Court had increased in the last few years and one interviewee was of the view that union density had been declining in some areas. If collectivism were to be seriously eroded, the Swedish system of employment rights adjudication would be threatened. At present, however, there are only a few wispy clouds on the horizon.

12
United States of America

Introduction

In contrast to the other countries covered in this book, the adjudication of individual employment disputes in the United States is increasingly taking place through private arbitration, with awards normally remaining confidential to the parties only, rather than adjudication in a public institution with publicly accessible judgments. This growth of private arbitration over alleged infringements of statutory employment rights stems from the US Supreme Court's rulings requiring the courts to defer to arbitrators' decisions both in unionised and non-unionised workplaces. Moreover, the US Supreme Court has held that an employer/employee agreement to arbitrate a statutory claim, rather than litigate it, does not entail any waiver of an employee's statutory rights; rather it is simply the substitution of an arbitral forum for a court forum.

Where employment disputes are adjudicated by a court, however, they are determined in an 'ordinary' civil court, not a labour court. Moreover, the court system in the United States, unlike the other countries in this book – and even highly federalist Germany (Chapter 4) – is made up of two different systems: alongside a federal court system, which has a national presence and enforces federal employment legislation, each state also has its own state court system and state legislation. This is because state legislatures, if they so wish, can enact legislation expanding on the federal provisions (but not detracting from them) and this results in some variation between states.[1] Moreover, in many civil cases, for instance where employment discrimination cases are adjudicated in the federal courts, the plaintiff can opt for a jury trial. This again distinguishes civil courts in the United States from the civil courts adjudicating employment disputes in other countries dealt with in this book, where one or more professional judges adjudicate in civil courts without a jury (see, for instance, Chapter 7, Italy; Chapter 8, The Netherlands; and Chapter 11, Sweden).

The plan of this chapter is as follows: after outlining the background, we first look at arbitration and at the civil court system. Next we consider the provisions regarding public employees and the pros and cons of arbitration versus the civil courts, before looking briefly at enforcing authorities and, finally, offering some concluding observations.

Background

The United States has very few statutorily protected employment rights compared to the other countries delineated in this book, either at the federal or state level; for instance the United States is notable for the absence of unfair dismissal legislation. Moreover, a foundation stone of US employment law is the notion that the employer and employee are equal and free contractors. Accordingly, employment is 'at will', terminable by the employer or the employee for any reason whatsoever, good cause, bad cause or no cause (Muhl, 2001). There are exceptions however: where the employment contract or a collective agreement, which normally has contractual status in the United States (and is often called a collective bargaining contract) provides otherwise; where a public employee is covered by special statutory provisions (see below); or where it can be shown that dismissal has been effected in violation of a specific statutory protection.

Although the Fair Labor Standards Act, which has provisions on the minimum wage and overtime pay of many employees, dates back to 1938, the growth in federal statutory employment rights really began in the 1960s with a raft of legislation initially dealing with civil rights and discrimination issues and extending to health and safety, disability and medical leave.[2] As noted above, this federal legislation has been enhanced by some state legislatures. This growth in statutory regulation has resulted in 'dramatic increases in the number of employment disputes litigated in federal and state courts' (Seeber and Lipsky, 2006: 720), and in the growth of private arbitration.

Moreover, while statutory employment rights have increased over the past half century, the number of unionised employees has decreased (see Table 1.1 on p. 2), leading to a fall in the number covered by collective agreements. This has had a direct impact on how employment rights are currently adjudicated, as we explain below. For this reason, we begin this chapter on the United States with an overview of the rapid growth in arbitration as an alternative to the courts.

Arbitration

Arbitration, which is much used in the United States for commercial contracts, is also used for contracts of employment and collective agreements.[3] It is usually final and binding, and may be voluntary or mandatory. Where the contract provides for voluntary arbitration, the employee can choose whether to go to the civil courts or to arbitration. Where the contract provides for mandatory arbitration, employees have no such choice and cannot take their dispute to a court.

The US courts distinguish between labour arbitration and employment arbitration. Labour arbitration, which stems from the National Labor Relations Act (NLRA) 1935, resolves grievances and disputes in a unionised workplace arising from a collective bargaining contract, with the parties being the union and employer, with the union acting on behalf of one or more employees in the bargaining unit. Employment arbitration, which is governed by the provisions of the Federal Arbitration Act 1925 (FAA), is arbitration in a non-union workplace and the parties are the employer and one (or occasionally more) individual employees.

Labour arbitration

Although grievance arbitration was introduced into unionised workplaces in the garment industries in the first part of the nineteenth century, it was not to be found more generally until after the passage of the NLRA. That Act gave private sector employees statutory rights to organise and engage in collective bargaining. The ensuing collective agreements often provided for arbitration to resolve disputes of interest and disputes of rights. Moreover, during the Second World War, the War Labor Board, intent on securing stability of production, encouraged companies to introduce arbitration for unionised workers in return for a union agreement not to strike (Stone, 2004).

In 1960, the US Supreme Court, in three cases brought by the United Steelworkers of America and known as the *Steelworkers' Trilogy*,[4] held that the courts should generally defer to the decisions of arbitrators handling grievance disputes under collective bargaining contracts. Collective bargaining contracts/agreements were distinguishable from commercial contracts and if a unionised employee brought a claim to a court that an arbitrator could resolve, the judge should order the dispute to be submitted to arbitration under the procedure set out in the collective bargaining contract. This 'defined a privileged role for arbitration' within the collective bargaining system (Stone, 1996: 1021).

As a result, 'the volume of arbitration cases, already high before 1960, continued to expand and less than one per cent were challenged in the courts' (Stone, 2004: 36). Today, virtually all collective bargaining contracts contain provisions that allow the union to take an employee's grievance to arbitration, often in return for a no-strike provision during the life of the contract.

Freed from the constraints of the court system, unions and employers developed their own procedures, for instance how arbitrator(s) should be selected (normally the union and employer have an equal voice in arbitrator selection). Other process matters include whether an arbitration hearing should be transcribed, whether the case should be heard by a single arbitrator or a panel (mostly the former), and whether strict rules of evidence should apply (mostly not). Unions and employers normally share the arbitrator's fee and the union represents the employee in the arbitration hearing, so the grievant does not pay (Naimark, 2004).

Labour arbitration normally relates to contractual disputes, rather than statutory claims. For instance normally collective bargaining contracts contain a clause providing for no dismissal without just cause for employees who have passed probation, so a union (if it so decides) can take a case on behalf of a dismissed employee to arbitration. To take another example, many collective bargaining contracts have seniority provisions, so a union (if it so decides) can take a case to arbitration on behalf of an employee who alleges his seniority rights have been ignored by the employer. The notion is that there is a 'law of the shop', which provides an internal system of justice.

From the 1960s, however, as noted above, a parallel system of individual statutory employment rights emerged, but this was the external law and collective bargaining contracts did not extend to statutory claims. This position was endorsed in 1974[5] by the US Supreme Court when it held that a mandatory arbitration provision in a collective bargaining contract could not cover Title VII claims (that is, claims in respect of discrimination on grounds of race, colour, religion, sex or national origin). Accordingly employees in unionised workplaces had the right to pursue their individual statutory discrimination claims in a judicial forum, even if the union decided to arbitrate an almost identical claim under the collective bargaining contract, because increasingly collective agreements included non-discrimination clauses.

The US Supreme Court, however, altered its approach in 2009 in the case of *14 Penn Plaza LCC v Pyett.*[6] In that case, the union had refused to take Pyett's and colleagues' age discrimination claims to arbitration, so the issue was whether Pyett and colleagues could enforce their age discrimination rights in a civil court. The US Supreme Court held that if the union included in its collective bargaining agreement a clause that 'clearly and unmistakably' provided that all claims of individual employees that arise under discrimination statutes have to be arbitrated, not litigated, employees are barred from litigating in the courts. Moreover, this bar can apply even if the union has refused to take the case to arbitration.

The union has a common law duty of fair representation (DFR), but a union does not necessarily breach its DFR in declining to take an individual's discrimination claim, even a meritorious one. This is because unions are allowed to balance many considerations and interests, and provided that unions can show lack of animus against an employee and a reasonable basis for their decisions, they are allowed a great deal of latitude by the courts.

In the wake of the *Pyett* judgment, the position is far from clear at the time of writing. For instance some courts (but not others) have held that an employee may proceed to a judicial forum where a union has refused to support an individual's claim in arbitration, especially where the wording in the collective agreement is open to interpretation. For their part, unions on the one hand wish to preserve their right to decide which cases to take to arbitration, but on the other hand do not wish to extinguish an employee's statutory rights, or to take on responsibility for enforcing federal law. According to a lawyer interviewed for this study, unions have reacted in various ways, including removing discrimination clauses from collective agreements; providing 'muscular' mediation (evaluative mediation with recommendations); setting up special arbitration arrangements between the employee and employer for discrimination claims outside the arbitration provisions of the collective bargaining agreement; and allowing employees to go to the courts, if the union has refused to take their claim to arbitration.

In short, arbitration in unionised workplaces has a long history; the courts have deferred to arbitrators' awards and allowed unions to decide which cases to take to arbitration, even where an employee has a statutory right to litigate. Today, however, labour arbitration pursuant to a collective bargaining agreement is increasingly rare in the private sector because the number of private sector unionised workplaces has decreased. Accordingly, this chapter now turns to employment arbitration.

Employment arbitration

As noted above, employment arbitration is to be found in non-union workplaces and is governed by the Federal Arbitration Act (FAA) 1925 pursuant to the individual's contract of employment. Employment arbitration essentially dates back to 1991 and the US Supreme Court's judgment in *Gilmer*.[7] In that case, the US Supreme Court held that an employment arbitration agreement in a non-unionised workplace, like any commercial arbitration agreement pursuant to a commercial contract, is enforceable under the Federal Arbitration Act (FAA) as the claimant has not waived substantive rights, only the right to a judicial forum, with an arbitral forum in its stead.

The Court rejected challenges based on the inadequacies of arbitration and those based on the argument that discrimination legislation (in the *Gilmer* case age discrimination in employment) embodied statutorily based policy considerations and thus should not be adjudicated in a private forum. In another leading case a decade later, *Circuit City Stores*,[8] the US Supreme Court held that the FAA's exemption of workers engaged in foreign or interstate commerce was a narrow one; it only applied to transportation workers (Bloomberg BNA, 2012).

As a result of these US Supreme Court decisions, employers began increasingly to require non-unionised employees to sign an agreement to arbitrate any statutory claims arising in the course of employment as a condition of hire, so-called pre-employment mandatory arbitration agreements (PMAAs). The reasons for this growth of arbitration in the expanding non-union sector are unclear, but several factors have been cited by those interviewed for this study: employer fear of litigation and the potentially large damages awarded by juries; union avoidance and union substitution; and the discretion it gives to the employer over process matters.

Whereas in unionised workplaces there is a rough balance of power between the union and employer, and in non-unionised workplaces there is generally a rough parity between a senior executive and the employer, any such parity between a worker and employer is more often than not a fiction. Accordingly a non-unionised employee faced with a PMAA at the time of hire is in effect forced to assent to it and agree to be covered by procedures that the employer promulgates unilaterally on a take-it-or leave-it basis. As a consequence, although American workers have a number of de jure rights under federal and state employment statutes, often these rights cannot be enforced in the courts because of PMAAs, which Stone (1996) has called 'yellow dog contracts'.

Arbitral standards and outcomes

There is virtually no federal licensing or regulation of arbitrators and very limited state regulation, except in California, leading to considerable variations in practice and procedure. The American Arbitration Association (AAA) and the smaller JAMS, the two leading arbitration providers, have issued process protocols for employment arbitration which include requirements that employees:

- have the same remedies as they could obtain in the courts;
- are able to participate in arbitrator selection;
- are not precluded by cost or location from access to arbitration;
- have their claim arbitrated by an arbitrator who specialises in employment law;
- are allowed to be represented by counsel;
- have reasonable discovery prior to the hearing;
- are able to present evidence through testimony, documents and cross examination; and
- are given a written, reasoned award.

In most, but not all individual contracts of employment the employer alone pays the arbitrator; the arbitrator's fees are not shared between the parties, unlike labour arbitration under collective bargaining contracts (Seeber and Lipsky, 2006). Arbitrators' fees can be substantial, although they vary across the country. According to an interviewee for this study, fees for employment arbitrators (like fees for arbitrators more generally) range from $1,500 to $3,000 a day (approximately €1,140 to €2,280) or even more and a hearing can take several days, plus days for preparation and writing the award.

There is a maxim that he who pays the piper calls the tune and, in line with this, there is the concern that if the employer pays all the arbitrator's fees this may lead to arbitrator bias, if only unconsciously. Requiring the employee to pay half the fee, however, deters complaints and thus limits access to justice, particularly if the employee is low paid. In *Cole* and *Perez*, federal courts ruled that a fee sharing provision created an unreasonable barrier to a low-paid claimant seeking adjudication of a claim.[9] Accordingly the arbitration agreement's provision on fees was unconscionable: it was a contract of adhesion, that is a legally binding agreement in which the employer has all the bargaining power and uses it to write the contract to his advantage.

In other cases also the federal courts have found unconscionability, albeit on a case by case basis. In *Hooters*,[10] a federal court held that the arbitration agreement was egregiously unfair because it enabled the company to control the selection of arbitrators, provided certain advantages only to the employer, and placed certain restrictions only on the employee. There are also rare instances where state courts have invalidated an arbitration agreement or a clause of it, for instance where an employee was required to go to arbitration but an employer was not, or where the agreement limited the damages that an employee could receive.[11] Furthermore, while some federal courts have struck out limitation periods for bringing an arbitration case that are significantly shorter than that provided under the relevant statute, others have held that a limitation period shorter than the statute's is a question of contract interpretation to be decided by the arbitrator. Some employment arbitration agreements prevent class/collective actions and the US Supreme Court has yet to rule on the legality of such clauses at the time of writing.[12]

As noted above, the AAA and JAMS protocols provide that an employee has the right to representation by an attorney/counsel. If represented, the employee usually is responsible for paying his/her lawyer's fees, but the employer may reimburse at least a portion of the employees' legal fees if the arbitration agreement so provides.[13]

Labour arbitration is often somewhat less formal than employment arbitration, but both are more formal than that found, for instance, in South Africa, another common law jurisdiction (see Chapter 10). Hill (2004: 370) found that the win rate and the win/loss ratio of employees bound by a PMAA and who self-represented 'was comparable to those who proceeded with counsel'. On the other hand Colvin (2011), in a study of over 1,000 employment arbitration cases, found that employees in his sample self-represented in almost a third of PMAAs and that employees represented by counsel had a greater chance of success and a greater chance of receiving a higher award than self-represented employees.

The protocols also provide for joint selection of the arbitrator. Although in labour arbitration the union will have as much knowledge as the employer, in employment arbitration the employee will tend to have far less knowledge than the employer. Also in employment arbitration the employer is likely to be a repeat player, but the employee is generally a one-shot player (unlike the union in labour arbitration). A study by Colvin (2011: 15) concluded that 'there is a strong repeat employer effect in employment arbitration' to the advantage of the employer and 'a smaller, but significant, repeat-employer-arbitrator pairing effect'.[14]

If the employee's attorney is a repeat player, it may reduce the repeat employer effect. A claimant in employment arbitration, however, may not be able to secure representation, either because it is not permitted or more often because, given a likely low level of award, an attorney or counsel operating on a contingency fee basis may decline to represent. Furthermore, the employee's attorney is perhaps less likely to be an employment specialist, unlike the employer's attorney.

It is not clear whether arbitration providers other than those from JAMS and the AAA prescribe similar employment arbitration protocols, nor are there statistics on the extent of PMAAs, let alone the number of PMAAs observing AAA or JAMS protocols. Reportedly PMAAs are used in the larger companies. Colvin (2012: 469) estimates that PMAAs cover 'over twice as many employees as union representation, which currently stands at only 12.3 per cent of the American workforce'. Colvin also estimates that about 15 million employees with PMAAs are covered by AAA procedures.

There have been various studies examining the characteristics of arbitrators in employment arbitration and employee win rates. For instance, Colvin and Gough (2012) found that male arbitrators favour employees more often than female arbitrators; former judges award higher damages than arbitrators without judicial experience, and there are variations across the states with arbitrators in California most likely to award in favour of employees and arbitrators in Texas least likely to favour employees.

Using a hypothetical case and a questionnaire, Bingham and Mesch (2000) compared three groups: 188 employment arbitrators with 210 labour arbitrators and with 161 labour arbitrators who were members of the prestigious National Academy of Arbitrators (NAA). They found that employment arbitrators reinstated the grievant significantly less often than labour arbitrators, whether or not they were members of the NAA, but there was no significant difference in the award of back pay between the three groups.

Employment arbitration awards can be reviewed under the FAA, but the grounds for review are narrow (for instance for arbitrator fraud, corruption, duress, unconscionability or because an arbitrator exceeds the authority provided under the arbitration agreement) and some circuits have reviewed an award which manifestly disregarded the law.

It is in the interests of unions to have a narrow test for a review in labour arbitration (see the *Steelworkers' Trilogy* above) given that most judges do not understand the workplace or unions, but this does not necessarily apply to employment arbitration. Moreover Rabin (2010), on the basis of his examination of employment arbitration awards, found that where the courts held that an employment arbitrator manifestly disregarded the law, they did so only where an arbitrator ignored the law or paid no attention to legal principles. In other words an arbitrator's mistake of law did not provide a court with sufficient grounds for vacating an award if it could be shown that the arbitrator paid attention to the law even though he/she got it wrong. This contrasts with the wide grounds for the review of arbitration awards in South Africa (see Chapter 10).

The civil courts

Federal and state

The United States is a federal country, and both the federal government and each of the state governments have their own complete and parallel court systems. Under the federal system, the US District Courts (that is, courts of original jurisdiction), are at the base. There are 94 Districts Courts and either side is entitled under the US Constitution to request a jury trial in the federal civil courts under certain statutes, including the discrimination statutes. Otherwise, a judge sits alone. The next federal level is the US Courts of Appeals (otherwise known as circuit courts) of which there are 13. Appeals can only be lodged on an alleged error of law. The highest federal level is the US Supreme Court which comprises nine judges; parties can petition the US Supreme Court to hear a case, but the US Supreme Court decides whether or not to accept it. All federal judges are nominated by the President, confirmed by the Senate and appointed for life (see Figure 12.1).

No two state court systems are exactly alike. At the base are the state trial courts sometimes called District Courts and in most states either side is allowed to opt for a jury trial in respect of some statutes. Most states also have an intermediate appellate court. Appeal is on the basis of procedural mistakes and errors of law and a case is heard by two or three judges. All states have some form of highest court, usually called a Supreme Court.

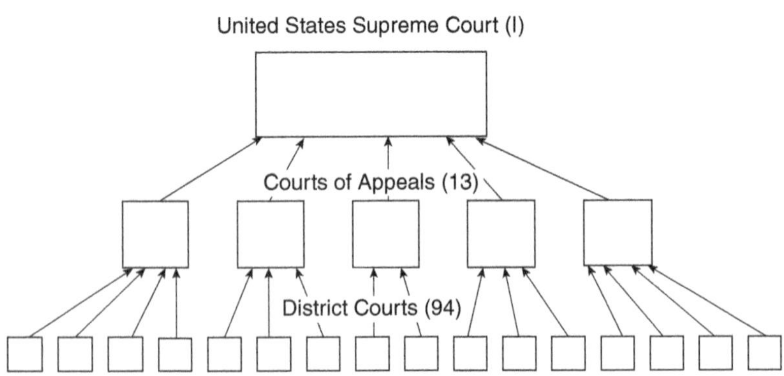

Figure 12.1 Federal court structure in the United States

In states with an intermediate appellate court, these highest state courts have discretion as to whether or not to accept a case. These highest courts often sit in panels of three, five, seven or even nine judges. Unlike federal judges, most state court judges are not appointed for life but are either elected or appointed for a certain number of years.

Essentially the state trial courts of so-called general jurisdiction hear claims relating to the contract of employment and to any state employment laws, while the federal courts hear claims relating to federal employment statutes, which – as noted above – have expanded considerably in scope since the 1960s. The two systems, however, can interact, for instance where there is both federal and state anti-discrimination legislation in place. Under the 'supplemental jurisdiction' doctrine, a federal claimant can attach a state claim (or a state claimant can attach a federal claim) with the result that the two claims are decided together in one court. Moreover, under the so-called Erie doctrine, a federal court, when exercising supplemental jurisdiction must apply the substantive common law of the state in which it is sitting, but is free to apply federal procedural law (Clermont, 2012).

The procedure at both federal and state trial courts is generally more formal than the procedure in arbitration, with discovery, motions, and depositions, and a plaintiff may find it difficult to navigate the system unless represented by a lawyer. As lawyers are unwilling to take on what they view as weak cases, they act as gatekeepers.

Discrimination

All federal US employment discrimination cases begin with a complaint to the US Equal Employment Opportunity Commission (EEOC) which must be filed within 300 days of the alleged act. Filing is free and the EEOC has 180 days to investigate the claim, after which the claimant can request the EEOC to cease to investigate and issue a 'right to sue' letter. If they do not, and the EEOC completes its investigation, there are three possible outcomes. First, the EEOC may find no reasonable cause to believe that discrimination occurred. Second, the EEOC may find that reasonable cause exists and that conciliation should be pursued. Third, the EEOC may find that reasonable cause exists, that conciliation should be pursued, but if that fails the EEOC will take up the lawsuit itself. Moreover, the US Supreme Court has held that the EEOC can bring an action or a class action and obtain equitable relief on behalf of an employee, even if the employee had previously signed a mandatory arbitration agreement precluding litigation.[15] The EEOC, however, essentially because of resource restrictions, only rarely litigates and where it does so, focuses on precedent setting cases. Accordingly, the overwhelming majority of claimants after 180 days either withdraw their complaint from the EEOC or receive a right to sue letter. Less than 1 per cent of claims become an EEOC lawsuit (US Equal Employment Opportunity Commission, 2013).

There are federal laws prohibiting discrimination on grounds of gender, race, national origin, ethnicity, colour, disability and age as noted above. In addition most states have similar anti-discrimination laws which may provide enhanced remedies, such as uncapped damages, whereas under federal law compensatory and punitive damages, although available, are capped according to employer size. Also in some states the protected characteristics under anti-discrimination law are broader than under federal law. For instance, some states prohibit discrimination on the grounds of sexual orientation.

In practice, a plaintiff normally joins a federal claim to a claim under a state statute (see above) and on receipt of the EEOC 'right to sue' letter has 90 days to file in the court. After filing there may be another gateway in the form of court-annexed mediation. In addition, there will be pre-trial screening and case management meetings, including a pre-discovery settlement meeting, and cases often settle during this process (Clermont and Schwab, 2004).

The Civil Rights Act 1991 entitles either side to demand a jury trial, as opposed to a judge trial, in a federal court. A plaintiff can also opt for summary judgment claiming that there are no material facts in dispute and so there is no need for findings of fact by a jury. According to Clermont and Schwab (2004), the plaintiff opts for a jury trial in the majority of cases. From EEOC complaint to trial can take three or more years (perhaps two years for summary judgment). The usual provision in courts in the United States is that each party bears its own costs, irrespective of who wins. Under certain statutes, however, including the anti-discrimination statutes, there are fee shifting provisions, whereby a winning plaintiff is reimbursed by the losing defendant, that is, the employer.

Clermont and Schwab (2004) compared employment discrimination claimants in federal courts with other categories of plaintiffs in federal courts. They found that employment discrimination plaintiffs obtained fewer resolutions early in litigation and so proceeded to trial more often than other plaintiffs. They won a lower proportion of cases at pre-trial and trial; more of their successful cases were taken to appeal; and on appeal employment discrimination plaintiffs had a harder time than other plaintiffs in preserving successes and reversing adverse outcomes. They describe this appeal success rate of the defendant below in employment discrimination cases as of 'extraordinary magnitude' and consider that the reason is judicial bias at the appellate level (Clermont and Schwab, 2004: 454).

Clermont and Schwab (2009) repeated this study adding five more years of data and concluded that the picture had not changed. Federal employment discrimination plaintiffs continued to fare worse when compared to plaintiffs in almost every other category of civil cases in the federal courts. Employment discrimination plaintiffs were usually unsuccessful at first instance and the results were affirmed on appeal. Where the employment discrimination plaintiff won below, the appellate courts were more likely to reverse this than they were to reverse defendant wins. Moreover, while employment discrimination plaintiffs fared better in jury trials compared to judge-alone trials, in both types of trials they fared worse than other categories of plaintiffs.

The main finding by Clermont and Schwab (2009), however, was the significant drop in employment discrimination claims since their study five years earlier and they speculated that perhaps employment discrimination plaintiffs are increasingly turning to arbitration. As noted above, however, PMAAs only cover a quarter of all US employees and many employers perhaps realise that a PMAA is unnecessary, given that the court system is daunting for plaintiffs and more likely to decide in their favour than for the plaintiff.

Controversy: arbitration or litigation?

This increased judicial deference to private arbitration to resolve employment claims is controversial. Critics submit that norms are not generated; employment law remains unelaborated; unfavourable publicity is circumvented; and arbitration, with its paucity of process regulation, is an inadequate substitute for the courts.

The critics of arbitration are particularly vocal in respect of pre-employment mandatory arbitration agreements in non-unionised companies, where normally the employer and employee are not on an equal footing: the employee has a greater desire to be employed than the employer has to hire and employees may not fully appreciate the value of what they are being asked to trade away.

The proponents of arbitration laud its finality as there are only limited grounds for the review of an arbitration award, whereas there can be an appeal from a judgment of a court on a point of law and in litigation the employer, more often than the plaintiff, has the financial leverage to mount an appeal. The proponents of arbitration also claim that arbitration produces a speedier resolution of claims, time to hearing and final decision, than litigation. There is considerable empirical evidence to support this (see Eisenberg and Hill (2004) and Delikat and Kleiner (2004)). Colvin (2007: 426) argues that:

> [i]n general, faster proceedings will be to the advantage of an employee claimant.... If the employee has lost his or her job and potentially had to take alternative employment at a lower salary level, the longer it takes to receive compensation, the greater will be the personal economic impact of the loss.

Nevertheless, as Colvin points out, a resolution of a dispute by arbitration still takes around a year.

Proponents of arbitration also claim that an arbitrator is more likely to understand the workplace than a generalist federal judge and jury.

In addition, proponents of arbitration maintain that a plaintiff is less likely to be 'out-lawyered' in arbitration than in the courts. Moreover, because the present court system is more costly for the parties than arbitration, this is likely to lead to employees bringing more claims under arbitration than through litigation and so arbitration can have a greater deterrence effect on employer behaviour than litigation (Hylton, 2004). Furthermore, even if in any single arbitration the employee concerned receives a lower arbitration award than he/she might have received in a court, the employer's lower process costs in arbitration overall as opposed to litigation overall may be passed on to consumers or employees, 'harming no one, except those (like lawyers) who sell process' (Ware, 2004: 493).

Defence lawyers, that is lawyers acting for the employer, are less likely to be motivated by the net cost of an individual case than plaintiff lawyers acting for employees because they have an on-going relationship with their clients who pay them, win or lose; their main consideration is whether their case handling is likely to lead to more work in the future. In contrast, plaintiffs' lawyers are normally paid on a contingency basis, so they weigh the potential value of each case before agreeing to represent a client. As damages are typically based on lost earnings, attorneys tend to favour the higher paid. Accordingly plaintiffs who are not supported by a union, may find it well-nigh impossible to engage a lawyer for the purpose of court litigation, particularly if they are low paid. According to Howard (1995) plaintiffs' lawyers accept only one in 20 cases offered, and focus on those where there is likely to be a high level of damages and the client can advance a retainer.

Of course low-paid employees may also have difficulty in securing a lawyer to represent them in arbitration, but the critical difference is that self-representation is in theory much easier for the employee in arbitration than in litigation. Estreicher (2001: 563) submits:

> In a world without employment arbitration as an available option, we would essentially have a 'cadillac' system for the few and a 'rickshaw' system for the many. The unspoken (yet undeniable) truth is that most claims filed by employees do not attract the attention of private lawyers because the stakes are too small and outcomes too uncertain to warrant the investment of lawyer time and resources.

In a similar vein, St. Antoine (2009: 126) maintains that it is easier to self-represent in arbitration and that the evidence shows that employees are often deterred from litigation because they cannot obtain counsel (see above). Arguing that PMAAs are better than they look, he maintains that 'recent studies show that lower paid employees still had quite respectable success rates in arbitration ranging from 21 per cent to 40 per cent'.

As noted above, however, arbitration is a formal process, and legal representation improves outcomes in arbitration (Colvin, 2011). Critics of mandatory arbitration argue, moreover, that if arbitration is speedier and cheaper than the court system, surely employees and employers will opt for arbitration in a *voluntary* post-dispute system and pre-employment mandatory arbitration agreements are otiose. Sherwyn and Sturman (2004), however, in their study of 1,300 cases lodged in Illinois with the Illinois Human Rights Commission and the Centre of Employment Dispute Resolution, found that there was not one case where both parties agreed to arbitrate post-dispute. They give some explanations for this, including the fact that neither side wants to appear weak by being the first to propose arbitration.

There have been several empirical studies of the results of employee success rates in arbitration and in court, and they point in different directions. Sherwyn and Sturman (2004: 435) maintain that all these empirical studies comparing plaintiff win rates before juries and before arbitrators should be disregarded: it 'is like comparing apples and oranges', because the cases going to arbitration and those going to litigation are unlikely to be comparable. Indeed, all the empirical studies can be critiqued methodologically and should be treated with caution, but scenarios and very large samples serve to mitigate the apples/oranges syndrome.

A survey by Howard (1995), looking at discrimination cases heard in the courts and by an employment arbitrator in the securities/stock exchange industries, found that employees won 28 per cent of non-jury trials, 38 per cent of jury trials and 48 per cent of arbitrations, but the mean damages received were significantly higher after a court verdict than after arbitration. He argued, however, that that might be because lawyers only act for a plaintiff where the potential recovery is significant and otherwise refuse to take on cases (see above).

Delikat and Kleiner (2004) compared the results of jury trials in the US District Court for the Southern District of New York between 1997 and 2001 with the results of employment arbitration administered by the National Association of Securities Dealers and the New York Stock Exchange 1989–2002. They found that claimants had a higher success rate in arbitration than they did in litigated cases in federal courts, that the median damages received in arbitration and litigation were broadly similar, and that arbitration was speedier than a court hearing.

A more sophisticated empirical study into arbitration/court wins was carried out by Eisenberg and Hill (2004) as they distinguished between civil rights (i.e. discrimination) and non-civil rights employment disputes and between higher-paid and lower-paid employees. They found that arbitrated outcomes differed little from trial outcomes for higher paid employees both in respect of civil rights and non-civil rights claims. Lower-paid employees fared less well in both civil rights arbitration and non-civil rights arbitration than in court. Looking only at discrimination cases, Eisenberg and Hill (2004) also distinguished between the federal courts, the state courts and employment arbitration, with employee win rates of 36.4 per cent, 43.8 per cent, and 26.2 per cent respectively. In other words, in discrimination cases employees were least likely to win in an arbitral forum and most likely to win in a state court.

Colvin (2011) in a recent study compared employment arbitration cases (that is, non-union arbitration) administered by the American Arbitration Association (AAA) with employment litigation trials. His study was based on a large scale data set (1,213 cases from 2003–7) and he found that employee win rates in employment arbitration were significantly less than win rates at trials; damages awarded at the median and mean were significantly lower than at trials; arbitration was speedier than litigation and was less expensive for the employee.

Colvin (2009) also compared the damages awarded after civil rights cases in employment arbitration with the damages awarded in federal courts and the damages awarded in non-civil rights cases in state courts with the damages awarded in non-civil rights cases in employment arbitration. In both sets of comparisons he found a large gap: the average damages awarded were significantly lower in employment arbitration than in litigation. He suggests, however, that this gap could perhaps be explained by the fact that only weaker cases reached arbitration, as stronger ones had been resolved through internal grievance procedures. Moreover high jury awards may be overturned on appeal.

Klaas et al. (2006) compared decisions by employment arbitrators (that is, arbitrators in non-unionised firms), labour arbitrators (arbitrators in unionised firms) and jurors. To avoid comparing apples and oranges, decision-makers were asked to respond to 32 scenarios where an employee challenged termination. The scenarios contained six variables either strongly or weakly: strength of evidence against the employee, evidence of discrimination, procedural compliance by the employer, employee work history, supervisor provocation, stress-inducing personal circumstances and procedural compliance. They found that labour arbitrators were more likely than employment arbitrators and jurors to find in favour of the employee and that jurors were more likely than employment arbitrators to rule in favour of the employee.

Public employees

Almost a fifth of all workers in the United States are in public sector employment, either with the federal government, a state or a municipality, and the relevant employment laws vary according to the employer, generating a

Byzantine web of statutes, ordinances, attorney general opinions and court decisions (Kearney, 2009).

The states differ in their statutory provisions. In a majority of states and municipalities, public employees in general or in certain specific occupations have collective bargaining rights, and a large municipality might have ten collective bargaining agreements. State law typically prescribes the grievances that civil servants in the states and municipalities can bring, often providing for some form of just cause for discharge (Kearney, 2009).

Police officers and fire-fighters are normally covered by collective bargaining but are generally not permitted by statute to strike. In return, typically they may have final and binding arbitration for disputes of interest. For disputes of rights in respect of a collective agreement there could be arbitration by a single arbitrator or by a panel including elected or appointed officials. The position varies from state to state and municipality to municipality.

Public employees at federal level have restricted collective bargaining rights with grievance procedures providing for interim administrative review by an agency, normally culminating in binding arbitration. These interim agencies include the Federal Labor Relations Agency if there is a contract dispute, the Merit System Protection Board if there is a dispute about promotion or discipline, and the Office of Special Counsel for whistle blowing. Moreover, certain federal public employees, such as the military and the Federal Bureau of Investigation (FBI), do not even have restricted collective bargaining rights and President George W. Bush extended this considerably to encompass, for instance, immigration and customs enforcement, including baggage screeners.

Enforcing authorities

For the sake of completeness this chapter briefly covers some enforcing authorities. A key enforcing authority is the Wages and Hours Division (WHD) of the United States Department of Labor, which enforces the Fair Labor Standards Act (FLSA) and some other labour laws, such as the Employee Polygraph Protection Act, the Contract Work Hours and Safety Standards Act, which sets overtime standards for service and construction contracts, and the Service Contracts Act, which requires payment of prevailing wage rates and fringe benefits on contracts to provide services to the Federal Government.

The FLSA, as noted above, establishes minimum wage and overtime pay for many workers, full-time and part-time in the private sector and in federal, state and local government. It also requires record-keeping and sets child labour standards.

WHD investigators conduct investigations and gather data on wages, hours and other employment conditions in order to determine compliance. Where violations are found they may recommend changes and require employers to pay a civil penalty. Wilful violations may be prosecuted criminally and the violator fined or on a second conviction may be imprisoned (WHD, 2011).

In addition, WHD may supervise the payment of back wages; the Secretary of Labor may bring a suit for back wages and an equal amount as liquidated damages; an employee may file a private suit for back pay and an equal amount as liquidated damages, plus attorney's fees and court costs and the Secretary of Labor may obtain an injunction to restrain any person from violating the FLSA, including the unlawful withholding of proper minimum wage and overtime pay. Statistics for 2001–8 inclusive show a decline in enforcement hours (WHD, 2008).

Other enforcing authorities at federal level include the Occupational Safety and Health Administration which has its own inspectors and the Equal Employment Opportunity Commission which can litigate in the civil courts (see above). In addition states may have their own, similar agencies.

Discussion and conclusions

Employees in the United States have few statutory employment rights compared to employees in all the other countries in this book. Such statutory rights as American employees enjoy essentially are based on anti-discrimination statutes, which can be litigated in the federal or state civil courts.

Litigation through the civil courts, where the procedures are lengthy and complex, often results in hefty payments to attorneys. Although employees are more likely to lose than to succeed in an employment discrimination civil case, if they win they receive large damages: a typical award might be $300,000 (€284,000).

Such litigation can be barred by the contract of employment or perhaps the collective bargaining agreement and the United States has a tradition of arbitration and a tradition of judicial deference to arbitration. Moreover, while this tradition stems from arbitration in a unionised setting, only a small minority of workplaces in the United States are unionised today. Most private sector employees work in non-unionised workplaces where they may be required to agree not to litigate their statutory claims, but instead to agree to arbitration before they start their employment.

Under arbitration, expense, complexity and delay are significantly reduced; arbitration provides simpler procedures, more informality, and greater accessibility than the courts which limit claimant access in practice. This is because it is daunting to litigate without legal representation and legal representation is often difficult for lower paid employees to obtain.

Arbitration, however, is no panacea and it is strongly arguable that it is not appropriate for statutorily based claims; it provides what even its proponents would call rough justice and its critics would call second class justice when compared with adjudication by the courts. Procedural shortcomings in arbitration include limited discovery, constraints on depositions, perhaps shorter limitation periods, while the standards of judicial oversight are narrow as arbitration awards can be reviewed only on limited grounds.

In short arbitration, whether employment arbitration or labour arbitration, is tantamount to a de facto privatisation of the adjudication of workers' rights and Finkin (2008) ascribes the judges' deference to arbitration to judicial shirking and to the US Supreme Court being motivated to reduce its workload. Moreover, even if arbitration provides an adequate procedural substitute for the courts (and it has been shown that essentially it does not), it enables companies to avoid adverse publicity and, because of its secrecy, hinders the propagation and development of legal norms.

13
Evaluation: Applying Yardsticks

Introduction

This final chapter seeks to evaluate the adjudicatory regimes that have been described in the previous ten chapters, assessing them against a range of yardsticks. We approach this chapter tentatively for a number of reasons. First, and notwithstanding our efforts to compare and contrast institutional features using comparative models in Chapter 2, comparisons remain fraught with difficulty as we noted in our introductory chapter, principally because comparison invariably entails some lifting of institutions out of context, ignoring the fact that a country's institutions reflect its context and history, as well as the political hue and public policy concerns of the country's government of the day. As such, the yardsticks against which institutions and procedures are evaluated may only be partly commensurable.

Second, institutions exercising comparable roles are in many cases very different and so are not always easy to match in terms of their characteristic features. For instance, in the United States employment rights claims are decided by private arbitration or the civil courts, while in Germany there are labour courts (see Figure 1.1 on p. 10 which depicts first-instance adjudication). Third, we have not always been able to find data on which to base an evaluation. Moreover, even when there are data and on the face of it there is commensurability, there can be differences, such as differing base years, annual fluctuations, or differences in what is included in a category. Readers are asked to bear in mind these caveats, particularly when considering some of the tables.

Importantly, any evaluation must take account of the different stakeholders, the worker and the employer who are parties to the dispute, the judges/adjudicators, and the legal and non-legal representatives. Moreover, the immediate participants are not the only stakeholders. The government of the day, civil society organisations and the public as taxpayers have an interest in whether an adjudicatory system, for instance, is speedy or slow, whether it is complex or simple and how much it costs and who bears these costs. Indeed when evaluating the features, we can only say that the institutional architecture in one country is 'better' than that in another in rather crude and overall terms. Judgements on the features depend on the standpoint of the stakeholder, which might conflict with that of other stakeholders. For example, there is widespread approval in Ireland for the replacement of an inordinately complex system with a much simpler system, but there is some dispute amongst stakeholders about certain features of these changes (see Chapter 6).

Taking the yardstick of accessibility, an institution is less accessible to a claimant if a fee is charged and a claimant is typically a worker not an employer; but if an institution is less accessible this may benefit the employer, who will have fewer claims to oppose and it may benefit the taxpayer if the user pays a fee. Ease of appeal, however, might benefit employers, if the majority of judgments at first instance are in favour of employees, especially as the employer typically has the greater resources and so can more easily afford to appeal. Similarly, if lawyers are given a monopoly of representation, this will benefit lawyers; but if lawyers are not permitted to represent (as in some types of complaint until now in South Africa) this may benefit the parties, because there is less formality and it may benefit the state, because it funds the hearings which may be shorter if lawyers are not present.

We are mindful of the fact that this is only an institutional comparison; we are not comparing employment laws themselves. The boundary between institutions and legal rights, however, is not clear cut. For instance the time limits for alleging that employment laws have been breached relate both to the scope of the laws and the remit of the institution concerned. De facto, they also determine access. Similarly, although the outcome of an adjudication will depend primarily on how the burden of proof and the legal tests are framed, the way that the adjudicatory institutions are constituted and operate can also influence the outcome.

The so-called Donovan Commission in Great Britain nearly half a century ago (Royal Commission, 1968: 156), when recommending labour courts for Great Britain, said that the objective was to establish 'a procedure which is easily accessible, informal, speedy and inexpensive and which gives [the parties] the best possible opportunities of arriving at an amicable settlement'. These criteria are not the only ones we adopt; we add other yardsticks for evaluating the institutions in the ten countries that we have covered as follows:

- accessibility;
- litigation rate;
- voluntary settlements through conciliation/mediation;
- the expertise of adjudicators;

- duration;
- the legal formality of proceedings;
- perceptions of users.

In assessing national systems against these yardsticks, we do not always touch on every country under every heading, often because the data are lacking, as noted above. Furthermore, where we give examples from countries, we only do so briefly; greater detail is provided in the preceding chapters where each country's regime is depicted much more fully.

Accessibility

There are a number of facets to accessibility. One facet is fees, which cross-cuts with the Royal Commission's criterion of inexpensiveness. Another facet is how easy it is to lodge a claim. Further facets are geographical accessibility and the time limits for making a claim. We look at each of these in turn.

Fees

A key determinant of accessibility is whether a claimant has to pay a fee to submit a claim to an adjudicatory body. As Table 13.1 shows, in Ireland, Sweden and South Africa, claims to the bespoke adjudicatory bodies for employment rights are free. In Great Britain a claim to an employment tribunal could be lodged free of charge until July 2013. Since then, there has been a charge which is by far the heftiest of all the countries considered here. As the claimant is usually the worker, not the employer, fees erect a barrier for workers. (As noted above, however, this may be to the employer's advantage as it can reduce the number of claims to which the employer has to respond.) In Germany, the deterrent effect is mitigated by the fact that the claimant does not have to pay fees up-front. The fee, which is based on a sliding scale according to the actual or notional sum claimed, is paid by the loser, which of course may not be the claimant, only after a judgment has been handed down. Moreover, fees are waived in the event of an agreed settlement, which is encouraged at all levels of the German system.

In France, the €35 fee payable at first and second instance (with an additional €150 payable on appeal) is primarily understood as a contribution to financing legal aid provisions, and therefore has an element of equity, rather than a deterrent to claims or a more general financing of the costs of administering justice. In 2013, the Labour Minister announced that the €35 fee would be abolished as a matter of social justice (Ministère de la Justice, 2013).

If there are fees at first instance, there are normally further fees for an appeal. For instance, in Great Britain, a fee to lodge an appeal at the Employment Appeal Tribunal is £400 (approximately €467) and a further £1,200 (approximately €1,401) for a hearing. In Germany the fees for an appeal are

Table 13.1 Fees for employment adjudication at first instance

Country **1st instance body**	**Issue fee**	**Hearing fee**	**Other**
Germany *Local labour court*	Free	Costs borne by loser *after* hearing, based on a sliding scale broadly related to the amount claimed. Scale from €50 to over €6,000, but typically around €390 for an unfair dismissal claimant on average earnings.	No court fee if amicable settlement reached. Judicial discretion to vary level of fee based on amount claimed.
Great Britain *Employment Tribunals*	€292	€1,111	Applies to dismissal/discrimination. Lower fee for wages/redundancy payments.
France *Conseils de Prud'hommes*	€35	Free	Issue fee to be abolished entirely.

Table 13.1 (Continued)

Country **1st instance body**	**Issue fee**	**Hearing fee**	**Other**
Ireland *Workplace Relations Commission*	Free	Free	
Italy *Tribunal (special chamber)*	Sliding scale according to amount claimed, starting from a fee of €18.50 if amount claimed up to €1,100, up to a fee of €733 if amount claimed over €520,000.	Free	
New Zealand *Employment Relations Authority*	€45	1st day free €96 for each subsequent half day	
South Africa *CCMA & Labour Court*	Free	Free	
Sweden *Labour Court*	Free	Free	

Notes:
1. Converted to Euros where Euros are not the local currency for ease of comparison.
2. In the Netherlands an employer may request official authorisation to dismiss using an administrative procedure – at no cost to the employee affected-rather than applying to the civil court.
3. The table denotes Ireland's proposed new system. In its many first-instance bodies currently, there is also no charge for making a claim or having a hearing.
4. In Italy no fee is payable if a claimant has an annual gross income of less than €21,256.332. The fees for employment claims before the Tribunal and the Court of Appeal are calculated at half the cost of other civil cases.
Sources: See dedicated country chapters in this book.

some 60 per cent higher than the first-instance fees, but on the same basis, for instance a sliding scale and only paid by the loser after the judgment.

Claim forms

Another aspect of accessibility is the ease of lodging a claim. There is a trade-off between having a simple claim form that a claimant can easily complete and providing fairly detailed information to the adjudicatory body. The more informed are the adjudicators, generally speaking, the better able they are to ascertain the issues before the hearing and identify the evidence needed, thus perhaps making the hearing shorter and thereby reducing the state's financial burden. Unusually in Sweden and Germany, there is no single prescribed claim form and in Germany a claimant can lodge a claim orally or in writing to a court official. Where countries have prescribed forms, the amount of detail that has to be given varies. In Ireland, until 2012, confusingly there were 30 different complaint forms, but they have now been amalgamated into a single complaint form (Bruton, 2012a: 8).

Location

An aspect of accessibility is geographical accessibility. Sweden's labour court is based solely in Stockholm, even though Sweden is a large country. It has a landmass of 450,000 square kilometres and is the third largest country by area in Western Europe. The former chair of Sweden's labour court, however, pointed out that workers could not bring claims themselves; their union or the Discrimination Ombudsman (DO) brought a claim on their behalf and both unions and the DO have their headquarters and legal services based in Stockholm.

In all the other countries covered in this book, however, there are either courts in the localities or the central court holds hearings in many areas to provide geographical accessibility. For instance in the Netherlands, which has a landmass of 33,900 square kilometres, employment rights cases go to the civil courts, and there are 11 District Courts, subdivided into 53 local (canton) courts (de Rechtspraak, 2013). In Ireland, one division of the Labour Court sits outside Dublin (except during the summer and Christmas holiday periods) and the other divisions spend one week out of three outside Dublin, according to the Labour Court chair.

Time limits

Time limits for filing a claim are set out in the relevant statutes. They vary from country to country and even in the same country the time limits may vary according to the type of complaint (see Table 13.2). The longer the time limit, the easier it is for the claimant, who is typically the worker, to lodge a claim. Memories fade, however, and if a considerable amount of time has elapsed, it might be difficult for either party to provide reliable evidence.

Table 13.2 Time limits for filing a claim at first instance

Country	Type of complaint	Time limit	Other
France	Dismissal	Two years	Discrimination = Five years
Germany	Dismissal	Three weeks	Statutory time limits only apply if one party invokes them & may be disregarded by the court
	Equal treatment	Two months	Statutory time limits may be superseded by contractual time limits
	Most other complaints	Three years from the end of the year when the claim arose	
Great Britain	Most complaints	Three calendar months	Exceptions: Equal Pay and Redundancy Payments – six months
Italy	Most complaints	Ten years	Five years for some pay and allowances complaints (e.g. occupational allowances, retirement benefits)
Netherlands	Dismissal	Six months	Five years for asserting rights under a contract or discrimination claims (but 20/30 years for some damages claims)
New Zealand	Personal grievance	90 days to raise grievance with employer Three years to file grievance with Employment Relations Authority	
South Africa	Dismissal	30 days	Discrimination = Six months
Sweden	Most complaints	Four months	
USA	Discrimination	300 days of alleged act to complain to EEOC 90 days to file in civil court from date of right to sue letter from EEOC	Discrimination claim cannot be filed without right to sue letter from Equal Employment Opportunity Commission (EEOC)

Note: Ireland is about to rationalise its time limits which currently vary considerably.
Sources: Employment rights legislation in relevant countries.

Litigation rate

Another yardstick is the litigation rate. A low litigation rate may suggest either an absence of employment disputes, or the resolution of disputes at workplace level without the need for adjudication, or barriers to accessibility so that even where workers consider that their employment rights have been breached, it is difficult for them to lodge a claim. Accordingly a high litigation rate is not necessarily to be decried as the more accessible are the employment rights institutions, the higher the number of claims is likely to be. For instance in Germany, fees were increased in 2004. In 2003 there were 630,000 claims. In 2005 there were 523,000 claims, a fall of over 100,000. Great Britain's litigation rate is based on 2011–12 figures, when submitting a claim to the first-instance body (employment tribunals) was free of charge. As we have already noted, substantial fees for submitting a claim and for a hearing were introduced in July 2013, but we do not yet know how this will affect the litigation rate. Of course, as we have noted, the level of fees is not the only factor determining the litigation rate, but the German example suggests a deterrent effect and bears out our intuitive understandings.

We first measure the litigation rate by the number of claims submitted as a proportion of the working population using figures for the working population rounded to the nearest million and we capture that in Table 13.3. These figures are only indicative, because the time period on which these statistics are based vary in line with the availability of the statistics from each country (see notes to Table 13.3).

Perhaps the most noticeable point to be drawn from Table 13.3 is that Sweden has comparatively few claims; it is probably no coincidence that its level of unionisation is significantly higher than that in the other countries in this book. In Sweden nearly seven in ten employees are unionised, a much higher rate than in any of the other countries in this study (see Table 1.1 on p. 2). Using data from a large-scale British survey, The Workplace Employment Relations Survey, 1998, Knight and Latreille (2000) examined disciplinary sanction and dismissal rates. Although they found an association between certain workforce characteristics, such as the percentage of employees in a particular occupational group, ethnicity, age and gender, they also found that unions 'play a major role in settling disputes between individual employees and their employers' (Knight and Latreille, 2000: 549).

We would point out that our figures differ from Gibbons (2007) who gives the German litigation rate at 1.5 per cent, the French litigation rate at 0.7 per cent and Great Britain at 0.4, whereas our rate is 1.2 (Germany), 1.1 (France) and 0.8 (Great Britain). This is because his figures are based on earlier statistics than ours (2005–6 we think) and there are changes over time.

Table 13.3 Employment litigation rates based on claims submitted

Country	Body	Claims per annum	Working population	Litigation rate %
France	Conseils de Prud'hommes	205,000	19 million	1.1(0.9)*
Germany	Local labour court	404,000	32.7 million	1.2
Great Britain	Employment tribunals	186,300	23.5 million	0.8
Italy	Tribunals (labour rights only)	158,000	17 million	0.93
New Zealand	Employment Relations Authority	2,000	2 million	0.1
South Africa	Commission for Conciliation Mediation & Arbitration/Bargaining Councils	200,000	13 million	1.5
Sweden	Labour Court	425	3.9 million	0.01

Notes:
1. The 'working population' figure embraces employees in employment and excludes the self-employed and civil servants in France and Germany, who may not use labour courts. (The French figure covers the eligible workforce as defined by the electorate for labour court elections, that is employees less those working under public law.) In some countries, some self-employed people may use the labour courts, depending on their contractual arrangements, but we have not taken this into account. We have excluded the unemployed, although a proportion of these might be added to reflect employees who are technically unemployed and who are contesting their dismissal.
2. Comparisons of litigation rates do not take account of the fact that there are barriers which vary cross-nationally, for instance whether or not there are dispute resolution gateways, whether there are fees for access and, if so, their level.
3. These statistics are the latest available at the time of writing but the time period on which these statistics are based varies. For instance for Great Britain it is 2011–12; for Italy it is 2010.
4. We have excluded the United States, Ireland and the Netherlands from this table. The United States is not included because many employment disputes are arbitrated privately and the number is not known, nor is the number of employment cases in the state courts. Ireland is excluded because a claim relating to the same set of circumstances, for instance discriminatory and unfair dismissal can be adjudicated by two separate bodies. The Netherlands is not included because half of all dismissal cases are handled through an administrative procedure.
*Excluding rapid procedure (référés) applications.
Sources: Calculations by the authors based on labour force statistics in EU – Eurostat Labour Force survey and national sources for civil servants (see Note 1). Claims figures based on statistics from the Ministère de la Justice, Statistisches Bundesamt, Ministry Of Justice/HM Courts and Tribunal Service, Ministero della Giustizia, Rasmussen and Greenwood, 2014, CCMA annual report and Tokisa Digest Claims statistics.

Conciliation/mediation

In all the countries in this book some claims, having been submitted, are then settled either by a formal process of conciliation/mediation, are withdrawn, or are settled outside a formal process. The number of claims that are adjudicated is, therefore, less than the number originally lodged, although there are significant variations by country. Accordingly this gives a different perspective on the litigation rate. We capture that in Table 13.4.

Table 13.4 Litigation rate based on adjudicatory judgments

Country	Hearings	Working population	Litigation rate %
France	86,680	19 million	0.45
Germany	28,505	32.7 million	0.09
Great Britain	61,400	23.5 million	0.3

Note: Hearings in France exclude rapid procedure applications.
Source: Calculations by the authors based on labour force statistics in EU – Eurostat Labour Force survey and national sources for civil servants (see Note 1 to Table 13.3). Claims figures based on statistics from the Ministère de la Justice, Statistisches Bundesamt, Ministry Of Justice/HM Courts and Tribunal Service.

It is a moot point whether conciliation/mediation benefits the parties. On the one hand, a voluntary settlement obviates a hearing which is often stressful, especially for a worker who, unlike an employer, is seldom a repeat player. Also the confidentiality of conciliation is often valued by both parties, whereas an adjudicatory hearing is normally held in public.[1] Moreover, a voluntary settlement may provide outcomes which could not be achieved by adjudication, for instance the provision of a reference. Nevertheless, legal norms are not propagated or developed and claimants might settle for less than they might obtain from a court if their claim were to be successful. Indeed, some unions are wary of alternative dispute resolution, adopting the view that only the courts can adequately protect workers' rights (see for example Chapter 7). Table 13.5 (p.216) reports the percentage of claims that are settled through conciliation/mediation, where we have been able to find statistics. As can be seen, the available statistics show a range from less than 10 per cent in France to over 80 per cent in New Zealand.

In some countries, an engagement with conciliation/mediation is a necessary step before adjudication. In some countries this is carried out by a separate agency, and in others it is carried out by the court, as noted in our introductory chapter (see Table 1.2 on p. 16 and the preceding chapters).

Expertise

Expertise is another yardstick that can be used to gauge one country's employment rights regime against another's. Intuitively, where there are

Table 13.5 Voluntary settlements obtained through conciliation/mediation

Country	Rate of conciliated/mediated settlements	Who provides it
France	7%	Lay judges
Germany	60–65%	Various
Great Britain	33%	Acas
Ireland	38%	Equality Tribunal cases
Italy	3% public sector 46% private sector	'Administrative' conciliation
New Zealand	81%	Mediation Service
South Africa	50%	CCMA
Sweden	50%	In court

Notes: 1. In Ireland: Rights Commissioners also conciliate but no figures are available.
2. In Italy there are other categories of conciliation – see Chapter 7.
3. In South Africa, in addition, there is a relatively small proportion of conciliation also carried out by bargaining councils and privately.
4. In Great Britain, in addition, there is small number of discrimination cases resolved through judicial mediation.
Sources: Ministère de la Justice, 2012; Statistisches Bundesamt, 2012; Ministry of Justice, 2012a; Equality Tribunal, 2012; Ministero del Lavoro e delle Politiche Sociali, 2013; Department of Labour, 2012; Estimate by Benjamin, 2009; Estimate by former Chief Judge of the Arbetsdomstolen.

professional judges sitting full-time[2] in labour courts or other bespoke adjudicatory bodies one would expect them to have more employment law expertise than the professional judges in civil courts who only occasionally deal with employment rights cases. We do not, however, know of any empirical studies that would corroborate this intuitive view.

As noted in earlier chapters, employment rights adjudication has to be seen in the context of the industrial relations of the country concerned. A proxy for this is whether lay judges representing employers and workers have a role in the adjudication of employment rights cases, so injecting a workplace perspective as opposed to the legal perspective of the professional judge. There are lay judges in first-instance labour courts of five countries in this book, see Figure 1.2 on p. 16, while Germany unusually has lay participation in all its appellate labour courts. There is, however, evidence that in all these countries the majority of decisions are unanimous (see, for example, Selwyn (2008); Koch (2002); Ministère de la Justice (2012); Bader et al. (2012)). This raises the question of how consensus is formed during deliberations, and whether and how underlying loyalties are shed when the professional and lay judges are tasked with jointly arriving at a judgment.

One approach to the issue of expertise is to consider how the decision-making parties assess each other. There is evidence for this for Germany and Great Britain. In Germany, information is available on how professional judges view lay judges as part of a wider study into how courts deal with employment protection cases (Höland et al., 2007).[3] The views of the professional judges were generally very positive. In all, 86 per cent of respondents stated that lay judges were of 'great benefit' in proceedings at first- and second-instance labour courts, 12 per cent stated they had 'no influence' and 2 per cent that they offered no benefit or were a hindrance. Overall, 66 per cent of presiding judges said that lay judges' knowledge was sufficient 'often or always', and only 11 per cent 'rarely or never'. However, presiding judges did not feel reliant on lay members for arriving at a judgment (in dismissal cases): only 13 per cent said they did so frequently or always, rising to 28 per cent where the judges sat in chambers for particular sectors (essentially in Berlin only); 43 per cent said this was the case sometimes; and 44 per cent said 'rarely or never'. In terms of the type of information that lay members provided, qualitative responses suggested that this turned on technical aspects of work, assessments of how seriously a particular type of conduct might be regarded, what discretion might be typical at workplaces, and 'assessments of the practical world of work outside the public sector' (ibid.: 228).

In Great Britain in 2011 both professional and lay judges in Britain's labour courts were asked for their views about the role of lay judges; (Corby and Latreille, 2011).[4] When asked to rate the overall contribution of lay judges to the hearing process on a 1 to 4 scale with 1 as the highest score, the mean for first-instance professional judges was 2.36, with second-instance judges giving a slightly higher, that is less favourable, scale point: a mean of 2.64. Unpicking this, nearly four in five of first-instance professional judges were of the view that lay judges were 'very useful' or 'quite useful' in assessing the evidence and making findings of fact in the decision-making process, but the same number were of the view that lay judges were not very/not at all useful in applying legal principles.

At the second instance in Great Britain only half of second-instance judges were of the view that lay members were very/quite useful in applying legal principles.

Interestingly, four in five of first-instance professional judges agreed with the statement 'a three person tribunal generally has a greater legitimacy for parties than a judge sitting alone'. As noted in Chapter 5, professional judges in Great Britain sit with lay judges in some types of complaints only. The survey found that 16 per cent of British first-instance judges 'always' preferred to sit alone, that is without lay judges, and over two-fifths (43 per cent), 'sometimes' preferred to sit alone. In France too, professional judges were held to be uncomfortable with lay judges' presence in a judicial setting (Bourdieu, 1987).

Further work on how and in what circumstances lay judges provide legitimacy has been undertaken by Burgess et al. (2013) comparing five countries: France, Germany, Great Britain, Ireland and Sweden. Applying a conceptual schema used to analyse the governance regime for developing transnational employment regulation (Novitz and Syrpis, 2006), they consider how lay judges provide performance legitimacy, that is, efficient performance; regime legitimacy, that is representativeness and accountability; and polity legitimacy, that is a reflection of the country's socio-economic and industrial relations arrangements. They conclude, however, that they are unable to measure legitimacy in a robust and quantitative way cross-nationally, but are able to offer some tentative comparisons (for a full discussion see Burgess et al. (2013)).

Duration

It is in the interests of both parties and other stakeholders, particularly the state, that employment rights disputes are adjudicated speedily and there is an old English adage, 'justice delayed is justice denied'. As can be seen from Table 13.6, the length of time an employment dismissal case takes in Italy, from the filing of a claim to the handing down of a judgment is significantly longer than in France and Germany and considerably longer than in the Netherlands.

This survey does not cover all the countries in this book as elsewhere we have not been able to find such robust data. In Sweden, for instance it took seven or eight months before a claim was heard (Labour Court, 2010). In Ireland, it used to take eight months in some cases for a claim just to be acknowledged. More efficient systems rectified this in 2012 according to the Minister, so now a claim is acknowledged, on average, within five working days of receipt (Bruton, 2012b: 5).

Of course, the time elapsing between making a claim and finality is much greater where appeals are made. Partly this depends on the number of courts to which appeals can be made in any one case, and this varies. For instance there is no appeal from the Swedish Labour Court or Dutch civil courts in respect of employment proceedings. By contrast in Great Britain,

Table 13.6 Average length of proceedings for employment dismissal cases at first-instance courts

Country	Days 2006	2008	2010
France	369	476	389
Germany	88	82	94
Italy	619	–	604 (public sector) 536 (private sector)
Netherlands	80	21	21

Source: European Commission for the Efficiency of Justice (2012: 219) Statistisches Bundesamt, 2012; Ministero della Giustizia, 2011.

Table 13.7 Appellate regimes for employment rights cases

Country	1st instance	Appeal 1	Appeal 2	Appeal 3	Other
France	Conseils de Prud'hommes	Court of Appeal (*fact and law*)	Court of Cassation (*point of law*)		See note below
Germany	Local Labour Court	Land Labour Court (*fact and law*)	Federal Labour Court (*leave to appeal*)		Constitutional Court See note below
Great Britain	Employment Tribunal	Employment Appeal Tribunal (*point of law*)	Court of Appeal (*point of law + leave to appeal*)	Supreme Court (*point of law + leave to appeal*)	
Ireland	Workplace Relations Commission	Labour Court (*de novo*)	High Court (*point of law*)	Supreme Court (*point of law + leave to appeal*)	This regime to be introduced in 2014
Italy	Tribunal	Court of Appeal (*fact and law*)	Supreme Court (*point of law*)		Special chambers in these civil courts
Netherlands	Civil court (employment)		None		
New Zealand	Employment Relations Authority	Employment Court (*de novo*)	Court of Appeal (*point of law*)	Supreme Court (*point of law + leave to appeal*)	

Table 13.7 (Continued)

South Africa	Commission for Conciliation, Mediation & Arbitration	Labour Court (*review*)	Labour Appeal Court (*leave to appeal*)	Supreme Court of Appeal (*leave to appeal*)	
	Labour Court	Labour Appeal Court (*leave to appeal*)	Supreme Court of Appeal (*leave to appeal*)		Constitutional Court
Sweden	Labour Court	None		None	
	District Court	Labour Court (*de novo*)			
USA (Federal)	District Court	Court of Appeals (*point of law*)	US Supreme Court (*leave to appeal*)		

Notes:
1. Germany, Great Britain, France, the Netherlands, Italy and Sweden are all in the European Union. Accordingly, where employment legislation emanates from a European directive, a reference can be made to the Court of Justice of the European Union.
2. In France there is a right of appeal to the Court of Appeal (social chamber) only if the amount at issue exceeds €4,000 (each claim taken separately) or in certain other instances where a claim has a non-monetary value. Otherwise the case can be appealed to the Court of Cassation on a point of law only.
3. In Germany, an appeal can be lodged at the Land Labour Court if the judicial amount exceeds €600 or if the case deals with the existence or termination of an employment contract. Also the first-instance court can give leave to appeal.
4. In New Zealand there is a suggestion that an appeal from the Employment Court should first go to the High Court and then to the Court of Appeal.
5. In South Africa where the dispute concerns dismissal for misconduct or incapacity there is arbitration by the CCMA. For dismissal on other grounds, and other employment rights issues, there is conciliation only by the CCMA and first-instance adjudication is by the Labour Court.
Sources: Dedicated country chapters in this book.

Ireland, New Zealand and South Africa there are three appellate levels (see Table 13.7). If a case is taken all the way up the appellate hierarchy it can take many years, particularly if a domestic court makes a reference to the Court of Justice of the European Union where European Union law is involved.

Typically, as noted above, the employer normally has greater financial resources than the worker, so a regime where there are many levels of appeal is likely to benefit the party with the greater resources – although an employer facing a claim that is likely to be protracted might not perceive the situation in these terms.

A comparison between appeal rates between different countries is constrained by the fact that the criteria for appeal differ. For instance in Great Britain, where an appeal can only be made on a point of law, the rate of appeal from the first-instance body to the first appellate court is 13 per cent (Ministry of Justice, 2012a), but in Germany, where among other things appeals can be made if the 'judicial amount' exceeds €600, the appeal rate is in the order of 40 per cent.[5] The comparable figure in New Zealand, where a decision by the first-instance body can be challenged de novo at the first appellate court is in the order of 10 per cent, according to the Chief Judge.

In France a decision by the first-instance *conseil de prud'hommes* can be appealed to the Court of Appeal (social chamber) only if among other things the amount at issue exceeds €4,000.[6] Otherwise the case can only be appealed to the Court of Cassation on a point of law. The French appeal rate from the *conseil*s to the Court of Appeal is 42.5 per cent according to the European Commission for the Efficiency of Justice (2012: 218), with appeals in the employment sphere higher than in other fields of civil law and accounting for around a quarter of the workload of the appellate court (Ministère de la Justice, 2012a). Both the French and German figures could be interpreted as considerable dissatisfaction by the parties to decisions by the first-instance body, and/or a reflection of the ease of appeal in those countries.

Legal formality

We now consider the extent to which legal formality, for instance rules of evidence, the conduct of the parties and witnesses, the drawing of analogies with previous published decisions and cross-examination are to the fore and we take as a proxy for that whether lawyers have a monopoly of representation, whether the costs of legal representation are refunded to the winning party, whether the adjudicator is legally qualified and whether the court proceedings are investigative or adversarial.

On the one hand, it could be argued that the dominance of legal formality is detrimental to the interests of parties not attuned to legal norms and values, especially if a party is not a repeat player (and employers are more likely to be repeat players than workers). On the other hand, it could be argued that evidence can only be properly tested if there is examination and cross-examination, where lawyers have expertise. The drift from investigative to adversarial procedures is observable in a number of countries, essentially due to the growth and increasing complexity of employment law, with employees navigating the 'single player' problem by hiring repeat players – that is, lawyers, or other experienced representatives. For instance, in Great Britain in 2008 two-thirds of claimants were represented at a hearing by a barrister, solicitor, or other representative; (see Corby and Latreille (2012: 395) for full details).

In the first-instance and appellate civil courts in the United States, apart from self-representation (pro se), one can only be represented by a qualified lawyer.[7] Even though in some cases the court can award costs to the winner under certain statutes, this monopoly deters American workers from taking a case to the civil courts as Chapter 12 indicates. In Italy it is mandatory for both parties to be legally represented.

In contrast, there are no restrictions on representation in the labour courts featured in this book, facilitating cost free representation, for instance if a worker is represented by a union official and an employer by a human resources manager or an employers' organisation official. Even if a party has to pay for representation, both workers and employers can be represented either by non-legally qualified advocates or by lawyers, and the fees of the former are normally below those of the latter. Interestingly, lawyers were only permitted in German trade and labour courts after 1926, and then not at first instance, gaining access at this level only in 1953. And up until 1979, they were only allowed to represent clients where the value of the claim was less than DM 300 (some £75 at that time) on application (Sawall, 2007: 293; Bundesarbeitsgericht, n.d.)

Unusually in South Africa's Commission for Conciliation, Mediation and Arbitration, which arbitrates on unfair dismissal for misconduct or incapacity, legal representation has not normally been allowed, albeit subject to the arbitrator's discretion, for example if the case was legally complex. This restriction on legal representation aimed to provide equality of arms and to prevent the formality that lawyers tend to inject, but it was successfully challenged in the High Court in 2012 on the grounds of constitutional invalidity.

If legal representation is permitted and costs are awarded to the winner, prima facie a party is more likely to be represented by a lawyer. On the one hand, this is likely to make proceedings more formal; on the other hand there is evidence that success is more likely if there is legal representation; (see, for example, Peters et al. (2010)).

In some countries legal representation, although permitted, is tacitly discouraged because costs are not awarded. For instance costs are not awarded in Germany's first-instance labour court, in Italy, or in Ireland's (largely appellate) Labour Court. In Great Britain costs are only awarded if, for instance, the labour court considers the case to be vexatious, mischievous or otherwise misconceived.

In some countries there is legal aid available, for instance in France and Italy, but not in Great Britain's first-instance court and only for discrimination cases in its appellate courts. It is beyond the remit of this book, however, to evaluate legal aid provisions which vary across several dimensions: whether legal aid applies to none/some/all employment rights cases in a country; the criteria for obtaining legal aid (and any analysis must relate to the average wage and purchasing power in the country), and the number of grants made.

Another way that legal formality is discouraged is if the adjudicator is not required to be legally qualified. As can be seen in Table 13.8, in the majority of countries covered in this book, the presiding judge has to be legally qualified. The exceptions are Ireland under its proposed system both at the first instance and first appellate level, in New Zealand at first instance,

Table 13.8 Legal formality

Country	1st instance		Appeal 1	
	Legal monopoly	**Presiding Judge required to be legally qualified**	**Legal monopoly**	**Presiding Judge required to be legally qualified**
France	No	Yes, but only presides if lay judges do not agree	No	Yes
Germany	No	Yes	No	Yes
Great Britain	No	Yes	No	Yes
Ireland	No	No	No	No
Italy	Yes	Yes	Yes	Yes
Netherlands	No	Yes	No appeal in employment cases	
New Zealand	No	No	No	Yes
South Africa	No	No for misconduct & incapacity dismissals. Yes for other complaints	No	Yes
Sweden	No	Yes	No appeal from Labour Court	
USA	Yes	Yes	Yes	Yes

Note: The proposed new system in Ireland is depicted, not the system current at the time of writing.
Source: Previous chapters in this book.

although in practice most adjudicators are legally qualified. In South Africa, France and the Netherlands some adjudicators are not required to be legally qualified.

Another way that legal formality can be gauged is if the hearing is conducted in an investigative or adversarial manner. This is not easy to measure cross-nationally as it depends on a range of factors such as the character of the judge(s) and whether the parties are represented by lawyers. For instance New Zealand's Employment Relations Authority is enjoined to adopt an investigative approach (Chapter 9), but if there is legal representation on both sides, some adjudicators allow the parties to drive the proceedings.

Outcomes

We noted earlier that that the outcome of an adjudication may depend primarily on how the burden of proof and the legal tests are framed, rather than how the adjudicatory institutions are constituted and operate. Having said that, 'who wins' is normally the most important consideration for the parties. Unfortunately, we do not have data on outcomes that is comprehensive and covers all the countries delineated in this book. We have some data for Great Britain and for the year to 31 March 2012 in 45 per cent of successful claimants in their unfair dismissal complaint (Ministry of Justice, 2012a).[8] In less than 1 per cent of these successful cases was reinstatement or re-engagement awarded; otherwise compensation was awarded with the median award £4,560 (approximately $6,970; €5,250). If the complaint was about discrimination the rate of success was lower. For instance claimants in sex discrimination claims were only successful in 19 per cent of the cases disposed of at a hearing, although the median award of compensation was slightly higher at £6,746 (approximately $10,313; €7,766).

South Africa's Commission for Conciliation, Mediation and Arbitration arbitrates cases of unfair dismissal for incapacity and misconduct and the employee won in 53 per cent of cases looking at the outcome over a three year period 2008–11.[9] As in Great Britain, overwhelmingly compensation, rather than reinstatement, is the remedy in South Africa (Venter and Levy, 2013).

In France, claimants win 73 per cent of all first-instance cases, and the vast bulk of claimants are employees. In Germany, Höland and Zeibig (2007: 143) in their survey of judgments found that 60 per cent of dismissal claims were upheld (that is the employee won) at first instance and 52 per cent at *Land* level (see Chapter 4 for details of that survey).

In short, although our figures are not strictly comparable, they provide evidence that in France, Germany and South Africa, a claimant is more likely to win a dismissal case than lose it, but not in Great Britain.

Perceptions of the parties

A criterion for the evaluation of employment rights institutions is whether those institutions deliver procedural justice. Do the parties, whether they have won or lost, believe that their case was handled fairly? One aspect of this is 'interactional justice'; do participants feel that they have been treated with dignity and respect and that the procedure and decisions were explained? Do the participants feel that the judicial process was a legitimate way of resolving a dispute? The presence of lay judges or representatives of the contending parties raises the potential legitimacy of judicial proceedings and we have briefly covered that above. Unfortunately evidence on procedural justice in the employment area is patchy.

A survey in Great Britain in 2008, based on a random sample of 4,027 cases, found that claimants' satisfaction with the outcome of their case was mixed. Perhaps not unsurprisingly satisfaction was related to the actual outcome. Three quarters of the claimants who won their case were satisfied with the outcome, while only 13 per cent of claimants who lost their case were satisfied. Satisfaction among British employers was also related to a successful outcome.

In New Zealand, a study by Shulruf et al. (2009) of employers who had experienced an employment dispute in the 12 months ending 31 March 2007 looked at satisfaction with the process and the outcome on a 1 to 6 scale with scale 1 very dissatisfied and scale 6 very satisfied. Employer satisfaction with the *process* of litigation was 2.6 and with the *outcome* of litigation it was 2.8. The comparable figures for mediation were 3.7 and 4. In addition the New Zealand government reviewed the system. The Department of Labour (2010) found that what little evidence there was suggested that the majority of employers were satisfied with the process and outcomes of the entire personal grievance system. There was, however, some indicative evidence that some employers and employees found that the system was not efficient and effective and this led to some minor amendments (Department of Labour, n.d.).

In Sweden, there is limited evidence of general satisfaction by stakeholders with the employment rights adjudicatory process as a government inquiry found general agreement by the social partners that labour disputes should continue to be heard by the Labour Court and not be transferred to the civil courts (Mål och medel, 2010).

In the Netherlands, some assessment of the views of participants in the official dismissal authorisation process was undertaken by the Dutch National Ombudsman in 2007, who also used satisfaction data collected from those who had passed through the dismissal procedure (Nationale Ombudsman, 2007). This process is an administrative process at which employers apply for permission to terminate an employee's contract (or make a collective redundancy) (see Chapter 8). Although employers felt the authorisation procedure could be improved and employer associations later supported its abolition, the procedure itself was considered fair. By contrast, employees reported that employers were seen as the 'the client' of the employment service and that the way in which information was presented favoured employers: for example, employers were briefed about the process on making an application but not, at that time, employees, except for collective dismissals. In addition, the procedure is based on written evidence. This lack of oral presentation and scope for challenge was also seen as a problem by the Ombudsman: the process was described by one participant as a 'black box'. Nonetheless, it was able to gain some legitimacy as it encompassed employer and employee members with legal expertise and workplace experience.

Further research

Which system is 'better' or more effective? As noted above, if crude generalisations are to be avoided, several yardsticks have to be adopted and there needs to be consideration of the standpoint of the stakeholder, for example the worker, the employer, both parties, the government, trade unions, lawyers. Accordingly, we have used a number of yardsticks and commented on the party/parties who might benefit. We have been stymied in this chapter, however, by the lack of evidence, and in particular data that can be scrutinised on a comparable basis, making it impossible to draw robust cross-national comparisons. Accordingly, we end this book with a plea for more research. Such research is important because the widespread decline of collective means for resolving workplace disputes has made the institutions for the adjudication of individual employment rights disputes both increasingly salient and socially significant.

Notes

1 Introduction: Issues and Overview

1. RES-00022-4154.
2. See Acknowledgements.
3. In New Zealand the Employment Relations Authority adjudicators, known as Members, are not now appointed unless they have some legal qualifications.
4. In the Netherlands there are professional judges in the civil courts who specialise in employment matters.
5. In both South Africa and New Zealand at the level below these courts the adjudicator need not be legally trained or qualified – see arbitration by the Commission for Conciliation, Mediation and Arbitration in South Africa and determinations by a Member of the Employment Relations Authority.
6. See Halford v Sharples and Ors [1992] ICR 146.

2 Employment Adjudication: Comparisons and Anomalies

1. P.J.A. Feuerbach (1810). Extract translated by the authors.
2. This consideration draws on theories of multi-level governance, in which second-order institutions either facilitate or are dominated by the resolution of 'first-order' problems (or conflicts). Roe (2007: 294) also terms some features of legal systems 'secondary institutions'.
3. Cross-cultural procedural justice theories would offer another avenue (Cohn et al., 2000). However, this approach leaves more unanswered questions about determination than the models chosen here.
4. It is perhaps worth noting that many of these studies emerged during the ascendancy of neo-liberalism and shareholder value approaches, with an implicit criticism of corporatism that, embodied in the 'German model', was then seen as in decline.
5. The classic exposition is the Introduction (Hall and Soskice, 2001), with contributions compiled in Hancké (2009).
6. Casey (2006) argues for a spectrum from CME to LME 'with others scattered in between', implying intermediate rather than alternative states. There is also a trade-off between multiplying business systems and the explanatory force of a simpler model – acceptable if the underlying model is sound.
7. For Germany, we estimate this is some 20 per cent of such contractual disputes in 2011.
8. For a discussion of national differences in the history and identity of lawyers in Europe, see Morgan and Quack (2010).
9. Williams v Compair Maxam Ltd [1982] IRLR 483 EAT.
10. Hepple (1988) refers to this procedure 'as the functional equivalent of the conciliation role of ACAS', but this would seem to omit the role of social partner representatives in advising public officials. Social partner representatives were not admitted until the 1950s, and before that the process was managed entirely by officials. One would need to reconstruct the decision-making process that led to

this change through historical research to explore whether and how it was connected with the type of institutionalisation characteristic of CMEs, of which the Netherlands was an emerging case.

3 France

1. These are Medef, a strong central organisation with some 750,000 company members, and organisations representing SMEs (CGPME) and craft workers (UPA).
2. Moritz (1987: 143) citing David (1974: 13) notes there was 'cross voting', with each side voting for the opposite side's representatives.
3. The Law of 13 July 1973 regulated the grounds for lawful ordinary and summary dismissal. Official authorisation was required for individual dismissal until 1986/87.
4. The appointment of staff representatives is mandatory in firms with 11 or more employees, although compliance is weak in small firms.
5. The creation of these chambers took place in the 1970s, in part in order to cut delays in the system (Napier, 1979: 273–4).
6. Judges are also elected in commercial tribunals, but the sheer size of the body of judges in labour courts, some 15,000 in all, is peculiar to the employment jurisdiction.
7. To have representative status at a workplace, a union must receive at least 10 per cent of the votes cast in elections for works committees (*comité d'entreprise*).
8. This also applies to claims for payment of severance pay, compensation related to the early termination of a fixed-term contract or any action for damages against the employer arising out of a breach of the employer's obligations. However, employees have a period of three years in which to submit a claim for any remuneration due. The time limit within which an employee must challenge an economic dismissal remains 12 months, provided this is expressly noted in the letter of dismissal, including the lack of a social compensation plan. A 12-month time limit also applies to termination by mutual agreement, *rupture conventionelle.*
9. The panel may make an exception if a public hearing could undermine individuals' private lives, if both parties request it, or if the peaceful administration of justice is at risk. Cases dealing with sexual harassment may be held in private at the request of one of the parties.
10. An individual is entitled to have all legal costs covered if they have a monthly income of below €929 (single person), with additions for other members of the household (€167 for the first two dependents, €106 for further dependents). A portion of costs can be covered for incomes below €1,393 (single person), with a sliding scale between the two levels.
11. Bourdieu (1987: 818ff.) noted in Roman law systems that 'the dominance of doctrine reproduces and reinforces the domination of the high magistracy'. He also noted that judges have an 'inventive' role that extends beyond applying the law, but that 'in granting the status of *judgment* to a legal decision which no doubt owes more to the ethical dispositions of the actors than to pure norms of the law', they add to the 'rationalising formalism' of the law. He argued that this clashed with the lay element, in which conciliation and agreement play a key role. This perhaps overlooks trade union aversion in Southern Europe to mediation over the application of the law.

4 Germany

1. 'East Germany' refers to the territory of the former German Democratic Republic, which joined the Federal Republic ('West Germany') in 1990.
2. Lay judges in all jurisdictions are subject to the Judges Law: this prescribes procedures for admission, swearing in, obligations and removal.
3. The term is '*ehrenamtlicher Richter*'. 'Ehrenamtlich' means an office held in 'honour', not for a fee. The presiding judge is the 'chair' (*Vorsitzende*), a role that can only be held by a professional judge (*Berufsrichter*), appointed by the relevant *Land* Justice Ministry (with the option of selection by a panel of employer and employee representatives).
4. Except North-Rhine Westphalia, where there is a '*Land* conciliator'.
5. This was a controversial aspect of the draft law as the professional body for mediators objected to the term 'judicial mediator' for judges acting in this capacity. As a consequence, these are now dubbed 'conciliation judges' (*Güterichter*).
6. *Länder* administer the system below the level of the Federal Labour Court.
7. Rehder emphasises the difference in the stance of labour lawyers in relation to civil (contract) lawyers. This has its roots in the influence of jurists such as Hugo Sinzheimer, who argued for the establishment of labour law, and in particular for the priority of collective agreements, as a means of redressing the structural imbalance between workers and employers that nullified formal contractual equality. This contrasts with the pragmatic and evolutionary emergence of employment tribunals in Great Britain.
8. Practitioners interviewed for this research stated that in their experience unions never submitted nominations for individuals who lacked appropriate experience. One issue that occasionally needed to be resolved at ministry level was whether nominees were correctly assigned to the employer or employee side, especially if someone had been promoted to senior management level.
9. According to Bader et al. (2012), the only *Land* that does so is Brandenburg.
10. There are 122 first-instance Labour Courts, of varying sizes.
11. The fee if a judgment is issued is calculated at double a 'base rate' set out in the statutory cost schedule. The multiple rises to 3.2 of the base rate on appeal.
12. See Greger and Unberath (2012). Intra-judicial mediation saw agreement on a wider range of issues than conciliation and lasted much longer, but with a net reduction in hours given the absence of case management for a full hearing.
13. The figure of 40 per cent is an inference from the number of judgments reached on dismissal in 2011 (c. 12,000) and the total number of cases heard on this issue in *Land* labour courts in the same year (c. 4,600), some of which would have been referred in previous years. However, the figure correlates with data from other sources from the early-2000s, which found that an appeal was lodged for around one-third of all first-instance judgments, with a higher rate in dismissal cases (see, for example, Höland, 2005).
14. The *Land* labour court for Hesse is one, rare, example of specialisation by area of law; there are also chambers for the public sector and for aviation. The court is large, with 19 presiding judges and 419 lay judges.

5 Great Britain

1. For instance Northern Ireland has Fair Employment Tribunals and no Employment Appeal Tribunal.

2. The Employment Rights (Dispute Resolution) Act 1998 renamed industrial tribunals as employment tribunals with effect from 1 August 1998.
3. Lay members are also called wing members, or non-legal members.
4. Other nominating bodies were later added including the Union of Democratic Mineworkers, the Council of Managerial and Professional Staffs, the Institute of Directors and the Federation of Small Businesses (Department of Trade & Industry, 1998).
5. The unions had great distrust of judges at that time as in a number of decisions, including Rookes v Barnard [1964] AC 1129, the courts whittled away at the legality of strike action.
6. Employment Tribunals (Constitution and Rules of Procedure) Regulations 2004, reg. 8.
7. For instance, any views of the parties and whether there is a likelihood of a dispute on the facts which makes it desirable for the proceedings to be heard by a full tribunal.
8. At the time of writing a professional judge can sit alone when hearing cases arising from claims for breach of contract, unauthorised deductions from wages, redundancy payments, interim relief applications, written statements of employment particulars, itemised pay statements, certain complaints under the National Minimum Wage Act, stage 1 hearings under the equal value provisions, holiday pay and unfair dismissal.
9. Approximately €212, $281.
10. An employer can counterclaim where the worker has complained of breach of contract.
11. Approximately $1,523, €1,173.
12. See ET Constitution and Rules of Procedure.
13. Approximately $30,460; €23,453.
14. These include a misdirection or misapplication of the law, inadequate reasons for a decision, bias, no evidence to support a tribunal's factual findings and perversity.
15. Approximately €370, $489.
16. For instance, increasing the qualifying period for unfair dismissal from one year to two years.
17. This research was funded by the Economic and Social Research Council, Award number: 000-22-4154.
18. At the time of writing the disposable capital test is £3,000 (approximately $4,712, €3,531) for a claimant under 61 and the monthly income test is £1,085 for a single person with no children (approximately $1,733, €1,280).
19. The cap on deposits was raised from £500 to £1,000 and the cap on costs was raised from £10,000 to £20,000.
20. Approximately £5,000 = $8,095, €6,117; £15,000 = $24,284, €18,332; £245 = $397, €299; £100,000 = $161,892, €122,352; £150,000 = $242,847, €183,518; £885 = $1,433, €1,083.
21. Approximately £25,000, €30,500, $40,316. Figures correct for December 2012.
22. The last appeal court must, and any court/tribunal may, refer a case to the European Court of Justice where European law is an issue.
23. These figures can be gleaned from a careful study of successive Acas annual reports.
24. Around €70,729 – Written Ministerial Statement to Parliament 24 May 2012. Also see http://services.parliament.uk/bills/2013-14/gangmasterslicensingauthority extensionofpowers.html

6 Ireland

1. Also protection of young persons, health and safety, information and consultation. For a full list see the Labour Relations Commission Annual Report 2011.
2. However, a Rights Commissioner may 'draw such inferences' as seem proper from a refusal to produce documents or respond to questions put by a Commissioner (Kerr and McGreal, 2009: 834).
3. Employment Equality Acts 1998–2011, Equal Status Acts 2000–2011 (which relate to the provision of goods and services), Pensions Acts 1990–2008.
4. The protected characteristics are age, disability, family status, gender, marital status, race, religion, sexual orientation and traveller community.
5. District Courts may also issue enforcement orders.
6. NERA also prosecutes for non-compliance with Labour Court determinations under the Industrial Relations Acts.
7. The Labour Court in its industrial relations role mainly provides a conciliation service and adjudicates in trade disputes. It also enforces national social partner agreements.
8. The Labour Court also hears appeals under the Pensions Acts 1990 to 2008, The Employees (Provision of Information and Consultation) Act 2006, The Protection of Employment (Exceptional Collective Redundancies and Related Matters) Act 2006, the Employment Permits Act 2006, Protection of Employees (Temporary Agency Work) Act 2012.
9. Visit by one of the authors.
10. It is rumoured that in making these appointments, the Minister is mainly guided by the interests of the social partners and currently one deputy chair comes from the trade union side and one deputy chair comes from the employer side.
11. The legislation will contain a provision to enable the Minister to impose a charge, although he has said he will not do so, at least for the time being.
12. The Registrar will have limited strike out powers and the Registrar's decision will be appealable at the Labour Court.
13. The parties will not be debarred from adjudication if they refuse to attempt conciliation.
14. According to the Director Designate of the WRC the time limit is likely to be six to eight weeks.
15. Level 8 of the National Framework of Qualifications in Ireland; as well as employment and discrimination law, the training will cover constitutional, administrative and human rights law, laws of evidence and workshop-type modules to enhance participants' skills in conducting hearings, dealing with the parties and writing up reasoned decisions.
16. In Great Britain, the Employment Appeal Tribunal can ask the Employment Tribunal for the judge's notes of evidence.
17. Also failing or refusing to provide an employee with written terms and conditions as prescribed by law, failing or refusing to maintain employment records in a prescribed manner and failing or refusing to record deductions on a payslip as required by law.
18. Where an appeal raises confidential or sensitive issues, for instance in relation to sexual harassment or Traveller status, the Court may decide to hold a hearing in private and a published decision will not contain the names of the parties.
19. Interview conducted by one of the authors on 9 July 2013.
20. See *Bryan v United Kingdom* [1995] 21 E.H.R.R. 342.

7 Italy

1. Law 3 April 1926, no. 563 and the related Regulation 1 July 1926 no. 1,130.
2. The workers' representation model at company level, as it was outlined in the Workers' Statute, has been recently altered (Constitutional Court no. 231/2013); this might indeed constitute a further element of uncertainty, calling for still more legislative intervention.
3. See also http://stats.oecd.org/Index.aspx?DatasetCode=LFS_SEXAGE_I_R. For a brief overview of the Italian industrial relations system see R. Pedersini, *Italy: industrial relations profile (online)*, in http://www.eurofound.europa.eu/eiro/country/italy.pdf
4. For a study of the evolution of trade union membership, see Regalia (2009: 123ff). Regalia suggests that trade unions have an opportunity to recruit two categories of workers: young people and white-collar workers. See also Carrieri (2011).
5. The total number of judges in Italy is 8,943, with 4,735 men and 4,208 women; see http://astra.csm.it/organicoOrdinari/orgord.php. There are no statistical data on the gender of the judges according to the level of the Court, but what evidence there is suggests that women are concentrated at the lower levels (such as in Tribunals or Court of Appeal), rather than in the Supreme Court. This is for two reasons: first because women were only allowed to compete to become a judge in 1966 (law of 9 February 1963, no. 66); second, even though the ranking of winners of the last 15 years' competitions contain many more women than men, women have not accrued the necessary service to gain promotion to the higher courts.
6. The court is composed of nine judges when they decide conflicting judgments in the Supreme Court (the so-called decision by *sezioni unite*).
7. See http://webstat.giustizia.it/AreaPubblica/default.aspx#
8. According to data from the Supreme Court it seems that the average length of proceedings before the Supreme Court has decreased by about 2.8 months. See 'Rapporto Statistico del settore civile, anno 2012', at http://www.cortedicassazione.it/Documenti/CCStatisticheCivile_2012.pdf
9. Workers are able to appeal to the judicial authorities against the certification.
10. There are only a few collective agreements that have enabled the parties to agree to this clause and they try to impose limits. For example, within the tertiary sector the clause cannot cover such matters as sexual harassment and illness.
11. See http://webstat.giustizia.it/AreaPubblica/Analisi%20e%20ricerche/Mediazione%20Civile%20al%2031%20luglio%202012.pdf
12. It was introduced as mandatory by law no. 28/2010, was then made discretionary as a result of the Constitutional Court's decision, but then Law 69/2013 made mediation mandatory again, except for employment disputes.

8 The Netherlands

1. At the time of writing, the FNV was undergoing an overhaul following internal disagreement between the confederation and two of its largest affiliates over policy towards concluding tripartite national accords, with some large affiliates hostile to neo-corporatist political exchange. As discussed below, the capacity of the FNV to obtain a mandate for central negotiations on reforms to dismissal law has been, and remains, a delicate issue within the federation.

2. In 2012, the main union confederations submitted a complaint to the ILO on the grounds that the current arrangements do not meet the Netherlands' obligation under the Conventions it has ratified.
3. Summary dismissal is possible without authorisation. Employees may contest this is in the courts. As a precaution, many employers simultaneously apply for authorisation for a normal termination.
4. UWV stands for 'Uitvoeringsinstituut Werknemers Verzekeringen' or 'Employee Insurance Service', an agency of the Ministry of Social Affairs. WERKbedrijf' is the 'Employment Service', a sub-division of the UWV.
5. Exceptionally, a payment may be offered voluntarily. There have also been – rare – circumstances in which a permit was conditional on compensation (van Arkel, 2007: 163).
6. In Spain, employers must obtain official permission for collective dismissals.
7. Van Arkel (2007) and Windmuller (1969: 268–9) discuss the tensions between the government-in-exile and the emerging, and clandestine, partnership between organised capital and labour from 1943.
8. This implied a revision of the prior legal position that emphasised freedom of contract and a right to terminate at-will in indefinite contracts. As such, the Netherlands might be seen as a case of a liberal employment regime yielding to a coordinated system as a result of the social partnership forged during the occupation.
9. In 2007, the National Ombudsman recommended that oral hearings be held as a matter of course. This was rejected by UWV WERKbedrijf, in part because much of its work during the crisis involved collective dismissals for which oral hearings were considered inappropriate.
10. According to one interviewee for this study, an attempt to conciliate was seen as strengthening an employer's position should the case come to court. ADR using trained conciliators was said to be increasing, but is still fairly limited in the employment field.
11. This also has a bearing on the wearing of gowns. One interviewee for this study noted that in some Cantons gowns were not worn by representatives in employment cases as representatives do not have to be lawyers, and only lawyers may wear gowns. They noted: 'You wear a gown to be equal. If one representative is wearing a gown and one not, then you are not equal.'
12. The only – and sole – exception to this has been where an individual CGB expert on job evaluation was called to present evidence in an equal pay case.
13. Havinga (2002: 85) noted: 'Half of the complainants were assisted by a lawyer, an anti-discrimination bureau or other person providing (legal) assistance... lawyers and unions rarely supply legal assistance in Commission cases concerning discrimination on grounds of race and/or nationality. Anti-discrimination bureaus play the most important role.'

9 New Zealand

1. S.4 Employment Relations Act, 2000.
2. S.49 Employment Tribunal Regulations, 1991. S.49 allows the Employment Tribunal to vary the procedure but that 'was not the norm at all' according to an erstwhile tribunal member interviewed.
3. Union Membership Return Report 2012 provided by registered trade unions in accordance with s.16 ERA 2000.

4. From 1 July 2011 all employees are entitled to a written employment agreement that must include certain clauses, including a clause on 'Resolving Employment Relationship Problems', with a suggested requirement that, after using internal procedure, the parties should go to the government's mediation service.
5. There is no such requirement in respect of ERPs which are not personal grievances, such as wage arrears, compliance and interpretation disputes.
6. A mediator may require the support person or adviser to withdraw if the mediator believes that their presence is not conducive to the prompt and effective resolution of the dispute. In practice this is not done.
7. The predecessor of the Ministry of Business, Innovation and Employment.
8. Mediation may be omitted if the Authority considers that it is not in the public interest, if mediation would not help resolve the matter, or if the case is urgent.
9. Internal statistics supplied to the author by the Chief of the Authority.
10. 'Whanau' is a Maori term that denotes the extended family.

10 South Africa

1. The CCMA has other powers, for instance to publish research and guidelines and provide advice and training.
2. Seven days if the parties to a dispute are engaged in an essential service.
3. An amendment to the LRA, yet to be promulgated, will prevent consultants appearing in proceedings before the Labour Court under the guise of membership or being an official of a trade union or employers' organisation, when in fact they appear in a professional capacity and seek to charge fees for that appearance.
4. Premier Gauteng & another v Ramabulana N.O. & others [2008] 4 BLLR 299.
5. See the LRA Amendment Bill which at the time of writing had gone through Parliament, but still had to go through the National Council of Provinces and then to be promulgated (i.e. by the President).
6. The Law Society of the Northern Provinces v Minister of Labour, Minister of Justice and Constitutional Development, Commission for Conciliation Mediation and Arbitration, Director for the CCMA case no 61197/11 HC.
7. This fee amounts to around $160, €115.
8. An amendment to the LRA not promulgated at the time of writing.
9. Venter and Levy (2013: 43), looking at successful unfair dismissal arbitration awards, found that reinstatement was awarded in 31 per cent of cases in 2011–12.
10. Email to the author, 9 October 2012.
11. Chirwa v Transnet Ltd and others [2007] ZACC 23; Gcaba versus Minister for Safety and Security and Others [2009] ZACC 26.
12. See s.77(3) BCEA.
13. See Law Society case above.
14. Sidumo & another v Rustenburg Platinum Mines Ltd and others [2007] 12 BLLR 1097 (CC).
15. Case no 701/2012 5 September 2013.
16. Information provided in an interview.
17. This does not look likely to change, whereas LC judges, if a legislative proposal becomes law, will be appointed until retirement or appointment to another superior court.
18. Emails to the author from L. Kley 11/12 October 2012.
19. Hoffmann v South African Airways [2000] ZACC 17.

20. National Education Health and Allied Workers Union v University of Cape Town [2002] ZACC 27.
21. Equivalent to roughly £5 or $9.
22. Similar administrative/civil enforcement procedures apply under the affirmative action provisions of the Employment Equity Act, while child labour and forced labour under the BCEA are criminal offences which may lead to imprisonment, as can breaches of the Occupational Health and Safety Act, although in practice criminal prosecution is extremely rare (Benjamin, 2011).
23. National Planning Commission, (2012: 34) quoted in Benjamin (2013).

11 Sweden

1. One of the principal explanations, among several, for the persistence of high rates of union density is the 'Ghent' system of voluntary unemployment insurance in which trade unions play a major role, of which there are a number of variants. Although trade unions in Sweden are no longer directly involved in the provision of unemployment insurance, and it is possible for individuals to affiliate to an unemployment fund without joining a union, the first funds were established and administered by unions and 'many workers still believe that trade union membership is a requirement for voluntary unemployment insurance coverage' (van Rie et al., 2011: 130). However, after peaking in the early 1990s at around 85 per cent, union density has since slipped back, in part due to broader social changes, but also as the cost of voluntary unemployment coverage has risen (Woolfson et al., 2010).
2. The Discrimination Ombudsman (*Diskrimineringsombudsmannen*) is the title of both a person and the organisation headed by that person.
3. The DO has to bring cases concerning goods and services and other non-employment matters to the District Court.
4. €170, $220, £140.
5. Prop. 2008/09:4, bet. 2008/09:AU6, rskr. 2008/09:43.
6. One option was that the District Court should hear all cases concerning discrimination, that is, including those relating to discrimination in employment, but the Government rejected that option.
7. Judge Michaël Koch, President Labour Court. Report to Tenth Meeting of European Labour Court Judges Stockholm, 2 September 2002.
8. Where European law is concerned, the Labour Court makes a reference to the Court of Justice of the European Union.
9. £42, $66, €51.
10. One interviewee was of the view that this was because of the growth of individualism and the prevalence of American TV with its many court-room dramas.
11. This can cause problems. See, for instance, *Laval un Patneri*, a Latvian construction company, which posted Latvian workers to work in Sweden and signed a collective agreement with the Latvian building sector's trade union.This undercut the pay rates applicable to building workers set out in the Swedish construction industry's agreement. The Swedish trade union then blockaded Laval's building sites in Sweden and Laval lodged a claim with the *Arbetsdomstolen*, which made a reference to the European Court of Justice (ECJ). The ECJ (C-341/05) determined that the Swedish union could not take industrial action to enforce the application of its collectively agreed terms and conditions to the posted Latvian workers. Only

if a country has statutory provisions on minimum wages or a collective agreement is generally applicable (*erga omnes*), can pay rates be prescribed for posted workers and this was not the case with the sectoral collective agreement in the instant case.

12 United States of America

1. It is beyond the remit of this chapter to delineate the similarities and differences between states.
2. The Equal Pay Act, 1963; The Civil Rights Act, 1964; The Age Discrimination in Employment Act, 1967; The Occupational Safety and Health Act, 1970; The Employment Income Security Act, 1974; The Employee Protection Polygraph Act, 1988; The Americans with Disabilities Act, 1990; The Civil Rights Act, 1991; The Family and Medical Leave Act, 1993.
3. Unlike Great Britain, collective agreements are normally contractual.
4. United Steelworkers v American Mfg. Co., 363 US 564, (1960); United Steelworkers v Warrior & Gulf Navigation Co., 363 US 574, (1960); United Steelworkers v Enterprise Wheel & Car Corp., 363 US 593, (1960).
5. Alexander v Gardner-Denver Co., 415 US 36 (1974).
6. 556 US 247.
7. Gilmer v Interstate/Johnson Lane, 500 US 20 (1991).
8. Circuit City Stores Inc v Adams, 532 US 105 (2001).
9. Cole v Burns International Security Services, 105 F.3d 1465 (DC Circuit 1997); Perez v Globe Airport Security Services Inc., 253 F.3d 1280, 1282 (11th Cir. 2001).
10. Hooters of America Inc v Phillips, 173 F.3d 933 (4th Cir 1999).
11. See California Supreme Court in Armendariz v Foundation Health Psyche Care Services Inc., 24 Cal.4th 83, 115–20 (2000) and the Texas Court of Appeals in Labor Ready Central III v Gonzalez, 87 FEP Cases 612 (2001).
12. Collective bargaining contracts are normally silent on this point, leaving it to the arbitrator to decide on a case-by-case basis.
13. Employment arbitration agreements often provide for reimbursement of legal costs to the employee in line with the fee-shifting provisions of federal discrimination statutes.
14. Perhaps this is because arbitrators, consciously or unconsciously, tend to favour the employer in the hope of further business.
15. In EEOC v Waffle House Inc., 534 US 279 (2002) the US Supreme Court held that the EEOC could litigate and obtain monetary damages for an employee, even if the employee was covered by a mandatory arbitration and so could not litigate him/herself, as such a provision did not bind the EEOC.

13 Evaluation: Applying Yardsticks

1. Under Ireland's proposed structure, first-instance adjudicatory hearings will be held in private. In Sweden the decision on whether to publish is a matter for the Labour Court to decide and less than half the decisions are published.
2. In Ireland's Employment Appeal Tribunal, the professional judges are part-time and as practising lawyers they rarely deal with employment cases and thus, according to some interviewees, lack expertise.

3. Questionnaires were sent to 912 first-instance presiding judges and 207 *Land* labour court judges. The response rates were 26 per cent and 32 per cent respectively.
4. This was a census, not a sample. At the first-instance level, questionnaires were sent to 424 judges with a 45 per cent response rate and 1,783 lay members with a 64 per cent response rate. At the first appellate level, questionnaires were sent to 20 judges with an 80 per cent response rate and 53 lay members with a 74 per cent response rate.
5. The grounds for appeal are complicated. See Chapter 4 for details. According to the European Commission for the Efficiency of Justice (2012: 218), the percentage of decisions subject to appeal in 2010 was 3.77 per cent, but this seems to be based on all claims lodged, not on cases where judgments at first instance were issued and then appealed.
6. See Chapter 3 for details.
7. There is no nationwide qualification for lawyers and each state sets its own rules for qualification.
8. This statistic relates to cases disposed at a hearing and includes default awards.
9. If default awards are excluded, the figure falls to 31 per cent according to Venter and Levy (2013: 42). They argue that 'the default figure should be disregarded. A proper view of the case can hardly be expected on one version alone, and it tends to be the practice of . . . Arbitrators to find for the party who is present'.

References

AA. VV. (2004) 'La giustizia del lavoro: disfunzioni, inefficienze, proposte di rivitalizzazione', *Rivista Critica di Diritto del Lavoro*, 3, 475–478.
Anderson, G. (2001) 'The Individual and the Employment Relations Act', *New Zealand Journal of Industrial Relations*, 26, 1, 103–118.
Anderson, G. (2011) 'Good Faith in the Individual Employment Relationship in New Zealand', *Comparative Labor Law & Policy*, 32, 685–727.
Arbetsdomstolen. (n.d.) http://www.arbetsdomstolen.se/pages/page.asp?lngID=7&lngLangID=1 [accessed 10 February 2012].
Bader, P., Hohman, R. and Klein, H. (2012) *Die ehrenamtlichen Richterinnen und Richter in der Arbeits – und Sozialgerichtsbarkeit*. 13th edition. Heidelberg: C.F. Müller Verlag.
Benjamin, P. (2009) 'Conciliation, Arbitration and Enforcement: The CCMA's Achievements and Challenges', *Industrial Law Journal*, 30, 26–49.
Benjamin, P. (2011) 'Enforcement and Sanctions to Promote Compliance with South African Labour Legislation', *Industrial Law Journal*, 32, 805–833.
Benjamin, P. (2013) 'Assessing South Africa's Commission for Conciliation, Mediation and Arbitration (CCMA)', *Working Paper 47*. Geneva: International Labour Organisation.
Benjamin, P., Bhorat, H. and Cheadle, H. (2010) 'The Cost of "Doing Business" and Labour Regulation: The Case of South Africa', *International Labour Review*, 149, 1, 73–91.
Bingham, L. and Mesch, D. (2000) 'Decision Making in Employment and Labor Arbitration', *Industrial Relations*, 39, 4, 671–693.
BIS. (2013a) *Trade Union Membership, 2013: Statistical Bulletin*. London: Department for Business, Innovation and Skills.
BIS. (2013b) 'Government to Simplify and Improve Employment Tribunals', *Press Release*, http://news.bis.gov.uk/Press-Releases/Government-to-simplify-and-improve-Employment-Tribunals-68966.aspx [accessed 23 March 2013].
BIS/HM Courts & Tribunals Service. (2011) *Resolving Workplace Disputes: Government Response to the Consultation*. London: Department for Business, Innovation and Skills.
Blalock, H. (1961) *Causal Inferences in Nonexperimental Research*. Chapel Hill: University of North Carolina Press.
Blanpain, R. (2007) 'Comparativism in Labour Law and Industrial Relations', in Blanpain, R. (ed) *Comparative Labour Law and Industrial Relations in Industrialized Market Economies*. Alphen aan der Rijn: Kluwer.
Blohorn-Brenneur, B. (2010) 'La mediation prud'homale', *International Conference of Mediation for Justice*, http://cimj.com/fr/base-documentaire/article/22-la-mediation-prud-homale-par-beatrice-blohorn-brenneur-fondatrice-et-vice-presidente-du-gemme [accessed 30 June 2013].
Bloomberg, BNA. (2012) 'Individual Employment Rights Law (Analysis) Jurisdiction and Procedure', *Labor & Employment Law Resource Center*, IERM 534, 901, 29 June.
Borghesi, D. (2010) 'L'arbitrato ai tempi del collegato lavoro', www.judicium.it [accessed 12 April 2013].
Bosch, C. (2013) 'An Evaluation of the Labour Court', in Venter, T. and Levy, A. (eds) *The Dispute Resolution Digest* 2013. Johannesburg: Tokiso/Juta.

Botero, J.C., Djankov, S., La Porta, R., Lopez-de-Silanes, F. and Shleifer, A. (2004) 'The Regulation of Labor', *Quarterly Journal of Economics*, November 2004, 119, 4, 133–1382.

Boulmier, D. (2011) *Conseil de prud'hommes*. Rueil-Malmaison: Lamy.

Bourdieu, P. (1987) 'The Force of Law: Towards a Sociology of the Juridical Field', *The Hastings Law Journal*, 38, July 1987, 805–853.

Bove, M. (2010) 'Art. 808 ter c.p.c.', in Menchini, S. (ed) *La nuova disciplina dell'arbitrato*. Padova: Cedam.

Brownlie, N. (2012) *Trade Union Membership 2011*. London: Department for Business, Innovation & Skills.

Bruton, R. (2011) *High Level Conference on the Resolution of Individual Employment Rights Disputes*, 1 July, Dublin: School of Law, University College Dublin.

Bruton, R. (2012a) *Blueprint to Deliver a World-Class Workplace Relations Service*. April. Dublin: DJEI.

Bruton, R. (2012b) *Legislating for a World-Class Workplace Relations Service: Submission to Oireachtas Committee on Jobs, Enterprise and Innovation*, July. Dublin: DJEI.

Bundesarbeitsgericht. (n.d.) 'Die Arbeitsgerichtsbarkeit' http://www.bundesarbeitsgericht.de/allgemeines/geschichte.html [accessed 20 August 2013].

Burgess, P., Corby, S. and Latreille, P. (2013) 'Lay Judges and Labour Courts', Paper presented to *the Industrial Relations in Europe Conference (IREC)*, Bucharest, Romania, 12–14 September.

Cabinet Office Economic Development Committee. (n.d) *Review of the Employment Relationship Problem Resolution System* Wellington: Department of Labour.

Calamandrei, P. (1968) 'Il significato costituzionale delle giurisdizioni di equità (1920)', in *Opere giuridiche*, III, Napoli: Jovene.

Canale, G. (2011) 'Arbitrato e collegato lavoro', www.judicium.it [accessed 12 April 2013].

Carrieri, M. (2011) *La regolazione del lavoro*. Rome: Ediesse.

Casey, T. (2006) 'Mapping European Capitalisms and the Challenge of Social Context'. Paper presented at the Fifteenth International Conference of the Council for European Studies, Chicago, IL, 29 March– 2 April, 2006, http://councilforeuropeanstudies.org/files/papers/Casey.pdf [accessed 10 January 2012].

CCMA. (2011) *Annual Report 2010–2011*. Pretoria: Department of Labour.

CCMA. (2012a) *Annual Report 2011–2012*. Pretoria: Department of Labour.

CCMA. (2012b) *Operations & Information Report September 2012*. CCMA: unpublished.

Cella, G.P. and Treu, T. (2009) *Relazioni industriali e contrattazione collettiva*. Bologna: Il Mulino.

CGT. (2010) *Médiation ou conciliation?* http://prudis-cgt.net/IMG/pdf/Articles-Droit_en_liberte-33.pdf [accessed 25 June 2013].

Charlwood, A. and Haynes, P. (2008) 'Union Membership Decline in New Zealand', *Journal of Industrial Relations*, 50, 78–110.

Chiovenda, G. (1923) *Principi di diritto processuale civile*. Naples: Jovene.

Chiovenda, G. (1930) 'Le riforme processuali e le correnti del pensiero moderno', in *Saggi di diritto processuale civile*, Vol. I, Rome: Società Editrice del Foro Italiano.

Ciocchetti, V. (1999) 'Crisi e paralisi nella giustizia del lavoro e previdenziale italiana', *Il Foro italiano*, 4, IV, 113–122.

Clark, J. and Lord Wedderburn. (1983) 'Modern Labour Law: Problems, Functions and Policies', in Lord Wedderburn, Lewis, R. and Clark, J. (eds) *Labour Law and Industrial Relations: Building on Kahn-Freund*, Oxford: Clarendon.

Clermont, K. (2012) *Civil Procedure*, 9th edition. St Paul Minnesota: Thomson/Reuters.

Clermont, K. and Schwab, S. (2004) 'How Employment Discrimination Plaintiffs Fare in Federal Court', *Journal of Empirical Legal Studies*, 1, 2, 429–457.
Clermont, K. and Schwab, S. (2009) 'Employment Discrimination Plaintiffs in Federal Court: From Bad to Worse', *Harvard Law and Policy Review*, 3, 1, 103–132.
Cohn, E.S., White S.O. and Sanders, J. (2000) 'Distributive and Procedural Justice in Seven Nations', *Law and Human Behavior*, 24, 25, 553–579.
Colvin, A. (2007) 'Empirical Research on Employment Arbitration: Clarity Amidst the Sound and Fury?' *Employee Rights and Employment Policy Journal*, 11, 405–447.
Colvin, A. (2009) 'Employment Arbitration and Research Needs', *ADR News*, August/October, 6–11.
Colvin, A. (2011) 'An Empirical Study of Employment Arbitration: Case Outcomes and Processes', *Journal of Empirical Legal Studies*, 8, 1, 1–23.
Colvin, A. (2012) 'American Workplace Dispute Resolution in the Individual Rights Era', *International Journal of Human Resource Management*, 23, 3, 459–475.
Colvin, A. and Gough, M. (2012) 'Individual Employment Rights Arbitration in the US: Actors and Outcomes'. Paper presented at the *International Labor and Employment Relations Association Conference*, 2–5 July, Philadelphia, USA.
Constitutional Court of South Africa. (2012) http://www.constitutionalcourt.org.za/site/thecourt/history.htm [accessed 8 November 2012].
Contrepois, S. (2009) *Changes in Conciliation, Mediation and Arbitration Services used in the Resolution of Labour Disputes in France*. Working Lives Institute, London: Metropolitan University, http://workinglives.org/fms/MRSite/Research/wlri/CAMS/France%20Report.pdf [accessed 25 June 2013].
Corby, S. (1999) *Resolving Employment Rights Disputes through Mediation: The New Zealand Experience*. London: Institute of Employment Rights.
Corby, S. (2000) 'Unfair Dismissal Disputes: A Comparative Study of Great Britain and New Zealand', *Human Resource Management Journal*, 10, 1, 79–92.
Corby, S. and Latreille, P. (2011) *Survey Evidence: ET and EAT Judges and Lay Members*, http://www2.gre.ac.uk/about/schools/business/research/centres/weru/publications [accessed 23 November 2012].
Corby, S. and Latreille, P. (2012) 'Employment Tribunals and the Civil Courts: Isomorphism Exemplified', *Industrial Law Journal*, 43, 2, 94–109.
Crouch, C. (1993) *Industrial Relations and European State Traditions*, Oxford: OUP.
Crouch, C. and Farrell, H. (2004) 'Breaking the Path of Institutional Development? Alternatives to the New Determinism', *Rationality and Society*, 16, 1, 5–43.
DARES. (2006) *La Couverture Conventionnelle et les Conventions Collectives de Branche du Secteur Concurrentiel non agricole*. Direction de l'animation de la recherché des etudes et des statistiques, http://travail-emploi.gouv.fr/IMG/pdf/Dossierno1_CouvertureConventionnelle_2004.pdf [accessed 21 June 2013].
DARES. (2013) *Les ruptures conventionelles de 2008 à 2012*. Dares Analyses, May 2013, No.031, http://travail-emploi.gouv.fr/IMG/pdf/2013-031_v2.pdf [accessed 21 June 2013].
David, M. (1974) 'Lévolution historique des conseils de prud'homme en France', *Droit Social*, Special, 9–29.
De Cristofaro, M. (2011) 'Il nuovo regime delle alternative alla giurisdizione statale (ADR) nel contenzioso del lavoro: conciliazione facoltativa ed arbitrato liberalizzato', *Lavoro nella Giurisprudenza*, 1, 19, 57–70.
De Luca Tamajo, R. (2008) 'Gli anni '70: dai fasti del garantismo al diritto del lavoro dell'emergenza', in Ichino, P. (ed) *Il diritto del lavoro nell'Italia repubblicana*, Milan: Giuffrè.

de Rechtspraak. (2013) 'Introduction', Official site of the Dutch judiciary, http://www.rechtspraak.nl/english/Pages/default.aspx [accessed 20 August 2013].

Deakin, S. (2009) 'Legal Origin, Juridical Form and Industrialisation in Historical Perspective: The Case of the Employment Contract and the Joint-Stock Company', *Socio-Economic Review*, 7, 1, 35–65.

Deakin, S., Lele, P. and Siems, M. (2007) 'The Evolution of Labour Law: Calibrating and Comparing Regulatory Regimes', *International Labour Review*, 146, 3–4, 133–162.

Deakin, S. and Sarkar, P. (2009) 'Assessing the Long-run Economic Impact of Labour Law Systems: A Theoretical Reappraisal and Analysis of New Time Series Data', *Industrial Relations Journal*, 39, 6, 453–487.

Défenseur des Droits. (2012) *Rapport Annuel*. Paris, http://www.defenseurdesdroits.fr/sites/default/files/upload/raa-ddd-2012_press02.pdf [accessed on 4 June 2013].

Delikat, M. and Kleiner, M. (2004) 'An Empirical Study of Dispute Resolution Mechanisms: Where Do Plaintiffs Better Vindicate their Rights?' *Dispute Resolution Journal*, Nov 2003–Jan 2004, 56–85.

Dendorfer, R. (2011) *Das Abeitsgerichtsverfahren*. Berlin: Berliner Wissenschaftsverlag.

Department of Labour. (1995) *Government Gazette*, 356, 16529, 10 February. Pretoria: Department of Labour.

Department of Labour. (2010) *Employer and Employee Views of the Personal Grievance Process; A Qualitative Study*. Wellington: Department of Labour.

Department of Labour. (2011a) *Employment Relationships: From Beginning to End*. Wellington: Department of Labour.

Department of Labour. (2011b) *Using Mediation Services Effectively*. Wellington: Department of Labour.

Department of Labour. (2012) *Annual Report for the Year Ending June 2012*. Wellington: Department of Labour.

Department of Labour. (n.d.) *Review of the Employment Relationship Problem Resolution System*, http://www.dol.govt.nz/publications/research/er-problems-cabinet/ [accessed 1 August 2013].

Department of Trade and Industry. (2003) 'Employment Tribunals: Lay Member Recruitment Exercise 2002, Evaluation Summary', http://webarchive.nationalarchives.gov.uk/+/http://www.berr.gov.uk/files/file11621.pdf [accessed 20 September 2010].

Department of Trade and Industry. (1998) *Appointment of Lay Members to the Employment Tribunals: A Consultation Paper*. London: Department of Trade and Industry.

DGB. (2005) 'Fachgerichte haben sich bewährt', *einblick* 7/05, 1.

Dickens, L. (2012) *Making Employment Rights Effective*. Oxford: Hart.

Dickens, L., Jones, M., Weekes, B. and Hart, M. (1985) *Dismissed: A Study of Unfair Dismissal and the Industrial Tribunal System*. Oxford: Blackwell.

Diskrimineringsombudsmannen. (2009) *Pay Surveys – Provisions and Outcomes*. Stockholm: DO.

DJEI. (2011) *Summary and Analysis of the Responses on the Reform of the State's Employment Rights and Industrial Relations Structure and Procedures*, October. Dublin: DJEI.

DJEI. (2013) *Workplace Relations Reform Programme, Ireland: Meeting with Professor Susan Corby*, 10 July, unpublished.

Dolder, C. (2004) 'The Contribution of Mediation to Workplace Justice', *Industrial Law Journal*, 33, 4, 320–342.

Donaghey, J. and Teague, P. (2007) 'The Mixed Fortunes of Irish Unions: Living with the Paradoxes of Social Partnership', *Journal of Labour Research*, 28, 1, 19–41.

Donnelly, E. and Dunn, S. (2006) 'Ten Years After: South African Employment Relations Since the Negotiated Revolution', *British Journal of Industrial Relations*, 44, 1, 1–30.

Dop, J. and van den Heuvel, L.H. (eds) (2008) *Handboek Ontslagsrecht*. Apeldoorn: Maklu-Uitgevers.

Duffy, K. (2012) 'Blueprint for Reform of Employment Rights Institutions', *Irish Employment Law Journal*, 9, 3, 81–84.

Ebbinghaus, B. (2005) *Can Path Dependence Explain Institutional Change?* MPIfG Discussion Paper 05/2.

Ebbinghaus, B. and Visser, J. (1997) 'Der Wandel der Arbeitsbeziehungen im westeuropäischen Vergleich', in Hradil, S. and Immerfall, S. (eds) *Die westeuropäischen Gesellschaften im Vergleich*, Leske+Budrich: Opladen.

EIRO. (2009a) *Italy: Industrial Relations Profile*, http://www.eurofound.europa.eu/eiro/country/italy.pdf [accessed 12 April 2013].

EIRO. (2009b) 'Cgil Refuses to Sign Agreement on Collective Bargaining Reform', http://www.eurofound.europa.eu/eiro/country/italy.pdf [accessed 12 June 2013].

EIRO. (2012) 'Unions Slam New Law Allowing Opt-Outs on Labour Rules', http://www.eurofound.europa.eu/eiro/country/italy.pdf [accessed 12 June 2013].

Eisenberg, T. and Hill, E. (2004) 'Arbitration and Litigation of Employment Claims: An Empirical Comparison', *Dispute Resolution Journal*, Nov–Jan, 44–55.

Ellgut, P. and Kohaut, S. (2013) 'Tarifbindung und betriebliche Interessenvertretung: Ergebnisse aus dem IAB-Betriebspanel 2012', *WSI-Mitteilungen*, June 2013, 66, 4, 281–288.

Elliot, C., Jeanpierre, E. and Vernon, C. (2006) *French Legal System*. 2nd edition. Harlow: Pearson.

Employment Appeals Tribunal. (2012) *Annual Report 2011*. Dublin: Employment Appeals Tribunal.

Employment Appeals Tribunal. (n.d.) Guidelines for Persons Representing Parties before the Tribunal, http://www.workplacerelations.ie/en/Publications_Forms/Guidelines_for_Persons_Representing_Parties_before_the_EAT.pdf, [accessed 14 October 2013].

Equality Tribunal. (2012) *Annual Report 2011*. Dublin: Equality Tribunal.

Equality Tribunal. (n.d) Frequently Asked Questions, http://www.equalitytribunal.ie/Employment-Equality/Frequently-Asked-Questions/ [accessed 20 July 2013].

Estreicher, S. (2001) 'Saturns for Rickshaws: The Stakes in the Debate over Predispute Employment Arbitration Agreements', *Ohio State Journal of Dispute Resolution*, 16, 559–570.

Eurofound. (2013) http://www.eurofound.europa.eu/eiro/country/ireland.pdf [accessed 14 July 2013].

European Commission. (2011) *Industrial Relations in Europe 2010*. Luxembourg: Publications Office of the European Union.

European Commission for the Efficiency of Justice. (2012) *European Judicial Systems*, CEPEI Studies no. 18. Brussels: Council of Europe.

Everett, W. (2012) *Looking Back and Moving Forward – The Viability of an Expanded Role for the CCMA in the South African Labour Market*. CCMA unpublished.

Everett, W. and Daphne, J. (2012) *Exploring the Full Use of Partnerships and A Multi-Faceted Job Saving Strategy to more Effectively Address Job Loss and Deepening Poverty*. CCMA unpublished.

Federal Anti-Discrimination Agency (2009) *Act Implementing European Directives Putting into Effect the Principle of Equal Treatment*. Berlin http://www.

antidiskriminierungsstelle.de/SharedDocs/Downloads/EN/publikationen/agg_in_englischer_Sprache.pdf?__blob=publicationFile [accessed 22 October 2013]

Feuerbach, P.J.A. (1810) *Blick auf die deutsche Rechtswissenschaft*. Munich: Fleischmann.

Finkin, M. (2008) 'Privatization of Wrongful Dismissal Protection in Comparative Perspective', *Industrial Law Journal*, 37, 2, 149–168.

Gangmasters' Licensing Authority. (2011) *Annual Report and Accounts 2010–2011*. London: Stationery Office.

Garofalo, G. (1993) 'Osservazioni sul sistema contrattuale e sulla giurisdizione', in Naccari, G. (ed) *La riforma del lavoro pubblico*. Rome: Ediesse.

Ghera, E. (1973) 'Interessi collettivi e processo del lavoro', *Rivista Giuridica del Lavoro*, 1, 4.

Gibbons, M. (2007) *Better Dispute Resolution*. London: Department of Trade & Industry.

Giugni, G. (2007) *Diritto sindacale*. Bari: Cacucci.

Glaeser, E.L. and Schleifer, A. (2002) 'Legal Origins', *Quarterly Journal of Economics*, 117, 4, 1193–1229.

Goetschy, J. and Jobert, A. (2010) 'Employment Relations in France', in Bamber, G.J., Lansbury, R.D. and Wailes, N. (eds) *International and Comparative Employment Relations: Globalisation and Change*. London: Sage.

Grassetti, C. (1950) 'La conciliazione delle controversie individuali', *Rivista Giuridica del lavoro*', I, 239.

Greger R. and Unberath, H. (2012) *Thüringer Projekt: Güterichter. Abschlußbericht*, http://www.thueringen.de/imperia/md/content/text/justiz/gueterichter/abschlussbericht_g__terichter_teil_1.pdf [accessed on 3 May 2013].

Greifenstein, R., Kißler, L. and Lange, H. (2010) *Trendreport Betriebsratswahlen 2010*. Hans-Böckler-Stiftung, http://www.boeckler.de/pdf_fof/S-2010-338-2-1.pdf [accessed 19 June 2013].

Hall, P. and Soskice, D. (eds) (2001) *Varieties of Capitalism*. Oxford: OUP.

Hall, P., and Soskice, D. (2009) 'An Introduction to Varieties of Capitalism', in Hancké, B. (ed) *Debating Varieties of Capitalism*. Oxford: Oxford University Press.

Hancké, B. (2007) *Beyond Varieties of Capitalism: Conflict, Contradictions, and Complementarities in the European Economy*. Oxford: Oxford University Press.

Hancké, B. (ed) (2009) *Debating Varieties of Capitalism: A Reader*. Oxford: OUP.

Havinga, T. (2002) 'The Effects and Limits of Anti-Discrimination Law in The Netherlands', *International Journal of the Sociology of Law*, 30, 75–90.

Health and Safety Executive. (2010) *The Health and Safety Executive Statistics 2009–10*. London: ONS.

Hepple, B. (1987) *Industrial Tribunals*. London: Justice.

Hepple, B. (1988) 'Labour Courts: Some Comparative Perspectives', *Current Legal Problems*, 41, 169–196.

Hepple, B. (2012) 'Workplace Equality', in Dickens, L. (ed) *Making Employment Rights Effective*, Oxford: Hart.

Herschel, W. (1980) 'Die ehrenamtlichen Richter der Arbeitsgerichtsbarkeit – Vorschläge zur Mehrung ihres Einflusses', *Arbeit und Recht*, 321–328.

Hill, E. (2004) 'Due Process at Low Cost: An Empirical Study of Employment Arbitration under the Auspices of the American Arbitration Association', in Estreicher, S. and Sherwyn, D. (eds) *Alternative Dispute Resolution in the Employment Arena*, New York: Kluwer.

Hirschman, A.O. (1987) 'The Search for Paradigms as a Hindrance to Understanding', in Rabinow, P. and Sullivan, W.M. (eds) *Interpretive Social Science: A Second Look*, 2nd edition. Berkeley/Los Angeles: University of California Press, 177–194.

Hodgson, G. (2001) *How Economics Forgot History*. London and New York: Routledge.
Höland, A. (2005) *Kündigungspraxis und Kündigungsschutz im Arbeitsverhältnis aus der Sicht des arbeitsgerichtlichen Verfahrens*. Hans-Böckler-Stiftung, http://www.boeckler.de/pdf/impuls_2005_09_hoeland.pdf [accessed 8 August 2013].
Höland, A. and Zeibig, N. (2007) 'Fairness bei Kündigungen des Arbeitsverhältnisses durch Arbeitgeber', *WSI-Mitteilungen*, 5/2007, 246–251.
Höland, A., Kahl, U. and Zeibig, N. (2007) *Kündigungspraxis und Kündigungsschutz im Arbeitsverhältnis*. Baden-Baden. Nomos Verlagsgesellschaft.
Howard, W. (1995) 'Arbitrating Claims of Employment Discrimination', *Dispute Resolution Journal*, October–December, 40–50.
Howell, C. and Givan, R.C. (2011) 'Rethinking Institutions and Institutional Change in European Industrial Relations', *British Journal of Industrial Relations*, 49, 2 June 2011, 231–255.
Human Rights Commission. (2012) *Annual Report for the Year Ended 30 June 2012*. Wellington: Human Rights Commission.
Hylton, K. (2004) 'Law and Economics of Mandatory Arbitration Agreements', in Estreicher, S. and Sherwyn, D. (eds) *Alternative Dispute Resolution in the Employment Arena*, New York: Kluwer.
Ianniruberto, G. (1999) *Il processo del lavoro rinnovato*. Padova: Cedam.
Ichino, A. and Pinotti P. (2012) 'La roulette russa dell'articolo 18', http://archivio.lavoce.info/articoli/pagina1002912.html [accessed 12 April 2013].
Ichino, A., Polo, M. and Rettore, E. (2003) 'Are Judges Biased by Labor Market Conditions?' *European Economic Review*, 47, 5, 913–944.
Ichino, P. (1996) *Il lavoro e il mercato*, Milano: Mondadori.
Ichino, P. (2010) *Intervento al Senato della Repubblica* http://www.pietroichino.it/?p=10402 [accessed 12 April 2013].
IDS. (2006) *Employment Tribunal Practice and Procedure*. London: Incomes Data Services.
IDS. (2010) *The Equality Act 2010*. London: Incomes Data Services.
Ijzermans, M. and de Roo, A. (2011) 'Dispute Resolution Inside and Outside the Courts', in Taekema, S., de Roo, A. and Elion-Valter, C. (eds) *Understanding Dutch Law*, 2nd edition. The Hague: Eleven International Publishing.
Incomes Data Services [IDS]. (2009) *Employment in France*. London.
International Labour Organisation. (2006) *International Labour Conference 95th Session, Report III (Part 1B)*, http://www.ilo.org/public/english/standards/relm/ilc/ilc95/pdf/rep-iii-1b.pdf [accessed 22 August 13].
ISTAT. (2013) *Employment rate*, http://dati.istat.it/?lang=en [accessed 12 April 2013].
Jäeger, N. (1935) *Diritto processuale del lavoro*. Padova: Cedam.
Judicial Appointments Commission. (n.d.) *Information Pack*. London: Judicial Appointments Commission.
Kagan, R. (2007) 'American and European Ways of Law: Six Entrenched Differences', in Gessner, V. and Nelken, D. (eds) *European Ways of Law: Towards a European Sociology of Law*, Oxford and Portland: Hart Publishing.
Kahn-Freund, O. (1977) *Labour and the Law*, 2nd edition. London: Stevens & Sons.
Kauff, J. and Putney, L. (2004) 'Negotiating Gilmer Agreements in the Union Sector', in Estreicher, S. and Sherwyn, D. (eds) *Alternative Dispute Resolution in the Employment Arena*, New York: Kluwer.
Kearney, R. (2009) *Labor Relations in the Public Sector*. 4th edition. New York: Taylor & Francis.
Kerr, A. and McGreal, C. (2009) 'Practice and Procedure in Employment Law', in Regan, M. (ed) *Employment Law*, Dublin/Haywards Heath: Tottel Publishing.

Kesting, S. and Nielsen, K. (2008) 'Varieties of Capitalism: Theoretical Critique and Empirical Observations', in Elsner, W. and Hanappi, H. (eds) *Varieties of Capitalism and New Institutional Deals*, Cheltenham: Edward Elgar, 23–51.

Klaas, B., Mahony, D. and Wheeler, H. (2006) 'Decision-Making about Workplace Disputes: A Policy-Capturing Study of Employment Arbitrators, Labor Arbitrators and Jurors', *Industrial Relations*, 45, 1, 68–95.

Klerman, D., Mahoney, P., Spamann, H. and Weinstein, M. (2011) 'Legal Origin or Colonial History', *Journal of Legal Analysis*, 3, 2, 379–409.

Knight, K. and Latreille, P. (2000) 'Discipline, Dismissals and Complaints to Employment Tribunals', *British Journal of Industrial Relations*, 38, 4, 533–555.

Koch, M. (2002) 'Report to Tenth Meeting of European Labour Court Judges', Stockholm, 2 September 2002, http://www.ilo.org/public/english/dialogue/ifpdial/downloads/lc_03/swe_1.pdf [accessed 6 July 2011].

Kovach, K. and Love, L. (1996) ' "Evaluative" Mediation is An Oxymoron', *CPR Institute for Dispute Resolution*, 14, 3, 31–32.

Labour Court. (2010) *Annual Report, 2009*. Stockholm: Labour Court.

Labour Court. (2012) *Annual Report 2011*. Dublin: Labour Court.

Labour Court. (2013) *Practice Manual of the Labour Court of South Africa*. Johannesburg: Labour Court.

Labour Court. (n.d.) *Guide to the Labour Court,* http://www.labourcourt.ie/labour/labour.nsf/LookupPageLink/HomeFrequentlyAskedQuestions [accessed 25 July 2013].

Labour Foundation. (2003) *The Labour Foundation*. The Hague: Stichting van de Arbeid.

Labour Relations Commission. (2012) *Annual Report 2011*. Dublin: Labour Relations Commission.

Levy, A. (2013) 'Strike Action: Will Things Ever Be the Same Again?' in Venter, T. and Levy, A. (eds) *The Dispute Resolution Digest* 2013, Johannesburg: Tokiso/Juta.

Liaisons Sociales. (2013) 'La future réforme des prud'hommes déjà contestée', 10 July 2013.

Licci, P. (2011) 'L'arbitrato', in Sassani, B. and Tiscini, R. (eds) *I profili processuali del collegato lavoro*, Rome: Dike.

Lieberman, R.C. (2002) 'Ideas, Institutions, and Political Order: Explaining Political Change', *The American Political Science Review*, 96, 4, 697–712.

Low Pay Commission. (2011) *Report – National Minimum Wage*. London: BIS.

Lucchetti, G. (2011) 'Il "collegato lavoro" alla prova dei fatti: conciliazione, certificazione arbitrato e welfare privato nel nuovo c.c.n.l. commercio', *Argomenti di Diritto del lavoro*, 4–5, 942–955.

Lucy, W. (2005) 'The Possibility of Impartiality', *Oxford Journal of Legal Studies*, 25, 1, 3–31.

Mac Cormaic, R. (2013) 'Court Braced for a Shake-Up, but Reforms Will Still Leave Important Questions Unanswered', *Irish Times,* 10 July, 6.

Mahoney, J. (2000) 'Path Dependence in Historical Sociology', *Theory and Society*, 29, 507–548.

Mahoney, P.G. (2001) 'The Common Law and Economic Growth: Hayek Might Be Right', *The Journal of Legal Studies*, 30, 2, 503–525.

Mål och medel. (2010) Ref: SOU 2010:44, http://www.regeringen.se/sb/d/108/a/148914 [accessed 11 April 2012].

Mallon, T. (2012) 'Employment Law Reform', *Irish Employment Law Journal*, 9, 3, 76–80.

McAndrew, I. (1995) 'The New Zealand Employment Tribunal: A Review and Assessment', *Asia Pacific Journal of Human Resources*, 33, 2, 36–49.

McAndrew, I. (2010) 'The Employment Institutions', in Rasmussen, E. (ed) *Employment Relationships: Workers, Unions and Employers in New Zealand*, Auckland: Auckland University Press.
Meeran, G. (2006) 'The Employment Tribunals', in Dickens, L. and Neal, A. (eds) *The Changing Institutional Face of British Employment Relations*. AH Alphen aan den Rijn, Netherlands: Kluwer.
Ministère de la Justice. (2012) *Activité des conseils de prud'hommes*. Statistique Judiciaire, http://www.justice.gouv.fr/statistiques.html [accessed 25 June 2013].
Ministère de la Justice. (2013) 'Retour de la Justice gratuite', http://www.justice.gouv.fr/la-garde-des-sceaux-10016/retour-a-la-justice-gratuite-25754.html [accessed 1 August 2013].
Ministère de la Justice et de la Liberté. (2012a) 'Chiffres clés de la justice 2010', http://www.justice.gouv.fr/art_pix/1_stat_chiffrescles10_20101213.pdf [accessed 4 July 2013].
Ministère des Affaires sociales, du Travail et de la Solidarité. (2002) *Le Conseil de Prud'hommes*. Paris.
Ministère du Travail, de l'Emploi, de la Formation professionnelle et du Dialogue social. (2013) *La Négociation Collective en 2012*. Paris.
Ministero del Lavoro e delle Politiche Sociali. (2013) *Prospetto riepilogativo delle controversie individuali*, http://www.lavoro.gov.it/NR/rdonlyres/75C010C9-6821-431C-BD5A-58D229E7066B/0/130306_2012.pdf [accessed 12 April 2013], 45.
Ministero del Lavoro e delle Politiche Sociali, Divisione generale per l'attività ispettiva. (2012a) *Rapporto annuale sull'attività di vigilanza in materia di lavoro e previdenziale*, http://www.lavoro.gov.it/NR/rdonlyres/E45EFA51-8217-4CBD-B52B-D0A77E9F8F76/0/Rapporto_annuale_vigilanza_2012.pdf [accessed 31 May 2013].
Ministero del Lavoro e delle Politiche Sociali, Divisione generale per l'attività ispettiva. (2012b) *Documento di programmazione per l'attività di vigilanza per l'anno 2013*, http://www.lavoro.gov.it/NR/rdonlyres/7A0A7C2A-0B66-4B91-A4AB-3308CBD3556D/0/Documento_programmazione_vigilanza_2013.pdf [accessed 31 May 2013].
Ministero della Giustizia. (2011) Direzione Generale di Statistica, http://webstat.giustizia.it/AreaPubblica/default.aspx# [accessed 12 April 2013].
Ministry of Justice. (2011) *Charging Fees in Employment Tribunals and the Employment Appeal Tribunal* consultation paper CP 22/2011. London: Ministry of Justice.
Ministry of Justice. (2012a) *Employment Tribunals and EAT Statistics April 2011 to March 2012*. London: Ministry of Justice.
Ministry of Justice. (2012b) *Charging Fees in Employment Tribunals and the Employment Appeal Tribunal*, response to consultation CP 22/2011. London: Ministry of Justice.
Ministry of Justice. (2013a) http://www.justice.govt.nz/courts/employment-court/role-and-structure-of-the-employment-court [accessed 19 April 2013].
Ministry of Justice. (2013b) *Annual Statistics Specialist Courts and Tribunals December 2012*, http://www.courtsofnz.govt.nz/fom/statistics/annual-statistics/december-2012/specialis-courts-and-tribunals [accessed 1 May 2013].
Ministry of Justice. (n.d.a) http://www.justice.govt.nz/courts/employment-court/how-cases-come-to-court/at-the-hearing [accessed 16 July 2013].
Ministry of Justice. (n.d.b) http://www.justice.govt.nz/tribunals/human-rights-review-tribunal/about-the-tribunal [accessed 16 July 2013].
Ministry of Justice/HM Courts and Tribunals Service. (2011) *Employment Tribunals and EAT Statistics April 2010 to March 2011*. London: Ministry of Justice.
Ministry of Labour and Social Affairs. (2013) 'Kabinet en sociale partners eens over sociale agenda voor arbeidsmarkt van de 21e eeuw', Press Release, 11 April

2013, http://www.rijksoverheid.nl/ministeries/szw/nieuws/2013/04/11/kabinet-en-sociale-partners-eens-over-sociale-agenda-voor-arbeidsmarkt-van-de-21e-eeuw.html [accessed 9 July 2013]. An English translation is available but the legal language used is not precise.

Montesano, L. and Mazziotti, F. (1974) *Le controversie di lavoro e della previdenza sociale*. Naples: Jovene.

Montesquieu, C. (1753) *L'esprit de loix*. Amsterdam and Leipzig: Arkstee & Merkus, http://babel.hathitrust.org/cgi/pt?id=nyp.33433007450186 [accessed 20 August 2011].

Morgan, G, and Quack, S. (2010) 'Law as a Governing Institution', in Morgan, G., Campbell, J.L., Crouch, C., Pedersen, O.K. and Whitley, R. (eds) *The Oxford Handbook of Comparative Institutional Analysis*, Oxford: OUP, 275–308.

Moritz, K. (1987) *Das französische Arbeitsgericht*. Berlin: Duncker & Humblot.

Morris, G. (2012) 'The Development of Statutory Employment Rights in Britain and Enforcement Mechanisms', in Dickens, L. (ed) *Making Employment Rights Effective*. Oxford: Hart.

Mortara, L. (1934) 'Il processo nelle controversie individuali di lavoro: passato, presente e futuro', *Giurisprudenza Italiana*, IV, 211.

Muhl, C. (2001) 'The Employment-at-Will Doctrine: Three Major Exceptions', *Monthly Labor Review*, January 3–11.

Naimark, R. (2004) 'The Uses and Interpretation of Research', in Estreicher, S. and Sherwyn, D. (eds) *Alternative Dispute Resolution in the Employment Arena*. New York: Kluwer.

Napier, B. (1979) 'The French Labour Courts – An Institution in Transition', *The Modern Law Review*, 42, 3, 270–284.

Napoletano, D. (1960) *Diritto processuale del lavoro*. Roma: Jandi Sapi.

Nascosi, A. (2007) *Il tentativo obbligatorio di conciliazione stragiudiziale nelle controversie di lavoro*. Milan: Giuffrè.

Nationale Ombudsman. (2007) *Naar een eerlijke ontslagprocedure*. 2007/260. The Hague: Bureau Nationale Ombudsman.

NERA. (2013) *Review of 2012*. Dublin: National Employment Rights Authority.

NERA. (n.d.) http://www.employmentrights.ie/en/aboutnera/ [accessed 20 August 2013].

Novitz, T. and Syrpis, P. (2006) 'Assessing Legitimate Structures for the Making of Transnational Labour Law: The Durability of Corporatism', *Industrial Law Journal*, 35, 4, 367–394.

NRW. (2009) 'Geschäftsstelle der ehrenamtlichen Richterinnen und Richter für die Arbeitsgerichtsbarkeit des Landes Nordrhein-Westfalen beruft 10.000en ehrenamtlichen Richter/in', 23 March 2009, [accessed 22 January 2011].

OECD. (2013) *Employment rate Aged 15–64 All Persons*, http://stats.oecd.org/Index.aspx?DatasetCode=LFS_SEXAGE_I_R [accessed 12 April 2013].

OECD and Visser, J. (2011) *ICTWSS database* (Institutional Characteristics of Trade Unions, Wage Setting, State Intervention and Social Pacts, 1960–2010), version 3.0 http://www.uva-aias.net/208 [accessed 12 April 2013].

Olszack, N. (2008) 'Invention de défense du caractère paritaire de la juridiction prud'homale', in Michel, H. and Willemez, L. (eds) *Les prud'hommes: actualité d'une justice bicentenaire*, 15–24.

Pedersini, R. (2010) *Trade Unions Strategies to Recruit New Groups of Workers*. Dublin: European Foundation for the Improvement of Living and Working Conditions.

Perone, G. (1975) *Il nuovo processo del lavoro*. Padova: Cedam.

Peters, M., Seeds, K., Harding, C. and Garnett, E. (2010) *Findings from the Survey of Employment Tribunal Applications 2008*. London: Department for Business, Innovation and Skills.
Picardi, N. (1979) 'Primi risultati di una ricerca sui tempi del processo del lavoro', *Rivista Trimestrale di Diritto e Procedura Civile*, 279–286.
Preti, D. (1977) 'La regolamentazione delle controversie individuali di lavoro in regime fascista', *Studi storici*, 2, 125–170.
Proto Pisani, A. (1983) 'Lavoro (controversie individuali in materia di)' *Novissimo Digesto Italiano. Appendice*. Turin: Utet.
Proto Pisani, A. (1987) 'Le controversie in materia di lavoro', in Branca, G. (ed) *Commentario della Costituzione*, Bologna-Rome: Zanichelli Zanichelli-Il Foro Italiano;
Rabin, R. (2010) 'Judicial Review of Awards in Mandatory Employment Arbitrations: Are We Getting it Right? *Proceedings of the 63rd Annual Meeting of the National Academy of Arbitrators,* 26–29 May, Philadelphia, USA.
Rapporto Statistico del settore civile. (2012) http://www.cortedicassazione.it/Documenti/CCStatisticheCivile_2012.pdf [accessed 12 April 2013].
Rasmussen, E. and Greenwood, G. (2014) 'Conflict Resolution in New Zealand, chapter 21', in Roche, K., Teague, P. and Colvin. (eds) *Oxford Handbook of Conflict Management in Organizations*, Oxford: OUP.
Rausei, P. (2012) *Ispezioni e nuovo sistema sanzionatorio*. Milan: Ipsoa.
Redenti, E. (1905) 'Il contratto di lavoro nella giurisprudenza dei probiviri', *Rivista di Diritto Commerciale*, 3, I, 356–380.
Regalia, I. (2009) *Quale rappresentanza. Dinamiche e prospettive del sindacato in Italia*. Roma: Ediesse.
Rehder, B. (2007a) 'Die fragile Erfolgsgeschichte der Arbeitsgerichtsbarkeit', Max-Planck-Institut für Gesellschaftsforschung, *Aus der Forschung*, http://www.mpifg.de/pu/ueber_mpifg/mpifg_jb/JB0708/MPIfG_07-08_07_Rehder.pdf [accessed 8 March 2013].
Rehder, B. (2007b) 'Normenwandel und Justizreform – Das Beispiel der Arbeitsgerichtsbarkeit', *WSI-Mitteilungen*, 8/2007, 448–454.
Relazione sull'amministrazione della Giustizia. (2012) http://www.cortedicassazione.it/Documenti/Relazione_anno_giudiziario_2012 [accessed 12 April 2013].
Renton, D. (2012) *Struck Out*. London: Pluto Press.
Richard, J. and Pascal, A. (2010) *Pour le Renforcement de la Légitimité de l'Institution Prud'homale: Quelle Forme de Désignation des Conseillers Prud'hommes?* Rapport au ministre du travail, de la solidarité et de la fonction publique. Paris, http://www.travail-emploi-sante.gouv.fr/IMG/pdf/VF_rapport_200510__2_.pdf [accessed 25 July 2011].
Rieble, V. (2005) *Zukunft der Arbeitsgerichtsbarkeit*, ZAAR Schriftenreihe, Band 3., Munich.
Rigby, E. (2013) 'Chancellors "Shares for Rights" Plan Flops', *Financial Times*, 28 June, http://www.ft.com/cms/s/0/6ec7934e-e005-11e2-bf9d-00144feab7de.html#axzz2ZIhuMnqL [accessed 17 July 2013].
Risak, M. E. and McAndrew, I. (2010) 'Who Mediates Employment Relationship Problems?' paper submitted at the 14th *Labour, Employment and Work Conference*, https://blogs.otago.ac.nz/mediation/files/2010/12/LEW14_Conference_2010_Risak_McAndrew_Mediation-ERP-final.pdf [accessed 10 May 2011].
Roe, M. (2000) 'Political Preconditions to Separating Ownership from Corporate Control', *Stanford Law Review*, 53, 3, 539–606.
Roe, M. (2007) 'Juries and the Political Economy of Legal Origin', *Journal of Comparative Economics*, 35, 294–308.

Romagnoli, U. (1973) 'Sindacati e diritto. Le origini del pensiero giuridico-sindacale in Italia' *Studi storici*, I, 3–60.
Romagnoli, U. (1974) 'Autorità e democrazia in azienda: teorie giuridico-politiche', in Romagnoli, U. (ed) *Lavoratori e sindacati tra vecchio e nuovo diritto*, Bologna: Il Mulino.
Royal Commission. (1968) *Royal Commission on Trade Unions and Employers' Associations 1965–68, Chairman: The Rt, Hon. Lord Donovan. Report*, Cmnd 3623. London: HMSO.
Rubery, J. (2010) 'Institutionalizing the Employment Relationship', in Morgan, G., Campbell, J.L., Crouch, C., Pedersen, O.K. and Whitley, R. (eds) *The Oxford Handbook of Comparative Institutional Analysis,* Oxford: OUP, 497–526.
Rycroft, A. (2012) 'An Evaluation of the Labour Court', in Levy, A. and Venter, T. (eds) *The Dispute Resolution Digest* 2012, Johannesburg: Tokiso/Juta.
Savage, K. (2013) 'Challenges in the Enforcement of Arbitration Award and Minimum Standards', in Venter, T. and Levy, A. (eds) *The Dispute Resolution Digest* 2013, Johannesburg: Tokiso/Juta.
Sawall, S. (2007) *Die Entwicklung der Arbeitsgerichtsbarkeit*. Aachen: Shaker Verlag.
Scheuer, S. (2011) 'Union Membership Variation in Europe: A Ten-Country Comparative Analysis', *European Journal of Industrial Relations*, 17, 1, 57–73.
Seeber, R. and Lipsky, D. (2006) 'The Ascendancy of Employment Arbitrators in US Employment Relations: A New Actor in the American System?' *British Journal of Industrial Relations*, 4, 4, 719–716.
Segni, A. (1927) *I tribunali del lavoro in Italia*, in *Studi di diritto processuale in onore di Chiovenda*. Padova: Cedam.
Selwyn, N. (2008) *Selwyn's Law of Employment*. 15th edition. Oxford: Oxford University Press.
Sgroi, V. (1989) 'Relazione del procuratore generale presso la Cassazione per l'anno giudiziario 1988. Parte seconda: la giustizia civile. Riflessi internazionali della durata dei processi. La situazione della Cassazione', *Giustizia Civile*, II, 73–76.
Sherwyn, D. and Sturman, M. (2004) 'Because It Takes Two: Why Post-Dispute Voluntary Arbitration Programs Will Fail to Fix the Problems Associated with Employment Discrimination Law Adjudication', in Estreicher, S. and Sherwyn, D. (eds) *Alternative Dispute Resolution in the Employment Arena*, New York: Kluwer.
Shulruf, B., Woodhams, B., Howard, C., Johri, R. and Yee, B. (2009) ' "Grievance Gravy Train Picking Up Speed": Myths and Reality Around Employment Disputes in New Zealand', *Journal of Industrial Relations*, 51, 245–261.
St. Antoine, T. (2009) 'Mandatory Arbitration: Why It's Better Than It Looks'. *Proceedings of the 62nd Annual Meeting of the National Academy of Arbitrators,* 20–23 May, Chicago, USA.
Statistisches Bundesamt. (2012) *Rechtspflege: Arbeitsgerichte*. Fachserie 10 Reihe 2.8. Wiesbaden: Statistisches Bundesamt.
Stipo, G. (2012) 'La risoluzione alternativa delle controversie in materia di lavoro: mediazione, conciliazione, arbitrato', *Nuova Rassegna di legislazione dottrina e giurisprudenza*, 6, 651–665.
Stone, K. (1996) 'Mandatory Arbitration of Individual Employment Rights: The Yellow Dog Contract of the 1990s', *Denver University Law Review*, 73, 4, 1017–1050.
Stone, K. (2004) 'The *Steelworkers' Trilogy*: The Evolution of Labor Arbitration', *Research Paper 04–29*. Los Angeles: University of California.
Sullivan, J. (2012) 'Innovation to Continue in Second Act', *Tribunals*, Winter, 2–4.
Supreme Court of Appeal South Africa. (2012) http://www.justice.gov.za/sca/aboutsca.htm [accessed 8 November 2012].

Swierczek, N. (2010) 'L'institution prud'homale: cette excentrique que l'on vouler rationaliser'. Doctoral thesis submitted to the University of Science and Technology Lille, https://iris.univ-lille1.fr/dspace/bitstream/1908/2177/1/50377-2010-Swierczek.pdf [accessed 4 August 2011].

Taekema, S. (2011) 'Introducing Dutch Law', in Taekema, S., de Roo, A. and Elion-Valter, C. (eds) *Understanding Dutch Law*. 2nd edition. The Hague: Eleven International Publishing.

Taruffo, M. (1980) *La giustizia civile in Italia dal '700 ad oggi*. Bologna: Il Mulino.

Tarzia, G. (2008) *Manuale del processo del lavoro*. Milan: Giuffrè.

Taylor, S. and Amir, A. (2009) *Employment Law: An Introduction*. Oxford: Oxford University Press.

Teague, P. (2009) 'Path Dependency and Comparative Industrial Relations: The Case of Conflict Resolution Systems in Ireland and Sweden', *British Journal of Industrial Relations*, 47, 3, 499–520.

Teubner, G. (2001) 'Legal Irritants: How Unifying Law Ends up in New Divergences', in Hall, P. and Soskice, D. (eds) *Varieties of Capitalism*, Oxford: OUP.

Thelen, K. (2003) 'How Institutions Evolve', in Mahoney, J. and Rueschemeyer, D. (eds) *Comparative Historical Analysis in the Social Sciences*, Cambridge: CUP, 208–240.

Thelen, K. (2010) 'Beyond Comparative Statics: Historical Institutional Approaches to Stability and Change in the Political Economy of Labour', in Morgan, G., Campbell, J.L., Crouch, C., Pedersen, O.K. and Whitley, R. (eds) *The Oxford Handbook of Comparative Institutional Analysis*, Oxford: OUP, 41–62.

Tombs, S. and Whyte, D. (2012) 'Reshaping Health and Safety Enforcement', in Dickens, L. (ed) *Making Employment Rights Effective*. Oxford: Hart.

Treu, T. (1975) 'Azione sindacale e nuova politica del diritto', in Treu, T. (ed) *L'uso politico dello Statuto dei lavoratori*, Bologna: Il Mulino.

Treu, T. (2007) *Labour Law and Industrial Relations in Italy*. The Netherlands: Kluwer.

Treu, T. (2010) *Intervento al Senato della Repubblica*, http://www.pietroichino.it/?p=10402 [accessed 12 April 2013].

Treu, T. (2011) 'Il futuro delle relazioni industriali', in Bordogna, L., Pedersini, R. and Provasi, G. (eds) *Lavoro, Mercato, Istituzioni. Scritti in onore di Gian Primo Cella*, Milano: Franco Angeli.

Trisorio Liuzzi, G. (2001) 'La conciliazione obbligatoria e l'arbitrato nelle controversie di lavoro privato', *Rivista di Diritto Processuale*, 56, 4, 948–1005.

Turner, J. (2001) 'Sociological Theory Today', in Turner, J. (ed) *Handbook of Sociological Theory*. New York: Springer.

Turner, R. (2008) *Neo-Liberal Ideology, History, Concepts and Policies*. Edinburgh: Edinburgh University Press.

US Equal Employment Opportunity Commission. (2013) www.eeoc.gov/eeoc/statistics/enforcement/all.cfm [accessed 28 May 13.]

UWV WERKbedrijf. (2010) *Ontslagsprocedure UWV WERKbedrijf: Beleidsregels en regelgeving*. Den Haag: Sdu Uitgevers.

Vallebona, A. (2011) 'Introduzione al Trattato di diritto del lavoro', in Persiani, M. and Carinci, F. (eds) *Il diritto processuale del lavoro*, IX, XXVI, Padova: Cedam.

Van Arkel, E.G. (2007) 'A Just Cause for Dismissal in the United States and the Netherlands'. PhD Thesis. Erasmus University of Rotterdam.

van Niekerk, A., Christianson, M., McGregor, M., Smit, N. and van Eck, B. (2012) *Law @ Work*. Johannnesburg: LexisNexis.

van Rie, T., Marx, I. and Horemans, J. (2011) 'Ghent Revisited: Unemployment Insurance and Union Membership in Belgium and the Nordic Countries', *European Journal of Industrial Relations*, 17, 2, 125–139.

Venter, R. and Levy, A. (2009) A. *Labour Relations in South Africa.* 3rd edition. Cape Town: Oxford University Press South Africa.

Venter, T. and Levy, A. (2012) 'Disputes at the CCMA, Bargaining Councils and Tokiso', in Levy, A. and Venter, T. (eds) *The Dispute Resolution Digest* 2012, Johannesburg: Tokiso/Juta.

Venter, T. and Levy, A. (2013) 'Disputes referred to the CCMA, Bargaining Councils and Tokiso', in Venter, T. and Levy, A. (eds) *The Dispute Resolution Digest* 2013, Johannesburg: Tokiso/Juta.

Visser, J. (2008) *The Quality of Industrial Relations and the Lisbon Strategy, in European Commission, Industrial relations in Europe 2008.* Luxembourg: Office for the Official Publications of the European Commission.

Visser, J. (2011) *ICTWSS: Database on Institutional Characteristics of Trade Unions, Wage Setting, State Intervention and Social Pacts in 34 Countries between1960 and 2007.* Amsterdam Institute for Advanced Studies, http:// www.uva-aias.net/208 [accessed on 28 June 2013].

Visser, J. (2013) *Database on Institutional Characteristics of Trade Unions, Wage Setting, State Intervention and Social Pacts in 34 Countries between 1960 and 2012.* Amsterdam: University of Amsterdam.

Vitols, S. (2001) 'Varieties of Corporate Governance', in Hall, P. and Soskice, D. (eds) *Varieties of Capitalism*, Oxford: OUP, 337–360.

von Bergh, M., Siesling, M. and van Rijs, A. (2009) *Ontslagzaken via de kantonrechter 2003–2008.* Tilburg: IVA.

Ware, S. (2004) 'The Effects of *Gilmer*: Empirical and Other Approaches to the Study of Employment Arbitration', in Estreicher, S. and Sherwyn, D. (eds) *Alternative Dispute Resolution in the Employment Arena*, New York: Kluwer.

Wedderburn, K. (1986) *The Worker and the Law.* 3rd edition. Harmondsworth: Penguin.

WHD US Department of Labor Wages and Hours Division. (2008) *Employment Standards Administration.* Washington D.C.: US Department of Labour.

WHD US Department of Labor Wages and Hours Division. (2011) *Handy Reference Guide to the Fair Labor Standards Act.* Washington D.C.: US Department of Labour.

Whitley, R. (1999) *Divergent Capitalisms: The Social Structuring and Change of Business Systems.* Oxford: Oxford University Press.

Windmuller, J. (1969) *Labor Relations in the Netherlands.* Ithaca, N.Y.: Cornell University Press.

Woodhams, B. (2007) *Employment Relationship Problems: Costs, Benefits and Choice.* Wellington: Department of Labour.

Woolfson, C., Thörnqvist, C. and Sommers, J. (2010) 'The Swedish Model and the Future of Labour Standard after *Laval*', *Industrial Relations Journal*, 41, 4, 333–350.

Zoppoli, L. (2010) 'Certificazione dei contratti di lavoro e arbitrato: le liaisons dangereuses', in Aa. Vv. (ed) *Sull'arbitrato. Studi offerti a Giovanni Verde*, Naples: Jovene, 927–948.

Zweigert, K. and Kötz, H. (1998) *An Introduction to Comparative Law.* Translated by Tony Weir. 3rd edition. Oxford: OUP.

Index

Printed and bound by CPI Group (UK) Ltd, Croydon, CR0 4YY